Between Sky and Ground

By Marrico Gordon

One

Fats came to work an hour late, parked, and sat in his car eating his breakfast burrito. He was listening to sports talk radio. It was Monday. The first Monday after the opening week of a new NFL pre-season. They interviewed callers.

"I don't like the kneeling during the anthem," a caller said. "And I get that there's an issue. I just think there's a better time and place for that. Go Hawks."

Fats shook his head and killed the motor, checked his yellow teeth in the rearview mirror, wiped the sleep out of his eye, and snorted hard. He stepped out, littered the parking lot, and shuffled to the brick building. There were more cars than usual—five lined up at either bay, totaling a car count of ten. He heard shouting as he came near the mechanic's pit. Dad was downstairs in the lower bay where the motor oil was drained. Sometimes, auto parts were hard to remove. Fats imagined that's what the shouting was about. Or maybe the wrench had slipped as Dad turned it, causing him to bust his knuckles. Fats noticed the new kid, Duck, wiping the windshield of a car parked in the first bay.

Fats approached him. Dad had made his way upstairs.

"Busy already?" Fats asked Duck.

"Yeah, and you smell like alcohol," Dad said, cleaning his dirty hands with a rag.

Fats pursed his lips. He'd overslept but had no more than a six-pack last night, so he knew he didn't smell like alcohol. He followed Duck to the driver's side, not apologizing to Dad for being late. Mondays were usually slow. Plus, Dad had Duck to help.

"So, what's going on with these cars?" Fats asked.

"They both need oil changes," Duck said.

Fats nodded. He was referring to the status, not the service. He hated that the boy had a smart mouth.

Duck adjusted the seat cover and slipped inside the Fiat.

Fats stepped back ten feet to guide him out. He stared at Duck and waited. The boy looked awkward in the small car. Six feet and lean like a swimmer. Brown eyes. Wheat-colored complexion. Large black rings of poodle-like hair.

Fats thought if they fought, he would take him. All he would have to do is wrestle him down.

Duck leaned forward and started the motor. Fats raised his hands and motioned him forward. Duck drove out slowly and parked.

An hour later, they were down to one car. Dad turned on the radio he kept in the lower bay. It stayed on 94.9 F.M, National Public Radio.

Fats was adding motor oil to the engine when he heard the segment. The volume was faint, but he could hear they were talking about the police shooting of an unarmed black man and why prosecuting officers was hard to do. He trashed the empty bottle, grabbed another quart, and opened it. Duck finished his duties and came around to watch him. Fats glanced at him. "Say, man, what d'you think about all these police shootings?" Fats asked, pouring the oil in.

Duck looked at the customer who was outside smoking a cigarette, then back at Fats. "What do you think about you losing weight," Duck asked. "Is this ready to start?"

"Yeah, it's ready."

"Ready to start!" Duck chimed.

"Go 'head and fire it up," Dad said.

Duck climbed in and started the motor. He had just graduated from high school—and never talked about anything regarding his race. Fats shook his head in disappointment. With that thin nose and fair skin, Duck couldn't be black enough to care.

He's probably not even black, Fats thought. *He's probably an Arab mixed with white or something else.*

"Pressure's up," Duck said.

"Go 'head and shut it down," Dad said.

Duck shut off the motor.

Fats looked at Duck again. Maybe the kid was skirting the subject because of the white man smoking near the bay. But Fats didn't care. He wanted the man to hear. "You hear about the brother they killed last week for jaywalking? And then in Philly, they choked that one brother to death."

"Cool it," Dad said from the lower bay. "Not at work. Now change the subject."

Fats saw that the customer had gone back inside.

Fats hand-tightened each cap, closed the hood, and guided Duck out of the bay.

Dad came upstairs, wiping his hands, then went into the lobby for the customer, who followed him to the register. Dad had been running his own business for the past fifteen years. A lube shop in Renton, Washington. He was a veteran who had served in the U.S. Air Force as a military police officer. When he came home, he'd joined the Nation of Islam, then became a Black Panther, and then a Muslim again. Now, he was just a strong old man who worked daily. He liked to talk about politics, just not in places where customers could hear.

They took a break after, sitting in the downstairs office. Dad made coffee, the machine brewing a pot of Folgers as dark as he was. A pair of dings sounded, alerting them that a customer was on the lot. Duck grabbed the stair rail, swung himself in a half circle, and ran up the stairs. Fats followed, as did Dad.

A girl stood outside her car, holding the door open with one hand, blocking the sun with the other. She had on a floppy straw hat and a summer dress. The warm afternoon breeze made it whip like a flag. She smiled as Duck approached her. Fats stopped at the cash register and watched them. Duck said something that made her laugh, and then she said something back. Now she smiled, listening to Duck, her big, bright eyes sparkling as though she were watching a magic trick.

Fats had seen eyes like those before, in fifth grade, belonging to a girl named Tatianna. But he was fond of her because of her hair. He would stare at it all during class, wanting to comb his fingers through it. It fell like a waterfall down her back. Sometimes, she'd brush it over her shoulder, showcasing the base of her neck. One day, in the schoolyard, Fats asked if he could touch it. Her friends giggled and whispered to each other when they heard him ask. Tatianna's large eyes rolled around, and then she said yes. Fats twisted the strands between his fingers, and for a moment, he thought he had all the evidence needed to prove there was a God. He forgot the hair belonged to a person until she pulled away.

A few weeks later, Tatianna and her friends brought him cookies. Homemade chocolate chip cookies. Not flat. The kind of cookies that come with a hump. Fats was sitting by himself in the cafeteria when they approached him. They were grinning and sat around until he finally took a bite. He ate three of the cookies. Within five minutes, his stomach reacted. He hurried to the bathroom, hoping he wouldn't mess his pants. When he ran, it felt like water was sloshing inside of him. Then something leaked out and stuck to the back of his underwear. He burst through the door and rushed inside a stall without locking it. He yanked down his pants, and liquid quickly shot out of him. He sat on the toilet for hours. He found out later the girls had baked the cookies with Ex-Lax as a joke.

He shook himself out of the memory, thinking he could never get a girl like that. He looked at the goddess before him. She was so beautiful that it made him mad. Light skin. Plump lips. Round cheeks. No bra supporting her breasts. The girl's eyes darted to his. He broke his gaze and pretended to be searching for receipts by the register. He watched through his peripheral. She pulled on the top of her dress, then crossed her arms. Duck turned and stared at Fats, then walked the girl to the lobby.

Fats went to the lobby window. The girl sat down and crossed her legs, adjusted the hem of her dress, and then scrolled through her phone. It looked to him like she was starting to play a game.

She likes games.

Duck honked. "You gonna guide me in or what?"

Fats collected himself, then did as requested. He lifted the hood to check the fluids but kept thinking about the girl. He walked around the car, getting a picture of her lifestyle and personality. "Hey, let's switch."

"Switch?"

"Yeah, I'll vacuum," Fats said. "You add oil and check fluids."

Duck peered at him. "Whatever, man." He then shuffled to the front of the car.

She wasn't perfect at all, Fats thought. He vacuumed and tossed the fast-food paper bags from the back of her car. There were old fries and crumbs everywhere on the seats and floorboards. He continued vacuuming, throwing the girl's trash into the industrial garbage can behind him. He moved quickly until he found an old bank statement of hers. He opened it and read the upper left corner.

Alexa Davis. She's probably married. She doesn't live too far from here, either.

"Ready for oil," Dad said.

Fats folded the paper and stuffed it in his breast pocket.

After the service, Duck introduced the girl to Dad. "This is my friend, Alexa," Duck said. Her eyes glittered as she took Dad's hand. "She wants to know if we're hiring."

"You know her?" Fats asked.

The three of them looked at him. "This guy," Duck mumbled. "Why are you even over here? Ain't you supposed to be working?"

Fats said nothing.

"You sure you wanna work here?" Dad asked.

"Just part-time," the girl said, smiling.

Fats went into the restroom and locked the door behind him. An intense thumping was in his chest. He pulled out his phone, searched her name, took screenshots of every image he could find of her, and then double-checked the lock on the door.

He came out thirty minutes later, glancing around for the girl, but she had already left.

"You always in that damn bathroom, using up all the toilet paper," Dad said.

Duck chuckled.

Fats walked away.

"What are you, incontinent?" Duck asked.

Two

Fats leaned by the cash register, daydreaming about the two weekends he'd spent working with Alexa. He'd learned she took ballet classes in grade school, was a foodie, and wanted to travel but hadn't gone anywhere except Vegas, where her grandfather was from. She liked music. Her favorite album was Beyonce's *Lemonade*. She once quoted Roxane Gay. She enjoyed essays and uplifting poetry written by women. She dressed artistically and liked bright colors. She painted her nails daily, color-coordinating them with her clothes. And sometimes, she wore gold anklets with her dresses, like a young Indian girl.

She talked a lot with Dad and always laughed with Duck, but once he was gone, she became quiet. The first day that she worked, Duck hung around after his shift to keep her company, but then Dad made him go home. Alexa had gotten too distracted. Fats tried talking to her then, but her answers were short, and she always looked for something to do. Last week, Fats overheard her talking to Dad and learned that she worked full-time at a daycare and needed a part-time job to save money for an apartment. She was eighteen, lived with her mother, and planned on going to Cancun next summer.

"Wake up!" Duck said, slapping the counter. He had come from the lower bay unannounced. He stood playfully close to Fats, holding a Styrofoam cup of coffee. His third for the day.

Fats grumbled, wondering how Duck ever met Alexa. They must have gone to the same school, had the same classes, and been forced to sit by each other. Or maybe they were neighbors that grew up together like cousins.

Fats moved from the counter away from Duck.

Duck sipped his coffee and followed him.

Fats turned around and said, "Hey, how long have you known Alexa?"

Duck choked, then wiped his mouth with the back of his hand. "That's none of your business. You're like forty years old, and we're dating. So stop asking about her."

"Dating?"

"Yes, R. Kelly."

Fats straightened at the insult.

Duck tilted the cup to his lips and finished drinking the coffee. He tossed the cup into the garbage can, side-eyed Fats, and then went back downstairs where Dad was.

Alexa arrived at eleven.

Fats watched her intensely from the counter. She drove in and parked unevenly with her tires across the dividing line and got out smiling, as if she knew she had double-parked but had no control over it.

She waved cordially and said good morning to Fats.

He said good morning back and smiled.

"You aught a feed 'em a snack," Duck said when she approached. They embraced each other softly and kissed. *Kissed.* "He's like a damn dog. 'I'm so happy. I'm so happy my owner's here!'"

"Be nice," Alexa said.

Fats said nothing. Duck smacked Alexa's backside, then told her to get dressed.

She ran downstairs.

Duck turned to Fats. "Slow day today, huh?"

Fats hardened his face and pursed his lips.

Dad came upstairs. "I might have to send one of y'all home. But let's give it another hour."

Fats looked at Dad. *Alexa just got here, and now you're sending me home?* "You cut my hours last week. How am I gonna pay you rent?"

Duck scoffed.

"I said we'll give it another hour," Dad said.

Alexa came upstairs in the blue coverall uniform just as a car dove onto the lot.

They started service on the vehicle. Fats worked under the hood as Alexa vacuumed the interior. Dad spoke with the customer in the lobby. Duck drained the motor oil and replaced the oil filter from the lower bay. He came up when he finished, goofing around, watching Alexa jump for a roll of blue paper towels in the cabinet high above her head. She needed it to clean the car windows. Fats filled the engine with motor oil and started replacing the air filter.

"Fats," Alexa called out. "Can you get this roll of paper towels for me, please? Since you're not going to do it," she said to Duck.

Fats jerked his head up from under the hood. He dropped the new air filter and bolted over to the cabinet where the roll was. Duck cut in front of him and grabbed the towels.

Fats jumped, tried to take them from him, and missed. "She asked me to do it!"

"Calm down," Duck said. "I already have it." He lowered the roll down at his side.

Fats slapped it out of his hand.

They got in each other's faces.

"You guys, it's not that serious," Alexa said.

"Knock that shit off," Dad said, stepping out of the lobby, onto the bay.

Neither one of them broke their gaze. Duck called Fats a faggot, and that's when Dad decided to send Duck home.

Five minutes later, Fats stood outside with his hands in his pockets, looking down at the ground, listening to the traffic. Alexa came over and asked if he was okay. He kicked at nothing, keeping his head down. "I'm fine," he muttered.

Then he realized . . . she was speaking to him!

He looked at her, happy-faced. "So, how are you liking the job so far?"

But before she could answer, a car pulled in. Then another. And another. They were busy for the next hour. As they worked, Fats wondered if Alexa liked plants. *Nah. Girls like flowers. But plants last longer,* he argued with himself.

Finally, things slowed. Fats stood around watching Alexa work the push broom. The wind had blown trash all over the bay. In the background, a metal clamp was clanking against a flag pole.

This was his chance. She had already given him an opportunity with the conversation they had earlier. She showed that she at least cared mildly for him. He wanted to ask her what she liked more. Plants or flowers? But he could never get the question out. He couldn't think of how to approach her.

Maybe he'd start by asking for her advice under the guise of buying them for someone else. Maybe he'd surprise her. Yes. That'd be better. Women love surprises.

Dad came upstairs. "Get your ass out of La La Land and find something to do."

Fats turned toward his father, mumbled to himself, and grabbed a broom.

The shop closed two hours earlier on Saturdays, and it was now five o'clock. Dad had left to drop a deposit before it got too dark. Fats locked down the bays and then hurried to catch Alexa, who was heading out the door. "I got you something," he said. "Stay right here."

He returned with a hand behind his back, then handed her a vase of purple and white lilies, a bouquet he bought at Safeway while on lunch. He couldn't wait to see her expression. She made a face like she had stepped in something mushy and then smiled. She sniffed at the flowers and then turned for the door.

He stepped alongside her. "Wait a minute," he said. "I just wanna talk to you for a second."

"I'm sorry, but I have to get going."

"I'll make it quick. I just . . . I just wanna know if you wanna go out sometime?"

"Go out?" She set the vase down politely and looked at him. "I'm seeing Duck. You know that."

"We can go out as friends."

"Uh, I don't think he would like that."

"Well, what about what you like, huh? Earlier, you were talking to me. You're always saying hi to me and smiling at me and stuff."

"Oh my god. I need to go."

"I'll call you."

"I can't give out my number." She turned with her keys and rushed out the door. She made it to her car and unlocked it.

"You forgot the flowers."

She spun around, startled. Her eyes widened as he gave her the bouquet. He reached past her to open the door for her. She clutched the vase and then backed into the driver's seat.

"Drive safe," he said, shutting the door.

Three

Duck played a game of NBA 2K in the morning in his room at his grandparents' house. He showered afterward and then took Alexa's car to the car wash. He washed it, emptied it of garbage, vacuumed it, wiped the dashboard down clean, toweled the wheels, and waxed the tires to a glossy shine. Then, he drove to the daycare where his car was parked. He and Alexa had swapped cars the night before so he could pamper hers in the morning. It was Tuesday, his second day off for the week. He stepped inside the daycare.

"Hey, Duck," said Amy, the daycare owner, standing behind a desk—waving, smiling, and showing her white model teeth. She was five feet, eleven inches tall, wearing glasses with red frames and a tight, red dress to match. The daycare had four classrooms, with one teacher to four children in each room.

Duck greeted her back, then asked about the business. She said it was good.

Enough small talk. "Well, I'm a head back here and drop off her keys," Duck said.

"Okay. You know where to go."

"Thanks." He started for the classroom.

"Oh, hey." Amy clonked over from behind the counter. Duck turned back around.

"My car is making some weird noises, and I was wondering if you could look at it?"

"Sure, just bring it to the shop."

She smiled and rubbed her hands together nervously. "Well, I don't want to risk driving it. Couldn't you just come over and look at it? Pleeease?" She had leaned forward, showing her cleavage, bouncing her body and jiggling her assets.

Duck frowned, then shoved his hands in his pockets. "I'm not a mobile mechanic. Just get it towed or have Stan look at it." Stan was her husband and co-owner of the daycare.

Amy smiled again. "Right. Well, Stan isn't very competent in that department. He hasn't checked my oil in months."

Duck shook his head and shrugged. "Well, I don't know what to tell you. Sorry." He turned and continued to the classroom.

Alexa was in a chair reading to the children. He stopped at the doorway and quietly eased himself against the doorpost, hoping he wouldn't disturb them. The four children sat down around her. Silent. Elbows on their knees. Little chins in their palms. Alexa's voice was soft, flowing in a rhythm that could either put you to sleep or mesmerize you. She finished the story.

Duck walked in and waved to the children.

"Ducky!" The children popped up and mobbed him, tapping his legs and talking over each other to get his attention.

"I have an owie," a little boy said, raising his elbow. He pointed to the Snoopy Band-Aid covering the scab.

Duck looked at it and said, "Ouch!"

"My bruh-der," said a girl. "My bruh-der. He's sick."

"Well, I hope he gets better soon."

"I have a puppy," another child said—a small boy wearing thick eyeglasses.

"Oh yeah?" Duck asked. "What's his name?"

The boy giggled, then ran from him.

Alexa walked up to Duck. "Okay, you guys, settle down," she said to the kids.

Duck smiled, then he and Alexa swapped keys, as they had the night before.

"Miss Davis! Miss Davis!" said a girl. "Can Ducky read us a story?"

"Yeah!" the others cried, then gathered to sit in a semicircle.

Alexa glanced at Duck, smiling.

"Okay," Duck said. "One story. And what shall Ducky read to the children?"

They named various books at once: *Goldilocks. Henny Penny. One Teddy Bear Is Enough!*

Duck went to the cluttered bookshelf full of thin paperbacks, wide hardbacks, and thick board books. He fingered through them and smiled when he saw *The Snowy Day.* He selected it and one other book by Dr. Seuss called *The Foot Book.* He grabbed a chair and sat down next to Alexa.

When he finished reading, the children mobbed him again.

A girl climbed onto him and began playing with his hair. He turned his head playfully as she pinched at his scalp. "Ow! Ow!" he cried jokingly. She laughed hard, as if tickled, then giggled in anticipation of the next swivel of his head.

"Alexa, you have a visitor," Amy said, appearing suddenly. Duck looked at Alexa, who stared back at him, confused.

Alexa looked at Amy. "Okay," Alexa said. "Well, who is it?"

"I don't know. Some guy. He said it was urgent."

Duck playfully jerked his head away from the girl playing with his hair. The child giggled again.

"Can you stay here with the kids then?" Alexa asked Amy.

"Sure."

Alexa left the room and found Fats standing at the end of the corridor.

Fats straightened when he saw her.

Alexa stopped and then continued slowly down the hall.

"Hey," Fats said, meeting her. "I was on lunch and—" He handed her a plastic bag. "I thought you might be hungry. It's teriyaki." He rubbed his hands in anticipation of her gratitude.

Alexa received the bag without looking inside it. She looked shocked.

Fats heard the clonk of high heels and looked over Alexa's shoulder at Amy, who was staring at them.

Alexa turned to look at her, then faced Fats again. "You know, Duck has already brought me lunch." She handed the bag back to Fats.

He frowned, taking it, then peeked over her shoulder again. "Is he here?"

"Yes, he's here. He's my boyfriend, Fats, and this is not okay."

"Your boyfriend? I thought you guys were only dating."

She sighed. "I have to get back to work." She turned and walked off.

"Sorry, I was just . . . I'll see you later this week." He watched her disappear, glanced at the lady creeping toward him, winced in irritation, and left.

The classroom was loud, with screaming children chasing each other. They ran up to Duck repeatedly, panting, exclaiming that they were hungry. It was five minutes past their lunch-time. He guessed sack lunches were in the refrigerator but didn't know if any of the children had allergies or dietary restrictions. Where was Amy? he wondered. And what was taking Alexa? He got up and stepped into the hallway, almost bumping into her.

She jumped, alarmed.

"My bad," he said. "Who was that?" he asked, looking down the hallway.

"Nobody," she said. "Just a parent." Her hand touched his shoulder, then fell like water down his arm.

He nodded, unable to identify the person who'd just left, and then looked into her eyes. "Well, the kids are hungry. I didn't know what to do. Sorry." He checked the time on his phone. "All right." He sighed. "I'm a head out. Text me when you get off, though. I have a surprise for you."

"A surprise?"

"Yep." He hugged her, then kissed her, and said goodbye to the children.

Duck arrived at the apartment he had rented for the night from Airbnb, searched under the doormat for the key, and went inside.

It was a nice flat, well-furnished with a gas fireplace and a modern dining room set that looked expensive. Plus, there was a dimmer knob on the wall that controlled the lighting of the chandelier above it. *That's going to make it even more romantic,* Duck thought.

He checked the rest of the apartment, then went to QFC, where he bought groceries and paid a stranger to buy him a bottle of Cabernet. Duck cooked and set up the food. He then met with Alexa nearby and led her to the complex.

They climbed the stairs. "Where are we going?" she asked behind him.

"I told you, it's a surprise."

"Whose place is this?"

He stepped to the door and unlocked it, then let her in. She walked inside smiling. "What is this?" she asked.

"Airbnb. So tell your mom you're not coming home tonight."

She smiled harder and then studied the unit.

He watched her as she looked around, then took her coat and hung it in the closet.

He turned the dimmer knob, lowering the lights until there was a somber feel to the room. He started the music, playing Maxwell's "Lake by the Ocean." The music was softer than chocolate mousse, and the lights above dimmed like gold specks on a black shirt.

"Have a seat," he said, pulling out her chair. She sat down, grinning, then placed her hands in her lap.

He removed the silver plate cover, revealing two halves of eggplant stuffed with ground buffalo, topped with diced tomatoes and bread crumbs. Then he brought out the asparagus he had baked in olive oil. He put four spears on her plate, then dashed sea salt all over them. "Is that enough?"

She said yes. He poured her a glass of red wine and placed a garden salad beside her.

Maxwell continued to sing. *It's just you. Just us. Nobody but love. On trust. On us. Nobody now . . .*

Alexa forked her salad.

Duck asked if it was okay.

She smiled and nodded yes. Then she tried the eggplant.

"That's ground buffalo," he said proudly.

"Mm." She seemed impressed. "It's very fine," she said. "Not coarse like ground beef."

"It's not cold, is it?"

"No. Everything is perfect."

He smiled at that, then dug into his dish. He asked about Alexa's workday, then made a joke about Fats, comparing him to a horny panda.

"Hey," she said, setting her fork down. "I've been meaning to talk to you about that."

"About what?"

"That. Why do you do that? Talk about that guy like that?"

He didn't know what to say. Things were going well, and he just changed the mood.

Wait. "Are you defending him?"

"This isn't about him, this is about you. You tease him at work, and now you're talking about him when he's not even here. That's childish," she said. "Just like you playing that stupid *video game.*"

"You love my Xbox."

"No. I don't. And I'm serious. What did Paul say? 'When I was a child, I played as a child . . . but when I became a man I put away childish things.' You're a man, Carlos. And a good one, so show it."

He felt warm with guilt. Why did she always have to be so heavy? But then again, this is why he loved her.

Fuck her, a voice said.

He looked around, turned the music down with the remote, listening to the dining room.

"What?" she asked.

"Did you hear that?"

"Hear what?"

Maxwell sang, *Can we swim a lake by the ocean . . . You're wasting your time.*

Duck muted the music.

"You didn't hear that?"

"No. Hear what?"

She doesn't love you.

He pushed himself back from the table. "There's someone here."

She looked at him, confused. "There's nobody here, Carlos."

He got up, took a deep breath, and then crept into the hallway, around the corner into the bathroom. He slung the shower curtain back, surprised to see no one there.

An infant cried from one of the rooms. He stormed into the master bedroom, yanked the closet door open, then tore the bed apart, looking for the baby. The cry grew within the walls and boomed from the ceiling, wailing louder and louder and louder as if a giant infant were hungry or needed to be changed. He yelled for the baby to shut up. Then, the cry tapered into silence.

He breathed hard. He could feel his heart thudding in his chest—like a boulder tumbling down a cobblestone hill. He was sweating. His hands were shaking. He headed back to the dining room.

Alexa stood in the hallway, staring at him.

He walked past her, saying, "I heard a baby."

He sat down, scooting up to the table.

She followed, then stood gawking at him.

He picked up his fork. "C'mon. The food's getting cold."

She came to the table and sat.

He looked down at his plate and tried to fork a bite of salad with his trembling hand. He brought it to his mouth, but the food fell onto the plate. He tried again and again, then set the fork down, flustered.

"Duck, what's going on?"

He raised his eyes to Alexa. "I told you, I heard a baby back there." She stared at him with concern. He blinked, then looked away at a window.

She sighed, then pushed her food around on her plate. "How's your mom been?" she asked. "When's the last time you visited her?"

He glanced at Alexa. He hadn't seen his mom in months. She lived far north and had been diagnosed as a paranoid schizophrenic when he was in grade school. She locked them in their apartment once. Taped newspaper to every window and mirror and broke every electronic, calling them *wicked devices of the devil*. He was seven years old when it happened. He remembered hiding in his room after seeing her rave at invisible people. She was disheveled. Maddened. Her brown eyes were stripped of life. Her black hair was wild and beast-like. She looked derelict. The police were called three days later by his grandparents, who subsequently adopted him.

Mom became homeless afterward but eventually got housing through the state and now lives in a cluttered apartment. She had a boyfriend Duck didn't like. The boyfriend wore sunglasses in the dark and never said anything to anyone. The last time Duck visited, he spent two hours cleaning while the boyfriend sat in the recliner shelling peanuts. He tossed them into his mouth and grunted, swiping at the residue that flaked his sweater.

"It's been a while," Duck said, rubbing his forehead.

"Well, you should go see her."

He shut his eyes, humming to drown out the voices. They seemed to be rising in volume as if someone were slowly turning a knob up in his head.

"Have you ever thought about seeing a doctor?"

He opened his eyes and said, "A doctor for what?"

She cleared her throat softly. "You know it can be hereditary."

"There's nothing wrong with me, Alexa."

"You're hearing things, Carlos."

He stood up.

She doesn't respect you.

He grabbed his head. A pounding attack of chatter filled the space of the living room.

He rushed to the bathroom and locked the door. Ran the faucet, splashed his face, and prayed hard. "God, please make them stop. Make them stop!"

Alexa knocked. "Carlos?"

He looked in the mirror and screamed at himself.

She knocked again, then twisted the locked door knob, calling his name over and over.

He ran the tub water, threw his head under it, and then sat down on the toilet, rocking. He stepped out ten minutes later. His face was wet with tears and water.

Alexa hugged herself and stepped back.

He saw her frightened eyes, the living room, then the door.

Murmurs. Whispers. A high pulse and a crying need for silence.

She had asked him a question and was waving at him now. "Carlos, will you say something, please?"

Say something, please.

He giggled, then started to sing: "Father Abraham—had many sons. Many sons had Father Abraham. I am one of them. And so are you. So let's all praise the Lord." He laughed and clapped in rhythm.

"Okay. Why don't you sit down?" She reached out, slowly, took his hand, then guided him into the living room.

He sat down on the couch and then held his head. The words fast-forwarding inside his skull. Looping. Reverberating.

Stab yourself. Stab yourself right in the ear. Go ahead. Puncture your eardrum.

"Leave me alone," he groaned. It was worse than a migraine.

He wanted Alexa. He looked up to see her on her phone. Five minutes after she hung up, the medics arrived. The EMT's walked in and asked Duck several questions. They took his blood pressure, gave him water, and asked if he wanted to be admitted to a hospital.

"No," he said. "It's just a headache." He palmed his head and then looked up. "It'll go away soon."

"Sir," said the paramedic. "If you have a family history of—"

"I'm fine!"

Now fuck off.

"I'm fine."

The paramedics asked a few more questions, then zipped their black EMT bags and apologized for not being of more help. Alexa saw them out.

Duck rocked back and forth for an hour, sometimes laughing—other times crying. Alexa sat beside him and held him close, then went to the bathroom and returned with a hot towel for his forehead. He closed his eyes when she applied it. He felt the heat and moisture over his face and neck. Her tender hand rubbed his back. Then he felt her massaging his temples.

The voices quieted ten minutes later. But Duck was still too upset to drive, so Alexa took him home to his grandparents. She helped him to his room, where he climbed into bed. Finally, he was able to rest.

Four

Fats poured antifreeze into the coolant reservoir of the car. His stomach continued to bellow and gnaw on itself. Because of Duck, he'd been working all day without any breaks or lunch. Both bays had been backed up for hours, and every time they got a car out, more cars would come. Fats huffed and squinted up at the time. Another hour before he was off. Another hour before he could eat. Another hour before he could go home and have a cold beer. He skipped vacuuming and started cleaning the car windows.

Dad came upstairs and lifted the hood of the truck in bay two. He had just drained the old motor oil and was about to refill the engine when a familiar voice called out.

Fats stopped wiping the windshield, looked up, and saw Alexa standing by the register, waving to Dad.

"Baby Girl!" Dad exclaimed. "Get over here!"

She walked carefully across the oily surface to Dad.

Fats turned and said, "What's up?" as she passed him. She said nothing. Didn't even look his way.

She and Dad began talking.

Fats went around to the other side of the car, spraying and wiping the windshield, looking across at them. Dad continued working as Alexa talked. It was strange seeing her on a weekday. He wondered why she was here. Maybe Duck had been in an accident, and she was telling Dad about Duck's paralysis and how he'd never walk again. Duck's grandmother did call in for him this morning. Maybe he was in a coma. Or in a body cast. Alexa shook

Dad's hand, smiled, and mouthed, "Thank you," then left promptly, walking around Fats to her car.

He watched her climb in and drive away, then turned to Dad, asking, "What was that about?"

"Her quitting." Dad slammed down the hood of the truck. "Now, let's get these cars out."

Fats stared at him with his mouth open. Dad came up beside him, checking his work.

"You top off the fluids?"

Fats remembered what he was doing and said, "Yeah."

"All right then, let's roll it out."

Fats unlatched the hood prop and started to close the hood.

"Stop," Dad said. "Ain't you forgetting something?"

Fats re-propped the hood. He stared at the engine. Saw both the oil cap and the coolant cap were in the corners he'd left them in. He put them in their proper places, shut the hood, then climbed in the car. He drove out, watching Dad's arm signals. *She still has to pick up her check.* So he would talk to her on Friday.

But when he got home, he found he couldn't wait. He looked in his phone, pulled up the number he got from her job application, and texted: **What happened? I thought you were saving up for an apartment.**

She replied: **Who is this?**

He assumed she would know by the questions. He texted back his name, then waited, and waited, and waited. Then he tried to call. After two rings, it went to voicemail. He guessed he would see her Friday.

Dad put the checks in the cash register, underneath the black compartment tray, where he hid the big bills. Alexa wouldn't be able to pick up her paycheck, until after six o'clock, unless she decided to get it on her lunch break. Fats went to sneak her paycheck out of the register when Dad went downstairs. Fats saw that Duck's check was on top of Alexa's and thought: *He must not be coming back. Good.* Duck had called in two days straight, and today was a no-show. Fats wondered if it had anything to do with Alexa. Maybe they had broken up. Maybe they were avoiding each other.

Fats clocked out for lunch and sat in his car for five minutes to see if Alexa would show. She did not. He drove to her job. Walked in and saw the same vigilant white lady standing ready behind the counter.

"May I help you?" she asked.

"I'm here to see Alexa."

"I'm sorry, but she's busy at the moment. Are you a parent?"

"No, I'm not a parent," he said, knowing she remembered him.

He heard the commotion and turned, seeing a line of excited children being led across a distant hallway. The woman guiding them wasn't Alexa. And neither was the woman trailing them. He sighed and faced the lady again.

"I just need to give her something," he said. He reached in his front coverall pocket for the check, then presented it to the lady.

She kept her eyes on him and said, "You're welcome to leave it here with me if you'd like, but right now, she is busy."

Fats stepped away from the counter, looked about the hallway again, then peered back at the lady. "It's kind of important. I want to make sure she gets it."

"Well, sir, as I said, you can leave it here with me. My name is Amy, and I'm her employer." She smiled.

He smacked his lips, put the check back in his pocket, and then went to his car and sat. If Alexa is on lunch, she'd be free to come out and get the check. He wanted to see her and wanted to see her badly. Maybe she was wearing a pretty dress or skin-tight yoga pants. He remembered her saying she took ballet classes in grade school. He wondered if she was still flexible. She probably was, with that body. *I bet she could do the splits, or put her legs behind her head. Damn.*

He reached into his pocket for his phone and texted: **Here at your job. Trying to drop off your check.** He hit send and set the phone down in the center console. He watched his phone for a long minute. No response yet. He clicked on the radio, then clicked it back off. He stared at the phone again. Then pressed the side buttons to see if it was working. He set it back down. After six minutes, it buzzed. He snatched it and read the message.

Just leave it with Amy. But after this, you have to stop texting me, or I will be forced to block you.

"Stop texting you?" he muttered. "All I ever did was be nice to you. So what are you talking about?"

He texted rapidly: **Well, fuck you too, bitch. I hope somebody rapes you.** Then, five minutes later, he texted: **Sorry, I was mad.**

He returned to work and put the check back underneath the tray in the cash register. Dad interviewed people throughout the week. By Thursday, they had two new hires. One from Grease Monkey, and the other from Job Corps.

Fats was in the lower bay training the kid out of Job Corps when Dad came down.

"We need to talk when you're done," he said to Fats.

"About what?" Fats asked.

Dad didn't respond. He just stood with his arms crossed. Staring and waiting.

Fats shook his head. Side-glanced the kid. "All right, look," Fats told him. "All you have to do is tighten this thing on." Fats finished his work, then ducked out from under the truck. He followed Dad upstairs, wondering what he wanted. As far as Fats knew, he'd been doing everything right.

He stopped cold at the sight of the sheriff.

"Fasir Mansur?"

"Yeah?" Fats answered, confused.

"I'm here to serve you a protection order. As of today, you are not to have any contact with Alexa Davis. That includes text, email, and phone calls. You cannot be within five hundred feet of her person. If you violate any of these conditions, you will be arrested. Do you understand?"

Fats nodded.

"Good. You have a hearing on the date listed below. At the hearing, the court will decide whether or not to extend this order. At the hearing, you will be able to argue your case. If you decide not to show, the motion will automatically be granted and sustained for one year or more." The sheriff handed Fats the clipboard. "I need you to sign here saying you've received these documents."

Fats signed the form and gave it back to the sheriff.

The sheriff handed him four pages of conditions and left.

Fats glanced over the first page. The hearing was in ten days. He never even touched Alexa. All he ever did was exchange a few words with her. He turned to face Dad, who had gone to check out a customer. The kid who used to work at Grease Monkey was guiding the other kid out of the second bay.

Dad folded the customer's receipt into the shape of a legal envelope. Dad smiled and handed it to the man, pressed his hand, and clapped his back. Dad then asked the newbies if they would be all right for ten minutes. They said yes.

Dad bee-lined over to Fats and said, "Let's talk."

Fats followed Dad downstairs to the office, where he was told to sit.

Fats sat down at the table, five feet across from Dad. Fats rolled the restraining order up and squeezed it tight.

"What's going on?" Dad asked.

"Nothing."

"Something's going on. You're getting served a protection order at *my* establishment in front of *my* customers."

Fats looked away at the coffee machine, then down at the anti-slip mat beneath him. He leaned left with his elbow on the armrest. Thumb under his chin.

Dad went on. "You're constantly late and show up to work smelling like a bum. I hire people and lose them."

"I don't have anything to do with that."

"You've been harassing that girl."

"Harassing her? All I did was give her some fuckin' flowers."

Dad sighed. He tilted his head, left, right, and then looked straight at his son. "Look, I'mma have to let you go."

"Let me go?"

"You have a week to move out."

"What? And you're kicking me out?" Fats stood up and said, "Fuck you! You ain't never done shit for me. Never! You're kicking me out for what? Huh? Man, fuck you."

"Get your shit out of my house. *Now.* I've done enough for your sorry ass."

Fats yelled and swiped at the desk. Stacks of paper and pens hit the floor.

Dad rose.

Fats stormed out, stomped upstairs, threw himself inside his car, and swerved off.

He stopped by 7-Eleven, bought a six-pack of Steel Reserve 211 beer, sat in the parking lot, and drank can after can until he was done. He climbed out of his car and toddled to the back of a dumpster to make water. He saw specks of blood in his urine and looked away. Swayed. Shook. Zipped. Climbed back into his car and waited for four hours.

Fats parked a few blocks from the daycare, stepped out of the car, and walked. It was getting dark out. Alexa would be getting off soon. He leaned against a telephone pole. Saw her car in the parking lot. He sipped from a bottle of Burnette's vodka. Spilled some into his beard. He stayed behind the pole and watched. She came out with two other women. They chatted in the parking lot for five minutes and hugged each other before walking to their cars. He took another swig.

He drove home, stumbled into his room, and sifted through the pile of clothes on his bed. He threw dirty sweatshirts and sweatpants across the room. He got tired after three minutes and sat down to rest. Two minutes later, he passed out.

Dad kicked the mattress.

Fats woke up hazy but startled.

"I told you to pack your shit," said Dad.

Fats sat up. Saw a group of Dads hovering above him. Fats blinked and then dozed off again.

Fats woke up being raised like a fish.

"Get the fuck up!" Dad shouted.

He released Fats with a shove.

Fats stumbled sideways and fell onto a mound of dirty laundry.

"Start packing your shit," Dad said.

Fats groped through the clothes and pushed himself up. Dad was gone.

Fats grabbed toiletries, canned goods, and clothes, stuffed what he could inside his backpack, and put the rest into a garbage bag. He threw the garbage bag and backpack into the trunk of his car, then put his blanket and pillows on the passenger side.

He drove to Newcastle Library, saw the lot had too much lighting, and continued east, passing the apartments on his left, where plenty of tall trees and shrubbery were. He made a U-turn and parked close to the curb. He shut off the motor.

He zipped his coat over his sweatshirt, then covered himself with the thick blanket. He pushed the seat back and reclined with two pillows under his head.

He thought back to how many times he'd been homeless. One winter night, he'd slept in his car and woke in a cold sweat, shivering, drenched down to his feet. He didn't think that was possible until it had happened to him. How could you sweat if you were freezing? He still wondered about that. Fall was approaching. He needed to find work and shelter fast.

Fats drove to LA Fitness in the morning. He parked and watched the girl at the front desk work for half an hour. He studied how she answered the phone, her posture, where she looked as she held the receiver, and how much attention she paid to the members coming in. He observed how long and how often she texted. Then he waited.

Five minutes later, someone drove into the parking lot and parked across from him. Fats popped the trunk open, got out, took off his coat, and tossed it into the trunk. He snatched his backpack, closed the trunk, and climbed back into the car. He waited for the driver to step out. The girl raised her head and answered the phone. The man got out of his car and headed toward the building. Fats climbed out and covered his head with his hood. He carried his backpack over one shoulder and walked with his head down.

The man held the door open for Fats.

He thanked the man, half-smiling.

The girl hung up the phone. The man went right, Fats turned left, and the girl said nothing. Fats walked into the shower room, sat on a bench, and opened a locker. He got undressed and showered.

The next night, he slept at the National Cemetery, where he once worked replanting headstones one year. He remembered how big the property was, how dark and peaceful it was at night, and how they had no security for the grounds. He woke up at dawn before anyone arrived, then parked at the public library where he could wash up and use their computers to watch videos once it opened. He lived this way for a week, finding various spots to sleep where it was dark. Then Dad called him to pick up his final paycheck.

Fats picked it up and cashed it at Walmart, paid fifty dollars toward his prepaid cell phone, filled up his gas tank, and then drove to a laundromat to take a birdbath and do laundry. Afterward, he stopped by a diner. It was one of the few places a registered sex offender could find employment.

He walked in and approached the server behind the register. She had just finished cashing out a customer.

"Is there a manager available?" Fats asked.

The cute girl lost her smile, looking worried. "You want to speak to a manager?"

"About a job, yeah."

"Oh." Her smile returned. "Okay." She nodded, then sped off. Seconds later, a large white man appeared.

"May I help you?" the man asked.

"Yes, I was wondering if you guys were hiring."

The boss nodded. "We are actually. For a dishwasher. Any experience?"

"Yeah, I was a busser for Denny's a while back. And I also worked at Shari's."

"Great. Well, let me grab you an application." The man walked off to the office and returned with the application. Everything was working out smoothly.

"I'm sorry," Fats said. "I didn't catch your name?"

"Ron."

Ron. Fats committed the name to memory.

"My name is Fasir, but everybody calls me Fats," Fats said, extending his hand.

Fasir was the name his father had given him. A name most teachers had a hard time saying, even with a college education. By middle school, kids were calling him Fats. Short for Fasir, but equivalent to Fat Boy.

He sat down at a table, filled out the application, and handed it to Ron when he was done.

"Like I said, I worked at diners before," Fats said. "So I know what needs to be done."

Ron looked over the application and nodded. "Okay, when can you start?"

"I can start now if you want."

Ron laughed. "How 'bout we start you tomorrow night? Come in at ten. I won't be here, but the night manager will be. His name is Brian. You'll work from ten p.m. to six a.m. Wear black pants. There'll be a dishwasher here to train you."

"Thanks," Fats said, pumping Ron's hand. Fats left and stopped by Dollar Tree to get more food for the week, then lounged at the public library until it closed.

He showed up for work at 9:45 p.m. the next day.

"You're here early," Brian said, impressed. He was maybe fifty years old. Six feet, two inches tall. White with loose, reddened skin. Gimpy, as if he had a hip replacement. Overall he was kind. His handshake was gentle. "All right, well, let's get started."

Brian gave him a brown button-up. Fats went to the bathroom and put it on. After he came out, Brian introduced him to Adam, the tall white busser. Adam told him to put on an apron. Fats grabbed one and tied it on. They loaded the dishwasher and went to the dining area with a bus tub. They filled it with dirty dishes, washed them, sorted out silverware, wiped down tables, and filled the bus tub again.

Adam trained him for an hour, then took off his black apron. "You got this?"

"Yeah, I got it."

"All right then, buddy, it's all yours." Adam clocked out and left.

Fats filled the machine, pulled the lever, and pressed the start button. He liked the job already and felt good about keeping it for a while. He enjoyed working alone. He had his station, and nobody bothered him except Rita.

"Hi, how are ya?" she asked, approaching him. She was a slender old woman, around his height at five feet, four inches tall. She reminded him of Betty White. Aging but infinitely vibrant. Small but vitally large.

"I'm fine." He tried to be short with his words. He wanted to focus on work, not conversation.

She said her name was Rita. She asked if he had any experience as a busser, where he grew up, if he had any kids, and if he lived nearby.

He answered yes, Washington, no, and yes, sprayed down dirty dishes, and continued loading the washer.

She introduced him to Javier, the cook, and then introduced Fats to Kelsi and Olivia, the other two servers. The women happily greeted him and then went back to work. But Rita lingered and talked.

"You're so quiet," she said. "Well, if you have any questions, let me know."

He finished the dishes, wiped tables, and set the silverware for the servers.

He returned to the dishwasher.

Rita came back with a bus tub full of glasses.

"These glasses are still dirty," she said. She set down the bus tub on the stainless steel table, picked up a glass, and held it up. "Is that soap, ya think?"

"I don't know. Just leave it."

Rita left it and came back three minutes later. "There's been an accident in the women's bathroom. Can you take care of it, please?"

Fats went to the women's bathroom and mopped the vomit someone had spewed.

He came back to three bus tubs loaded with dishes.

"We need silverware right away," Rita said, blazing by with a plate of food in each hand.

Fats started on the silverware.

A minute later, she yelled through the pass-through. "They want it medium rare, not well-done." She left the plate at the pass-through window and vanished.

Javier, who was cooking an omelet, hash browns, French toast, and three eggs sunny-side up, asked Fats if he wanted the steak.

Fats nodded. Javier put it in a to-go box for him.

After work, Fats sat down at a booth and ate.

He passed out.

Rita slid in next to him. "What a night, huh."

His eyes popped open.

"So, how do you like it so far?" Before he could answer, she said, "The weekends are always busy. It's tough at first. But you'll get used to it."

Fats rubbed his forehead, sighed, and then clenched his jaw.

"You're tired, aren't ya? Well, good job tonight." She rubbed him on the back, then got up.

Fats watched everyone leave. As the night crew vanished, the morning crew arrived. First the cook, then the waitresses, then Ron. Ron came in carrying a briefcase. Fats wondered what was in it, then fell asleep again. He slept until he was tapped on the shoulder.

"You okay?" Ron asked.

Fats blinked himself awake and said, "Yes."

"Good. Well, this is a diner, not a motel. Go home now and get you some rest."

Fats nodded and slid out of the booth.

Home to rest? Home to a cold and cramped car, with windows that fog up and sweat. Home to poverty. Home to depression. He checked the time. It was ten minutes to nine a.m. The Liberty Park Library opened in little more than an hour.

He sat in the library parking lot until ten, went in, and slept in a comfortable armchair until the library closed at five. During the week, it closed at nine, except on Friday when it closed at six. He gathered himself up and thought about where to go next. He sat in his car, then brought out his phone to search for an apartment. He found a unit on Craigslist renting for six hundred dollars. Month to month. Right there in Renton, Washington. The place was close by, off of Edmonds. They wanted the first month's rent and a six hundred-dollar deposit. No credit check or background check. Only one unit was available. He called the number and spoke to Matthew. He invited him to look at the place. Fats stopped by the building.

He pulled up to see an obese white man who looked like he weighed about four hundred pounds. The man was standing outside the two-story building. Fats got out and looked at the complex. It was old and rickety. The second window on the right, below the triangle roof, was broken. The wooden stairs leading up to the entrance leaned. The left door had a drop slot, and the right door was missing.

The large man, who was Matthew, greeted Fats. Fats walked over to him, shook his hand, and then followed him inside the building.

They went up splintered stairs that creaked, then right, into a filthy hallway. Matthew began explaining the building's history. It was once a morgue, so every room was small and windowless. Two bathrooms were on each floor, but they only had sinks and toilets. Shower stalls were separate and shared.

"If you're going to move in," said Matthew. "I advise you to buy shower shoes." The halls reeked of weed and cigarette smoke. And at least one tenant had a dog. Fats could hear it yapping.

They stopped at a vacant unit. Matthew unlocked it and let him enter. The room was dreary, with no lighting and a stained carpet. There was a refrigerator and nothing else inside the unit. Not a sink. Not a stove. Not a window or a cabinet. Just four hundred square feet of floor space.

The large man said, "We've been getting a lot of calls. When are you looking to move in?"

Compared to where Fats lived now, the place was a mansion. "Uh, as soon as possible. But . . ." He considered how long it would be before he had twelve hundred dollars. He frowned, wishing he had saved something. "It might be another month before I have the money."

"It'll be gone by then."

"Is there any way you can hold it for me? I get paid next week."

"I can't make any guarantees, boss. A lot of people are looking for cheap places."

Fats sighed.

"Just check back with me next week."

Fats nodded, then squeezed the man's hand again.

A week went by. Fats came to work two hours early on Friday to pick up his paycheck. He stood in the office, upset. He listened to Ron explain how pay periods and lag time for new hires worked. Fats tramped out of the office, balling his fists. Now he had to call Matthew and tell him he didn't have the money.

For two days, Matthew didn't answer. It was the weekend. Maybe he was busy. Fats decided to stop by on one of his days off, which were Tuesdays and Wednesdays. He stopped by Tuesday morning. Matthew said the unit was still available. Fats drove by again on Wednesday, imagining he had a home there. He'd buy a floor mattress from Walmart or see what he could find at Goodwill. He'd buy a microwave, a small table, and a hot plate. Matthew agreed to hold the unit for him if he paid the deposit. Fats guessed his first check would be over six hundred dollars. He just had to wait.

He then went to Starbucks on North East Fourth Street. Dad's shop was near, and the daycare was down the street. Fats sat in a leather armchair, dragged over the matching ottoman, and kicked up his feet. He crossed his arms, thinking. He had found a job quickly. Now, he'd soon have an apartment. He fell asleep daydreaming. The manager woke him and then asked him to leave.

He left and drove by the daycare. Soon, he'd be back on his feet. No matter what the court decided. He slowed down, saw Alexa's car in the parking lot, and gave it the finger. The driver behind him honked impatiently. Fats pulled over to let the agitated woman blow by.

He glared at the entrance to the building, then eased off, continuing toward the park on Eighth Street. As he approached the park, he saw a woman leading a line of four small children. They toddled along the sidewalk, holding hands. He slowed again, peering. As he cruised by, he and the woman exchanged glances. It was Alexa.

He continued down Union past Twelfth Street. Turned left onto Sunset. Saw the Renton Highlands Library was open and pulled in. He went in with his backpack stuffed with underclothes and toiletry. He went into the bathroom, lathered a wash towel, and hid inside a stall to wash. He went out to rinse the towel, half-naked at the sink with white foam under his armpits.

A white man entered the restroom, holding an infant. A large diaper bag was strapped over the man's shoulder. Fats turned and grunted as the man laid the baby down at the changing station. Fats returned to the stall to finish washing, using the cold toilet water to complete his ablution. Soon after the man left, a librarian entered the bathroom.

"Sir, is everything okay?" the librarian asked.

"Yeah, man, everything is good," Fats answered from within the stall. He pulled up his pants, having just changed his underwear.

"Sir, you have to leave when you're done."

"Yeah, yeah," Fats mumbled under his breath. He then left and drove back to the park on Eighth Street. He parked under a tree and fell asleep.

He woke up to a hard tap on the window. Blinded by the bright light, Fats held his hand up, blocking it.

The officer moved the flashlight away from Fats's face and shined it on the passenger side, then around the backseat where Fats's backpack and bags of vittles were.

"Roll down your window," the officer said, shining the light back into Fats's face.

He slowly rolled down the window.

"Have you been drinking?" the cop asked.

Fats squinted and said, "No."

"You wanna tell me what's going on, then? Why you're sitting out here?"

"I'm homeless," Fats said in a groggy voice. "But I work close by. At a diner. I was just trying to get some sleep."

"Do you have a paystub?"

Fats hesitated. "I have a paystub but—"

"All right, let's see it, along with your driver's license, registration, and insurance."

Goddamn, man. Shit. A $550 ticket is just what he needed right now. Fats slowly opened the glove box, then carefully picked out his registration and the check stub from Dad's shop. He then cautiously reached into his back pocket for his license. He didn't want to be shot. He looked up at the officer passively. "Uh, I don't have any insurance, and this is a check stub from my last employer. I just started this other job."

The officer took the credentials. "Keep your hands on the dash." He walked back to his squad car.

Several minutes went by. Fats imagined the cop was checking for warrants, then wondered what was taking so long. He tried to see in the sideview mirror, but the spotlight from the squad car was too bright for him to make out anything.

The officer returned and yanked the door open. "Get out and place your hands on your head."

Fats glared at the officer, perplexed.

The officer grabbed him by the arm and pulled him out of the car. Another cop seized Fats by the wrist. Together, they pushed him against the car, bent his arms back, and cuffed him.

He craned his neck and spoke over his shoulder. "What am I being arrested for? I didn't do anything."

"You're under arrest for violation of a no-contact order."

"But I didn't do anything."

They pushed him inside the squad car. The arresting officer slid in and typed on his computer.

"I just got this job, man. Please."

The officer continued typing, then eased out into the street.

This is some bullshit. I didn't even do anything. Fats writhed around on the hard plastic seat. He lowered his head. He wanted to kick at the officer's backrest, but there was no room for him to lift his feet. He felt tears forming with the anger. He huffed, growled, scowled, and quivered his lips.

They arrived at the jail, where Fats was fingerprinted and photographed.

He paced inside the holding cell and then sat down on a bench. He stood again, then returned to his seat. He waited until a female guard appeared. She tossed him folded prison garments, then stood by as he changed into them.

He stripped out of his street clothes and put them into a paper bag as commanded. He put on the used underwear, blue scrubs, loose socks, and rubber flip-flops, then waited thirty minutes before being transferred to population.

He stood at the solid door, facing a tank full of inmates. The sack lunch in his right hand felt weightless. The bedroll and cot under his left arm started to slip. He hunched his shoulder forward to restore the balance. There were over thirty men inside. Most sleeping. Those awake were sitting at the wooden tables playing spades or dominoes. Those without bunks slept on cots laid out on the floor. They were all in there for misdemeanors. That was about the only thing that made Fats feel halfway comfortable, but even then—

The steel door started wheeling itself open. Fats flinched and blinked, recalling the last time he was here. The door clanged, slamming against metal. He walked in slowly and laid his cot in a corner close to the entrance. He glanced around. One of the inmates playing dominoes was staring at him.

Fats cringed. Shit. It was Terror, a forty-year-old Black Gangster Disciple. Crack addict on the streets. Shot caller in prison. Six feet and five inches tall. Gorilla-like arms and chest. Palms the size of helmets. He and Fats were cellmates at Washington Corrections Center in Shelton, Washington, during Fats's first stint.

Terror used to make him sweep out the cell and clean the toilet with a toothbrush. And whenever they gambled, he cheated so that Fats always owed him something.

Terror rose from his seat. Monstrous. Gigantic. Six months healthy in jail, he was no longer crack-head skinny. He was now ripped and athletic.

Fats turned and unfolded his bedding.

"What's up, G?" Terror said, approaching Fats. "Don't I know you?"

Fats knelt and tied the sheet over one end of the plastic mattress. With his back to the man, he said, "No, I don't think so."

"Yeah, I remember you. We were in Shelton together." The man paused, then turned, addressing the prison tank. "Yo, this dude a pedophile!"

Hot fear filled Fats's body. Three inmates got up and surrounded him. He lowered his eyes and cowered. Terror took Fats's sack lunch. The other inmates took his bedding.

He lay on the bare cot with his eyes open until dawn.

Inmates filed by the door, where two correctional officers handed out bulky trays of skimpy breakfast. Fats got in line, took one, and then sat on his cot to eat.

The guards wheeled the food cart away.

The gangster approached Fats, took his tray, and walked off.

At lunch, the GD took his food, again. By dinner, Fats was ready to die.

When night came, he tried to sleep but couldn't. He lay on his cot thinking about how much he hated the inmates and how much he hated life.

The heavy door clanged open again.

The inmates stood and lined up for breakfast. Fats remained on his cot, mentally broken. The officers handed out trays and then wheeled the cart off. When they were gone, an inmate strode over and punched him to the ground. Others joined in and stomped on him.

When he woke up, he was barely able to see. His left eye was half-closed, and his right eye was swollen shut. He held his ribs and hobbled to the panic button by the door. He pressed it three times and breathed hard with his mouth ready by the speaker grille.

"Yeah," a voice said from the speaker.

"I've been assaulted. Please, help me." He wheezed, holding his ribs, and winced when he tried to draw in a deep breath. The sharp pain almost buckled him. The inmates were—no doubt—staring at him, wagging their heads at the idea of him pressing the panic button, and were probably calling him a snitch.

Fuck them. He should snitch on all of them. They were the ones who jumped him. But he dared not to. He stretched his sore mouth open and felt an outrageous clicking in his jaw. He touched his lips. They were fat and bloody and split. His front tooth was chipped—and two of his bottom teeth were loosened. He spat out blood.

Ten minutes later, a troop of guards rushed to the door. They handcuffed him, then took him to the infirmary, and then to solitary confinement.

A guard asked if he had eaten, then brought three sack lunches to his cell.

He ate and rested, then woke up, lying on his back, staring at the concrete ceiling. He was battered all over, aching in his face, thinking. Would he still have a job when he got out? And what about his car, which held all his worldly possessions? He thought about his past and how much he hated Alexa for this.

The clink of prison keys caught his ears. The entrance gate to the cellblock creaked open, then slammed shut again. Every sound echoed. There was an exchange of words between the guard and another man. Then the guard left, leaving the man alone on the cellblock. In a kind voice, he greeted an inmate at the head of the tier. It was the prison chaplain making his way down, preaching the gospel.

Fats stirred in his bed as he heard the man praying for prisoners.

"It doesn't matter what you did," the chaplain told a neighbor. "God loves you."

Fats tore out of bed, disgusted. "Fuck God!" He clenched the bars, yelling. "God don't give a shit about us! What kind of a God lets a child get molested? What kind of a God doesn't protect children?"

The cellblock grew quiet.

"These motherfuckers sell drugs to kids and pregnant women. They shoot and kill each other and then beat me up? Fuck God! I don't wanna hear shit about a god!

Five

Duck lay curled in bed, buried under a heavy comforter with his back to his bedroom door. Secured by warmth and darkness, he intended not to move.

Someone knocked softly and then entered. "It's ten o'clock," Grandmother said. "Why don't you get up? I made you some breakfast."

The mattress sank where she sat down. Ice clanked against the glass loudly, and the smell of turkey links turned Duck's stomach. He imagined her holding a tray of food. He moaned under his pillow and said, "I'm not hungry."

"You're not hungry because you haven't eaten."

He heard footsteps behind her voice. "You've been in this room for two weeks," Grandpa said. "Now get up."

Grandmother shook Duck gently. "Come on now, get up and eat."

He squirmed, then removed the pillow from over his head. He sat upright and felt a spinning vertigo that made him grip the side of the mattress. It passed through him quickly.

Grandmother set the tray on his lap. Breakfast was to be a plate of grits, salted with a pool of melted butter; two plump turkey links; scrambled eggs with cheese; and a glass of orange juice with light ice.

"Eat, and you'll feel better," Grandmother said, rubbing his back. "And when you're done, you can sit with me."

Duck ate a turkey link and a bite of eggs, set the rest of the food on his bed, then went into the living room. He plopped down on the sofa, still wearing his flannel pajamas. Exhausted, feeling like wet cement was pouring out of his eyes, ears, and nostrils. Grandmother was in her rocking chair, watching *The Price is Right,* crocheting.

"How was your breakfast?" she asked, looking at him.

Grandpa had gone to an appointment or to play pool at the senior center, Duck assumed. He glanced at her. "Good."

He looked at the television. A heavyset black woman yanked down a spin from the Big Wheel. The audience applauded and cheered crazily, then moaned when the wheel stopped. Drew Carey expressed sympathy, holding a wand in his hand, then merrily addressed the next contestant. Grandmother spoke faintly as the TV blared over her voice. Words twisted with one another as the host spoke louder and louder.

And then: *Carlos Duckworth, you've just won a brand new car!* Drew Carey shouted, pointing at Duck. The audience clapped hysterically. Drew Carey clapped with them, still holding the thin mike in hand. Grandmother was beside Drew Carey, jumping up and down with excitement.

Duck giggled. "I just won a brand new car!" He looked at Grandmother, who was back in her rocking chair. "Grandmother, you see that? I just won a brand-new car!"

She turned and looked at him, then turned off the TV. "Why don't you shower now that you're feeling better?"

Yeah, you stink, a voice said. He shook his head at the voice, then did as she suggested. By the time he got out of the shower, both his grandparents were in the living room waiting for him.

Grandpa pointed toward the dining room. "Sit down." His tone was harsh and sharp. His demeanor demanding.

"What's going on?" Duck asked.

His grandparents passed him, leading the way into the dining room. Duck turned and followed them to the dining table.

"We need to talk," Grandpa said, pulling a chair.

Talk? About what?

Duck stood at the table, studying their faces. Grandmother's eyes were weary, while Grandpa's showed impatience.

They all seated themselves at the table. Grandmother folded her liver-spotted hands. Grandpa adjusted his hearing aid and then leaned forward, glaring at Duck.

Duck wanted back in his room. The last time they sat him down like this, he was a freshman in high school. Grandmother had found condoms in his room.

"We think you need to see a doctor," Grandpa said.

"A doctor?" Duck asked. "For what?" He looked at Grandmother. She was the more compassionate of the two. Her ageless, round face peered back at him. He wasn't crazy. He wasn't covering windows like Mom or thinking the FBI was out to get him.

"We think you might be sick," Grandmother said, touching his hand.

The gesture fell on him like the kiss of Judas. "There's nothing wrong with me," he said, pulling away from her.

"It's still early," said Grandpa. "The sooner you get help, the better."

"You're not sending me to a hospital!"

"You need help," said Grandmother.

"I don't need any help!"

"This is how it starts," said Grandmother. "Remember how your mom thought she was fine, but the voices kept controlling her?"

"Shut up!" Duck stood up and gnashed his teeth. "Shut up! Shut up! Shut up!" He pointed at himself. "Nobody controls me but me!"

He stormed off to his room, grabbed his hand-grip strengthener, and squeezed it, over and over, as he paced.

Listen.

He stopped to listen. He could hear them arguing.

"He's telling you to shut up in our house!" Grandpa said.

"Well, what else are we going to do?" Grandmother asked, almost crying.

"I'll tell you what we can do," answered Grandpa. But then Duck couldn't make out the rest.

He heard heavy footsteps, the jingle of keys, and then the front door slam.

They're going to send you away to a psych ward. Mechanical restraints and shots in the buttocks. Just like they did to Mom.

They've been watching me, he thought.

He looked over his room, surveying every inch and corner. He snatched the fork he used earlier for breakfast, fell to his knees, and tried to unscrew an outlet.

He realized he needed a flat-headed screwdriver and spent the next twenty minutes in a frenzy searching for one in his room. Then he thought of grabbing a table knife from the kitchen, but the idea of leaving his room troubled him—almost as much as needing to find that hidden camera.

He gave up, sat on his bed, and remembered the fingernail file on his nail clippers. He snatched his keys off the dresser and returned to unscrewing the outlet. He tore off the panel, pulled out wires, and repeated the process until every outlet in the room was dismantled. None of them had a microphone or camera hidden inside.

He lay flat on his bed, looking up.

It's in there! he thought. He quickly stood on the mattress and reached for the light fixture.

Nothing was in it.

He collapsed into a skeletal ball and wept. Weakened by confusion. Distraught in terror.

Hours later, there was a knock.

"Open the door, Carlos. It's me." It was Alexa. For the past few weeks, she'd been coming by after work. She even stayed the night over the weekends.

He lay coiled under the sheets, half wishing she'd go away. Half wishing she'd come in and help him. He listened as she tried the knob. She knocked again. "Carlos, open the door so we can talk." She sighed when he didn't respond. "If you don't unlock the door, we're breaking up."

He got up and answered, then crawled back into bed with his back to her.

He felt her glancing over his room, then forced himself to sit up and face her.

She stood over him, her concerned eyes examining him.

"I can't control 'em," he said, rubbing the back of his neck. "They won't stop!"

She sat down beside him, then squeezed his shoulders and rubbed.

He looked down at his hands.

"Look at me," she said.

He looked at her, trying to manage his thoughts. He was normal, but something horrible was happening to him. Spirits possessed him. A mad circus of faceless beings now lived inside his mind, making him a slave to suggestion. A puppet controlled by impulse. A vessel for demon life.

"You have to get help," she said. "Talk to your mom at least. She can tell you what to do to get better." She said this, caressing his back, and then kissed him. "I can go with you. Whenever you decide."

He expected her to lecture, but she didn't. He wept beside her, shuddering. She started massaging the nape of his neck, gradually working her way up to his temples.

He closed his eyes and visualized seeing his mom. Two days later, he got well enough to visit her.

He stepped out of the elevator into the hallway. It was a big building. A high-rise apartment that housed low-income families and disabled people, twenty-three miles north of Renton, in Shoreline, Washington. He passed by units, carrying a loaded paper bag and a bouquet. Inside the bag were four coloring books, a bag of ginger snaps, and two jigsaw puzzles. Ginger snaps were his mom's favorite snack, and the coloring books and puzzles helped keep her mind busy.

He made it to the apartment and knocked. To his surprise, the door was ajar.

"Who is that?" he heard his mom ask someone inside.

"It's me, Mom," Duck answered.

"Me? Well, come on in, Me."

He pushed the door open and entered. The place was gloomy. Curtains closed. TV flickering without sound. Mom sat on a couch with her knees close to the coffee table, hunched over. She held a jigsaw piece, staring down at a nearly completed puzzle. She looked frail, and her light skin was blotchy. Her black hair was thick and disheveled.

He swallowed what felt like a spud. "Hey, Mom, it's me."

She looked up finally. Her quiet boyfriend grunted. He was sitting in a recliner, watching TV. *Jerry Springer* muted with captions.

Mom wore a bleak expression on her face and then brightened. "My little Ducky," she said, rising. They met each other smiling. Duck hugged her gently, kissed her soft cheek, and squeezed her tighter. She was like a pillow of feathers.

They stood back and observed each other.

"I got you something, Mom."

"Really?" She took the bouquet and explored it.

"And your favorite, ginger snaps," he said, showing her the bag.

She set the bouquet down on the table and received the rest of the gifts he handed her.

"Look at my son, all tall and handsome. Are you hungry? There's Cornish game hen in the fridge."

"No, thank you, Mom. Maybe later."

She set the coloring books and puzzles aside, then tried to open the bag of ginger snaps.

"I got it, Mom." He took the bag and pried it open for her. She sat down on the couch with it, then asked if he could put the flowers in a vase that was somewhere in the kitchen. He did, then returned to the living room.

"How have you been, Mom?" He sat down beside her. She leaned forward with a jigsaw piece, examining the voids of the puzzle.

"I've been okay," she said, concentrating on the puzzle. "I have my off days, you know."

"Well, you're looking good."

"Thank you." She smiled. "The Seroquel helps."

Seroquel?

He thought he remembered the name of the medicine. Then he thought back to when she started taking it. Three years ago, when she had complications with the previous drug. What was it? He couldn't remember.

He didn't like that her hair was unkempt and excused himself to the bathroom to look for a hairbrush. The sink was caked with a gray ring, and the mirror was spotted with white dots. He found a brush but started cleaning the restroom, including the tub.

He returned half an hour later and saw that his mom had completed the puzzle. He sat down beside her and started brushing her hair.

He felt guilty for not visiting sooner and more often. He hoped when he and Alexa had a family that she and the kids would not leave him to be on his own, if he, too, lost his mind. And if he had to be on his own, he hoped he wouldn't have to rely on his children. And that if he was going to be sick, his illness would not frighten them in the way it had scared him into shamefully neglecting his mom. In fear, he promised to build a better relationship with her. In fear, he swore he'd visit her more often. Whether he had the illness or not.

He held a patch of her hair and brushed it. Mom relaxed, tilting her head with the stroke.

He drew in a deep breath. "Mom, I want to ask you about something."

"Okay."

He noticed gray flakes on her scalp and thought about shampooing her hair. He continued brushing. "I wanted to ask you—" He paused, hesitating. "I wanted to ask you about schizophrenia."

There was silence. Long seconds of silence. So long that he wondered if she had even heard him. But then he could feel her thinking. Her frail body stiffened under the hairbrush.

Finally, she said, "What do you want to know about it, Carlos?"

He stopped brushing. "How do you manage it?" he asked. "Or fight it?"

"Fight it?" She turned and looked at him, laughing. "If I knew how to fight it, I wouldn't be on medication."

"I don't wanna take medication."

She frowned. He read her face and knew she understood him. "Have you been diagnosed?" she asked.

"No. Not yet."

"But you're having symptoms?"

He nodded, then shared his experience in detail.

She sighed. "Well, you can talk to the voices, I suppose."

He couldn't tell if she was joking or not. "Talk to them?"

"If you don't want to take meds, talking can help. Just don't give in to them. And talk with someone you trust—to see if what the voices are saying is true because they can be convincing. But you have to see a psychiatrist, Carlos. The sooner, the better. And join a support group. We attend one every Saturday and every second and fourth Wednesday of the month."

"A support group?"

"Yeah. You'll meet people like yourself there. They talk about their own experiences and share ways to cope."

A support group, he thought. *That should help.*

Six

"Fasir Mansur, it's time to roll it up!" a guard said, approaching the cell.

Fats rose from his bunk, quickly rolled his sheets, then stepped up to the cell door. The steel gate motored open. He hefted the bedding over his shoulder, followed the two officers down the cellblock, went through a few corridors, tossed the bedding into a dirty-clothes bin, and took the elevator up with the guards.

They stepped off onto the main floor, where he followed the two officers to a reception station. A female guard with long extension braids gave him a sheet of paper and told him to sign it. He signed and returned it like he'd done so many times before. The excitement of being released was long dead to him. He was merely transitioning from one hell to another now.

She handed him a brown paper bag full of his belongings. He did a quick inventory over the counter and noticed his car keys were missing.

He looked up, stunned. "Where are my car keys? What's going on with my car?"

The guard popped a chewing gum bubble. "Have you been in jail for over thirty days?"

He blinked. "Yeah."

"Well, then it's probably been auctioned off."

What?

His meaty fists clutched the paper bag. "What do you mean it's been auctioned off?"

The officer beside him said, "Hey, buddy, do you want to stand here and argue or go home?" Fats felt his eyes well up with tears of anger, but he said nothing.

Fats got dressed in a holding cell and walked out wearing loose, wrinkled clothing. His black hoodie, his black coat, and his blue jeans fit him as if they were two sizes bigger than the last day he'd worn them.

He handed the county wear to the guard waiting, who then escorted him out into the cold, drizzling rain. Fats looked up at the sky of falling drops, then down at the wet pavement, then across at a car cruising by. The city, the air, the weather—was all new to him again. It was dark and just after two a.m. October thirty-first, according to the calendar he'd seen in the police station. So far a wet Halloween.

He covered his head with the hood of his sweatshirt, shoved his hands in his coat pockets, and headed north, shifting his broad shoulders, and sliding his wide feet. The diner was eight miles away.

He made it to Renton three hours later. He entered the diner, drenched from head to foot. Exhausted.

"Fasir!" Rita ran up as if she were going to hug him, but then stopped. "Oh my god. You're all wet. What happened?"

He pushed back the hood of his sweatshirt and then wiped down his face. "Is Ron here? Or Brian?"

"Sure. Have a seat. I'll get you some coffee." She hurried off.

Instead of sitting he stood and watched, soaked as a dog locked out in the elements. He stamped his feet on the rug and unzipped his heavy, rain-sodden coat.

"Brian, Fats is here," he heard Rita say at the end of the hall.

Brian stepped out of the office and signaled for Fats to come.

Fats met him in the office.

"Have a seat," Brian said.

Fats sat down with his hands in his pockets.

"What happened?" Brian asked.

"I apologize," Fats started. "I got into a situation. Some warrant I didn't know about."

"A warrant?" Brian asked, widening his eyes. "Christ. Well, did you get it cleared up?"

"Yeah, I did." Fats lowered his head, then looked up. "I'm sorry, but . . . is there any way I can get my job back?"

Brian shook his head. "You've been gone for over a month, Fasir. We've already filled your position."

"I can do something else." He leaned forward with begging hands. "I can be a cook . . . or even a server."

"I'm sorry," Brian said. "If anything changes, we'll give you a call."

Fats dropped his head again, then stood to go to the door.

"Hey, you still have a paycheck, remember." Brian reached under the desk into a drawer, then rose with the check. He handed it to Fats, then squeezed his shoulder lightly, saying, "Stay out of trouble now, will you?"

Fats nodded, then left, passing Rita, who pretended to be sweeping outside the office.

He stormed through the double doors of the diner and shouted up at the rain.

Rita stepped outside behind him. "Is everything okay?"

He turned around and faced her, his muscles tense, knotting in the back of his head.

"What happened?" she asked. "Did you ask Brian about your job? Other places are hiring, you know. And you can put me down as a reference."

"Go back inside and leave me the fuck alone!"

She gasped, blinking in horror. "I understand you're upset, but you don't have to curse at me." She snatched the broom and long-handled dustpan and stomped back inside.

Bitch.

He lurched onward to Fred Meyers and waited half an hour for the supermarket to open. His check was seven hundred and twenty-eight dollars. He cashed it at the customer service center, paid on his prepaid cell phone, and then called Matthew about the apartment Fats had planned to rent before going to jail.

It was quarter past seven in the morning, but Big Matthew was up. He answered and told Fats the unit was no longer available. Fats groaned but thanked him anyway, then went to a gas station, where he could buy cheap beer and wine.

He placed a can of Two-Eleven on the counter, along with a carton of Vendange chardonnay. He paid and then asked the clerk if they were hiring. The man said no. Fats cursed him mentally, then walked out with his bag of alcohol.

He stood outside, against the wall of the store, a few feet left of the entrance. He took out his beer and popped it open, then took a sip. A loud group of teenagers dressed in Halloween costumes turned the corner. They passed by him laughing and talking, wearing masks. He took another sip, then turned his attention to them. They stopped at the entrance, staring at the hand-written sign that had been taped to the glass door. Fats recalled what it read.

No Mask Allowed.

The kid leading the group said, "Hey, we have to take off our masks." He and his friends complied, removing them. They went inside.

Fats sipped his beer and grinned wickedly. The teens had just given him an idea.

He caught a bus to Goodwill, in Renton Highlands. It was crowded with a frenzy of last-minute Halloween shoppers. Parents watched their children decide on one disguise, just to watch them change their minds at the sight of another.

Fats grabbed a hand-basket and walked around. He stopped at a display of rubber gorilla heads, took one and slipped it over his face, looked in a mirror, and then down at a blond-haired toddler. The frightened boy grabbed onto his father's leg and then hid behind it. Fats smirked, then pulled off the mask.

He tried the face of the President next, then saw how he looked as a Power Ranger. Dissatisfied, he continued his hunt. He saw a green mask with two black hollow eyes as wide as the mouths of shoes. The face had a murderous darkness to it as if it belonged to a minion of Satan. Fats touched the mask, caressing its felt cheek as if it were the flesh of a woman. He took the mask from the metal rod and tried it on, then found a mirror to examine himself in. The mouth was a thin slit through which he tried to stick his tongue.

He breathed inside the mask slowly, feeling the birth of wickedness tingle throughout his cerebrum. Behind the mask, he felt invisible yet more alive than ever. He peeled it back and placed it inside the handbasket, thinking he needed something to go with it. He browsed around the store to see what else he could find.

Everything was outdated. The electronics he sifted through were mere junk. The sporting goods section was limited to bicycle helmets, tennis rackets, and a few under-inflated balls. The only item that caught his eye was a set of golf clubs. He set down his basket and picked out a nine-iron, holding it tight in his hands. He swung it as if it were a baseball bat and found it too awkward and uncomfortable in his hold. He put it back and left the sporting goods section, then leered around aimlessly, spying on young girls shopping with their parents.

He stopped at the music section, spotting a girl sifting through CDs. Her blond hair stopped at her waist, and she was wearing a blue-and-yellow Hazen High School sweatshirt with black leggings. He inched along closer to her, pretending to browse through the section.

A tall white man entered the aisle and approached the girl. "Find anything?" he asked her. Fats quickly surmised the silver-headed man was her father, and took off in the opposite direction to the men's clothing section. He searched through the racks of woven shirts, button-ups, and sweaters. He found a black hoodie that would fit him better, then a pair of black sweatpants to match. He stepped in line to pay for the items.

He went to Lowe's Home Improvement right after. Passing through the parting doors, he saw an available employee trotting off into the aisle ahead of him. Fats rushed to catch him, moving swiftly by paint products.

He was about to shout to get the man's attention when he saw, through his peripheral, a display of 3M tekk-protection chemical gloves. He stopped. Grabbed the first package he saw and read the labeling: *Cotton lining, anti-slip, durable. Long lasting, good dexterity, heavy duty. Resistant to most chemicals.*

What chemicals? he wondered. He read the chart on the back. The list included acetone, chloroform, and sulfuric acid. Then, glowing with satisfaction, Fats strutted to the checkout stand to purchase the gloves. They cost eight dollars and seventy-six cents after tax. He added them to his Goodwill bag of clothes and headed to AutoZone.

While on the bus, he realized he was lucky he didn't ask the Lowe's employee if they sold battery acid. That might have raised suspicion. Plus he was on camera.

He stepped off the bus with his bag and saw that a man was seated at the weather-protected bus stop, sheltering himself from the torrent of heavy rain. The man was resting his head against the glass. His pale face was hooded and full of red sores that looked freshly picked at, raw, and possibly even infected. He had glassy blue eyes and thin, splintered lips. He wore fingerless gloves and blue jeans with soot smeared at the thighs, and a filthy, gray-hooded sweatshirt. His black shoes had Velcro straps (instead of laces) to secure his feet, and the clear soles had been worn to a slant at the bottom. Fats recognized the pair as state-issued Bob Barker tennis.

The bus roared off.

The man lifted his head off the glass and looked at Fats. "Can you spare a dollar?" he asked.

Fats pondered a bit, marveling at the fact that he was seeing someone worse off than himself. He fished in his pocket for currency, then gladly slipped the man a tattered one-dollar bill.

"How long you been wearing them shoes?" Fats asked.

The man gazed down at his feet, then shrugged and said: "I don't know, man. You know where I can get some bubble?"

Bubble was meth. Meth was a hard drug that kept people up for weeks. One of its key ingredients was battery acid.

Fats nodded in answer and headed toward the parking lot behind the bus stop. The man hurried to his feet and followed after him. They walked across the parking lot toward AutoZone.

"I want you to get me a quart of battery acid," Fats said, nodding toward the building. "Should be no more than ten dollars." He reached in his pocket and handed the tweaker a ten, and then a five-dollar bill. "You can keep the change, and I'll give you ten more when you're back."

The man hustled off as Fats waited several feet away, out of view of the cameras.

It was noon. Everyone in the support group was chatting, waiting for the meeting to start. Duck and Alexa followed Mom. She was busy introducing them to others who suffered from mental illness. Everyone was friendly and seemed normal on the surface except for a few tics. One man blinked rapidly as he spoke to Duck, while another man conversed without ever making eye contact at all. But overall they were interesting people. And not all were schizophrenic. The peer group welcomed anyone suffering from any mental illness, including depression and bipolar disorder.

Duck excused himself from Mom and the third family she had introduced him and Alexa to. He went to the snack table, where refreshments had been set up by members of the peer group. He started to reach for a bottle of water when a tall, burly white man seized his hand.

"How are you doing?" the man asked. "I'm Eddie Blodgett." Eddie held a strong grasp and shook vigorously. His beady eyes were wild and deep and his cheeks were fat and clean-shaven. He looked to be in his fifties, and his voice was loud. "You're new here, aren't you?"

"Yes, sir, I'm new," Duck said, rolling his shoulder once his hand was free.

"Drop the sir crap, call me Eddie. Name?"

"Carlos. I'm Carlos Duckworth."

"Duckworth?" Eddie said, jerking his head back. "I saw you come in with Leah."

"Yeah, that's my mom."

"Well, I'll be . . . you look just like her! She never said she had a son."

"All right, everybody, sorry I'm late," a small white man announced. He dragged a chair toward the center of the room. A folder was under his arm, and he was holding a cup of coffee.

Everyone jockeyed for seats. Duck lost track of Mom and her boyfriend and Alexa. He wound up in a chair next to Eddie Blodgett. The group sat in a large circle—thirty persons in total.

The facilitator, as he was called, removed sheets of paper from his folder and handed them to the man on his right. That man took a sheet and then passed the stack to the woman beside him, who repeated the process.

Duck saw Alexa across the room, sitting between Mom and her boyfriend, who was wearing his dark sunglasses, staring straight ahead. Alexa looked out of place between them, but Duck thought she was trying her best to appear comfortable.

"All right, let's get started," the facilitator said. "For those of you who are new, welcome to the Hearing Voices Support Group Meeting. My name is Bert. I, too, suffer from mental illness. I was diagnosed with schizophrenia twenty-one years ago."

Eddie leaned into Duck's right ear and whispered, "Bert? Where's Ernie?"

Duck leaned forward to show that he was paying attention to Bert, then noticed through his peripheral, Eddie repeatedly jerking back his head in involuntary tics.

"We're passing around a sheet of paper with today's topics," Bert said. "Some of you are here with friends and family, who are all welcome to ask questions."

Someone elbowed Duck and handed him the thin stack of papers. He took a sheet and passed it along to Eddie, who passed it along without taking one.

"Okay, topic one," Bert said. "How do we manage our voices?"

A hand shot up.

"Yes, Norman."

"I manage my voice by listening to music."

"Thank you, Norman," Bert said politely. "Now—"

"I talk to mine," a lady said.

"I like to sing," another woman said.

"I like to sing, too!" Mom said.

"I tell mine to shut up, and then I take my meds," a man said loudly across the room.

Everyone laughed.

"All right now, let's establish some order here," Bert interjected.

Duck sat up straight. A man leaned into his left ear and said, "I suffer from bipolar syndrome." Duck glanced at him and then nodded.

Eddie's left arm jerked. Duck flinched, then watched Eddie curl it as if he were flexing out a bad cramp. Eddie stopped, then fidgeted, and threw up his right hand.

"Yes, Eddie," Bert said.

"Binaural beats," Eddie said. "Binaural beats. Binaural beats. Binaural beats."

"What's that?" a woman asked.

"Binaural beats," Eddie continued. "Low-frequency noise waves that cancel each other out. You just slap on the headphones, and boom! Voices are gone."

"That's a load of crap, Eddie," a man said.

"Okay, I'm telling you," Eddie said, leaning back in his seat. "Best thing since Clozapine."

The room stirred with commotion.

Bert held his hand up and asked Eddie to continue. Eddie went on about the science of binaural beats, then half-confessed that there was nothing better than medication. "The meds help, but it's the side effects I don't like."

Side effects?

"What type of side effects?" Duck asked.

Eddie faced him, turning with his hand on his thigh. "Well, for starters, you're jittery all the time, can't sit still, and you get these spasms."

Bert took notes. "Have you spoken to your psychiatrist about changing medication?"

"I'm fifty-three years old and have been on meds since I was eleven," Eddie said. "I've taken everything. I change meds every three months! Can't stay well for more than eight. I'm a damn guinea pig!"

"What do you mean?" Duck asked.

"What do you mean, what do I mean?" Eddie asked peering at him. "They give you pills for anxiety. Pills for depression. If five milligrams isn't working for you, they up the dose to ten, or switch you to Clozapine or some other creation. Now don't get me wrong. I appreciate the meds. But when you try to explain things to your p-doc they just nod, like you're an idiot or something. They don't understand things, like how you can't keep a job because you can't make sense of simple demands. How words spoken to you get jumbled up and you have to think about what's being said. And people see you in the streets panhandling and say, 'Get a job.' Like it's easy." He sighed. "The assholes out there!"

Duck knew exactly what he meant. Throughout the recent weeks, Alexa and his grandparents would sometimes bombard him with a blend of questions, and he would nod, or say nothing when he couldn't understand them. More experiences were shared, and soon everyone forgot about the initiating subject. Twenty minutes later, Bert interrupted.

"All right, everyone," he said, clapping his hands for attention. "Now we're going to split into groups. On the right side of the room will be friends and family members. You will break up into groups of threes and fours and discuss how your loved one's illness has affected each of you, what adjustments you've made, and what remedies you have found to be most useful in helping you cope with the illness. On the left side . . ."

Everyone got up and moved, dragging their chairs to various areas of the room. Duck felt Eddie clap him on the shoulder. "All right, partner," Eddie said. "We just need a third party." A small woman, white as Ivory Soap, walked over to join them. They pulled their chairs together, and Eddie broke the ice, beginning with his last hospital stay. They were instructed to talk about what stigmas they faced and how they dealt with them.

"The last time I was in the mental hospital," Eddie said, "I was there for three days before they kicked me out to make room. I've seen them do that to people who later committed suicide the same week. Anyhow, I was doing okay the day they released me. But I stayed off my meds once I was out. Later that week, I went down to the church to get some grub and exposed myself to the ladies serving the food. Someone called the cops, and I was arrested. The jail's got my medical records, but they kept me there anyway when I should've been back at the hospital."

He paused. "You see what happened to that guy, who was off his meds downtown? He got killed, wielding a knife at the police. You see, I got off my meds thinking I didn't need 'em. The mind can play tricks on you like that. So now I take my meds and do other things, like play the binaural beats or come to these group meetings."

Duck looked at the woman, then focused on the carpeted floor. He clasped his hands. He tilted his shoe. He examined the sole of it. Then, the woman began. She didn't talk about stigmas but followed up on suicide. She said that her voice once told her to set herself on fire. It had been drilling her, and she had been begging it to stop, so then it bargained with her, saying if she lit herself on fire, it would be quiet for her. She was dousing herself with gasoline at the gas station. Two witnesses stopped her. Consequently, she was admitted to the state hospital for twenty-four weeks.

Duck was digesting all this when Bert made them re-form the circle. Once they were settled, Bert asked if anyone wanted to share what they had learned. Up went the hands, then came the questions from family members and friends of the afflicted.

"Do your voices have faces?"

"What's the scariest thing you've ever seen?"

"How do you cope with thoughts of suicide?"

"How often do you take medication?"

"Friggin' normies," Eddie whispered to Duck. Normies, he learned, were normal people. Schizophrenics regarded themselves as schizos.

The meeting ended after two hours. Duck and Alexa waited for Mom and her boyfriend to be picked up by the Access bus. Access was a King County Metro Transit program that provided transportation services for disabled people. The driver arrived on time. Duck hugged his mom goodbye, then got in his car with Alexa to drive her home in the rain.

During the drive, he thought about what Eddie had said about not taking his medication. Jail sounded scary, but what about the side effects of the meds? He remembered how Eddie jerked involuntarily and had an intense Charles Manson-like gaze. Duck didn't want to look that way or feel like a zombie. But then he thought about how the short white lady almost set herself on fire. That, too, was scary. The idea that voices could push him to suicide started to frighten him.

"Are you okay?" Alexa asked.

A wild torrent of rain spattered over the windshield. The wipers swept back and forth, clicking rhythmically. Duck drove slowly and carefully, squinting out at the traffic.

Eddie said he couldn't live without the meds. And Mom got better, taking them. But the side effects . . .

"Babe, are you okay?" Alexa repeated.

Duck didn't respond.

The back of a cold hand reached over and stroked his cheek. The hand then fell on his lap and rubbed.

He came to a slow stop behind traffic. The light turned green, then eventually back to red. He leaned forward to see what was holding them up. Four or five cars were in front of them. He couldn't quite tell, but the waiting seemed abnormally long. He rolled down his window, stuck out his arm, and slapped the door three times in impatience, getting himself wet. He glanced around at the cars in the left lane, then at the one in front of him and Alexa. Then he noticed its license plate: KCD2448.

KILL CARLOS DUCKWORTH! WITHIN FORTY-EIGHT HOURS!

His eyes widened at death's forewarning. A knocking throb was in his chest. In his neck was choking pressure. He squeezed the steering wheel and tried to maneuver out of traffic. Traffic that wouldn't budge. He jerked his car forward and honked. Wheeled a few feet to the left and honked. Alexa braced one hand against the dashboard and reached for the steering wheel.

"Carlos, stop!" she said.

His heart was in his neck, running in punching circles.

"Talk to me, Carlos. Tell me what's going on."

They were going to shoot him. That's why there was a gridlock. But then the light turned green. And the traffic moved. He made a right at the next corner to escape the snipers.

"Carlos, stop the car," Alexa said, reaching for the wheel again. He knocked her hand away and looked at her wildly, still driving.

Woop! Woop!

He flashed a look at the rearview mirror. Red-and-blue lights were swirling behind them.

He's going to kill you.

"Shut up!" Duck said.

You don't run a business. You don't go to college.

"Shut up!"

You're the reason police kill black men!

Alexa palmed his knee. "It's okay, babe. Just pull the car over."

He pulled over slowly, clenching his jaw. Then doubled over, shaking his head. "No. No. No. No. No."

He raised his head and yelled, "Fuck!"

"Carlos, listen to me."

He felt Alexa's soft hand on his thigh again.

"Whatever you're hearing or seeing is not real," she said. "I just need you to communicate with me. Okay? Now tell me, what's going on?"

Don't listen to that bitch! a voice roared.

Duck banged his head three times on the steering wheel, then looked out the windshield, distraught. He wanted the demons out. Out!

Alexa placed her hand on his neck and rubbed it. "You have to talk to me," she repeated. "That's the only way I can help you. Talk to me, Carlos. Talk to me." Her voice was soothing.

He drew in a deep breath. "He's telling me not to listen to you," he said. "He's saying the police are going to kill me!"

"Nobody is going to kill you, Carlos."

He looked in the side view mirror at the officer climbing out of the squad car.

"Look at me." Alexa took him by the chin and looked him straight in the eyes. "Nobody is going to kill you."

"License and insurance," the officer demanded.

"He needs your license and insurance, that's all," Alexa said.

Duck looked up at the officer, who was jet-black and freakishly tall. He stood a foot away from the door and had a relaxed hand resting on the grip of a black gun. Duck gulped, reached for the sun visor, and then handed the documents to the officer. Duck's hand was trembling.

Alexa rubbed his leg as they waited.

The officer came back minutes later, returning the credentials. "Do you know why I pulled you over?"

"No." Duck glanced at the officer's gun.

Grab his gun, Lucky Ducky, grab his gun!

"No!"

The officer stepped back and grasped the handle of his pistol as if he had heard the murderous thought. He peered down at Duck. "First off, I pulled you over because you were reckless. Second, you failed to use your signal. Third, your tabs are expired." He received a call from dispatch and responded, then returned his attention to Duck. "Take care of those tabs, and remember to use your signal."

The officer rushed to his squad car, turned on his siren, and sped off.

Alexa seized the keys when Duck reached for the ignition. She got out of the car. Duck followed her with his eyes. She hurried over to the driver's door.

She pulled it open. "I'm driving," she said shakily.

He investigated her face, thinking they had fooled the cop.

She crossed her arms and looked at him angrily, waiting. Raindrops pelted her. "I'm getting wet."

Duck unlatched his seatbelt and climbed out of the car. He was barely out before she climbed in behind him. He went around and got in the passenger side, wet. "Where are we going?" he asked, fastening his seatbelt.

"We're taking you to a hospital," she said, pulling off.

"But I don't need a hospital," he said, gawking at her.

"Yes, you do. We're switching to my car and going to Harborview."

He wanted to protest but screams suddenly began to magnify themselves, like thousands of mad children running out at the sound of a recess bell. The joyful frenzy was replaced by tumult. His mind—a toxic playground for the lost. He squeezed his fists against his temples, closed his eyes tight, and rocked, then shrieked, scaring himself into a teary jitter.

His lips moved, possessed. Jabberwocky. He told himself the voices weren't real, even though they felt present. He felt powerless. Still trembling, he grew enough courage to face Alexa. He looked across at her like a sick and nauseated drunkard, begging with soft eyes. Helpless.

"I don't wanna see you like this," she said, controlling her sob. She sniffed, then wiped her face with the back of her sleeve. "There's no shame in needing help, Carlos. But you have to accept that you're sick."

He shook his head no.

"The doctors there will help you," she said.

He thought about taking medication, how people would call him crazy and label him worthless as they do with homeless cart-pushers deeply engaged in monologue. Like they do with Mom. Would the medication even allow him to function? And what was the evaluation process? Would they keep him overnight or commit him for several weeks? How would the psychiatrist treat him? Would she patronize him like Eddie Blodgett said or be understanding and supportive of him, like Alexa?

Alexa drove on.

Duck doubled over and massaged his temples, squinting from the constant throbbing. The voices continued to loop faintly, oscillating from ear to ear. He groaned. He groaned hard.

Alexa had parked in front of her mom's house, behind her own car, and had gone inside. Duck sat in his car and waited, staring out the passenger side window. Wet leaves swirled and scattered into the streets. The downpour had lightened into a steady rainfall. And the wind was no longer howling or whistling between trees. That afternoon was dark.

He went to click on the radio and realized Alexa had taken the keys. Suddenly, he saw a goblin flit by. Across the street on the driver's side. It disappeared out of view somewhere behind the car.

Duck turned and clutched the armrest. The goblin lurched onward, in the middle of the street, then turned around. Its face was green, and its eyes were hollow. Duck looked away and covered himself with his arms. "Leave me alone! Just leave me alone!"

Alexa knocked on the window. Startled, Duck nearly shat himself, looking up.

"My mom wants to see you before we leave," Alexa said outside the window.

Duck looked over his shoulder behind him at the street, making sure the goblin was gone.

"Are you coming?" Alexa asked, still standing at his door.

Duck nodded and climbed out reluctantly. What could Ms. Davis want to see him about? He followed Alexa inside the house.

Ms. Davis stomped over from the kitchen, wiping her hands on a kitchen towel. "Just a minute," she said. She tossed the towel over her shoulder and pulled out a small bottle of oil from the pocket of the kitchen apron she was wearing. She poured oil on her fingers and flicked it onto Duck's face. He blinked, flinching.

The woman whispered something in an unknown tongue, then laid a cold, greasy hand on his forehead. He felt the heel of her hand and her sharp fingers digging for grip. She shoved his head back. He fought to keep his balance.

Ms. Davis bowed her head and said, "Lord Jesus, we pray You remove these demons, these wicked, devilish demons from the mind of this demented child."

Duck felt his head being jerked around like a gear shift.

"Cast out these demons, Lord," she continued. "Satan, we command you out of this body, and demand you to leave! In Jesus's name, we pray. Amen."

She said the devil was a liar, then walked off.

Alexa had gone out and walked to the trunk of her car and unlocked it. She lifted the lid and tossed her backpack inside. The car shook as if someone had bumped it. She stiffened, still holding the trunk lid open. She looked around, listening. Someone sprouted out from the driver's side of the car, wearing a black hood over a green mask. She screamed as he came around the end of the car holding a bucket, wearing long, black gloves and black sweats. Immobilized by shock, Alexa could only blink in confusion and terror. The man lifted the bucket and then he doused her.

She grabbed at her eyes and screamed. A horrifying, whistling scream. She could feel the hot liquid seeping into her eyes, burning like fire on raw flesh. Biting at her tongue. Eating away at her lips. Chewing on her skin.

Duck had heard the scream from inside the house. He rushed out the door and saw Alexa doubled over, wiping at her face frantically. She was still screaming, and the goblin he saw earlier was standing over her, holding a bucket.

Duck ran off the porch, yelling at the creature. It raised its head and then took off.

Duck threw his long legs into a fiery sprint, chasing the goblin, and hearing the screams of Alexa. What had it done to her? Duck wanted to kill it but needed to check on Alexa. He stopped and doubled back to her. She was crying, guarding her face for reasons he didn't understand. He put an arm around her, and she trembled underneath it violently, shuddering with every shriek from her mouth.

"What happened?" he asked. "Alexa, what happened?" But she couldn't answer. She could only scream and writhe. And he could only see himself catching the monster who had done this to her. He saw himself beating the goblin, choking it, and crushing its larynx.

Ms. Davis, who had come out of the house, was beside Alexa now, speaking into her cell phone frantically, explaining to a 911 dispatcher what was happening.

Duck scooped up Alexa and ran her inside the house. Ms. Davis followed.

"Water," Ms. Davis cried. "You need water!"

He forced his way through the bathroom door, placed Alexa in the tub, and ripped her shirt open. He turned both faucet knobs on and pushed her head back with force. Alexa gagged under the water-gushing spigot, then turned her head away, coughing and then screaming again. She clung onto him, spewing, kicking her feet. He shoved her head back under the faucet.

Finally, the wail of sirens.

Alexa moved her head wildly as Duck forced it back under the running water again. Her face was red and pink, and her chest was raw where her skin was burned. He pulled her up to his body and cried out to God.

Kill yourself! You deserve to die! Kill yourself! You deserve to die! Kill yourself! You deserve to die!

Seven

The maid at Renton Inn knocked softly. "Ten minutes till check-out," she said in a rich, Latin accent. A moment later, the wheels of the maid cart squeaked off.

Fats sat on the foot of the bed, refolding the Monday paper he had borrowed from the front desk twenty minutes earlier. He had just finished reading an article about a girl who had suffered an acid attack over the Halloween weekend. No suspects. "A cowardly act," the reporter wrote.

Fats gathered his clothes, thinking of how his funds were depleting rapidly. He was already down to three hundred and fifty-four dollars. He had spent two nights at the motel and fifty dollars on a whore he had met the night before. Not to mention the food deliveries and alcohol. He'd be broke in less than a week, he thought.

He stuffed his belongings into plastic grocery bags, then opened the drawer nightstand drawer. He reached inside for the Gideon Bible and flipped to the book of Revelations, where he'd hidden his money. The money was gone!

He remembered putting it *right there*. Right there in between chapters one and two, and three and four. Right before he got undressed to have sex with the meth whore who was then showering. He closed the book and flipped through the pages again, huffing and puffing like a child about to throw a tantrum.

"Where the fuck is my money?" he yelled. He stood up. His eyes were hot with tears of anger and panic. He held the Holy Book by the spine, shook it hard, and then slung it across the room, screaming at the forces against him.

He paced, hyperventilating, then punched himself in the face three times. He stopped and then tried to slow everything down in his mind. Maybe he hadn't searched well enough. He swept his hand around the empty drawer, flipped over the pillows, and tore back the comforter and sheets, knowing the money was gone.

He sat down on the bed for a moment. He never thought a hooker would check the Bible. Maybe she felt guilty after sex and sought out a scripture, while he felt dirty and got in the shower. The maid knocked again, entering this time.

"Señor?"

"I'm leaving now!" Fats shouted. He grabbed his two bags and stormed out. Hoofed it to the 7-11 on Northeast Fourth Street, an hour-long walk.

As he climbed the final hill, he looked across the street at Dad's shop. Fats was exhausted and sweaty, yet relieved his feet were approaching flat ground. He shuffled across the parking lot to his left, where there was a Subway, a pizzeria, and the 7-11. He dropped his bags and stood against the wall of the convenience store, with one leg up and his arms crossed.

He watched his father, who was under the hood of a car. Dad appeared to be working alone. A moment later, he headed downstairs to drain the oil. Maybe his employees were on break. But it was after one p.m., so maybe they were on lunch. Maybe he no longer had anyone working for him.

Either way, Fats had to hurry before Dad resurfaced. Fats ran across the street and hurried along the left side of the building, then crept around to the rear of the first bay, where he could easily spot his father. Fats knew Dad's back would be turned. He was downstairs in the pit, working underneath the car. Fats hesitated for a moment, then pushed himself onward, knowing he had no time to be cautious.

He crept along the bay, moving without a sound. The customer in the lobby was focused on his phone. The radio downstairs was playing, and Fats hoped that would deafen the register's *ding!* He opened the register and grabbed every dollar, lifted the bed tray, and took every big bill underneath, then quietly closed the drawer. He snuck out the same way he came in, without any notice.

Fuck him, he thought.

He ran back to the 7-11 and went inside. Paid the clerk for a tall can of Hurricane High Gravity Lager. Fats asked what time it was.

The woman bagged his beer and looked at him as if to say it was too early to drink. "One thirty-two," she answered. He nodded and took his purchase, then stepped outside and popped the top. He tilted the can, guzzling beer. He wiped his lips and looked at the shop again.

Fuck him.

He finished his beer and then observed his surroundings. Ahead, traffic was stopped at a red light. And in the right outside turn lane, a long bus was idling. It would be going in the direction of the Newcastle Library. He picked up his bags and hustled over to the bus stop.

He got off four miles later, went into an AMPM, and bought a liter of chardonnay and a thirty-two-ounce fountain cup with a lid and straw. He crossed the street to McDonald's, strode inside the restroom, and filled the entire cup with wine. He drank what was left in the carton and then used the urinal before going back outside.

He went around the corner, up the block to the library, and stepped inside. He saw a book at the front display called *Kindred,* by Octavia Butler. On the cover was a dark black woman. Her head was lowered, and she looked sad. She wore a white blouse reminiscent of a slave garment.

Fats set a bag down, picked up the book, and read the back. It was about slavery and time travel. The slave narrative made him think about the home library Dad once had. Fats remembered being young and seeing books by James Baldwin and Eldridge Cleaver, and Dick Gregory. *Nigger*, Fats recalled, and *The Autobiography of Malcolm X*, which Fats had read in prison, and *The Confessions of Nat Turner*, which Fats later learned was fiction and not a true account of the slave revolt.

Some of those men were his heroes. He especially liked Nat Turner and how he'd fought back against his oppressors. That had always impressed Fats. He sat down and logged onto a computer, searching for videos of Malcolm X ministering before Malcolm made his trip to Mecca. Those speeches were more fiery and cutthroat. Fats believed Malcolm sold out and grew soft once he was silenced by Elijah Muhammed, who was the real savior of black Americans at that time.

Still, Fats liked Malcolm for his early venom. Fats spent two hours in a library cubbyhole, watching link after link, video after video. From Marcus Garvey to Jeremiah Wright to a new group of religious leaders Fats had never heard of before called the Israelites. Fats sipped his wine, then fell asleep in an armchair after his time limit at the computer was up.

"The library will be closing in fifteen minutes," a librarian announced over the PA system. Fats rubbed his face and realized he'd overslept. It was 8:45 p.m. He quickly removed his feet from the ottoman, rose from the lounge chair, and gathered his things.

He hurried out and caught the bus. He needed it to move fast. It was already ten minutes to nine. He kicked himself for oversleeping. He needed to make it to the Salvation Army Church on South Tobin Street. It was the closest homeless shelter, but the travel time on Metro made it seem very far.

When he arrived the church doors were locked. It was 9:15 p.m. He pulled on the metal handles, then peeked in through the door's slim window, seeing nothing but darkness. He yanked on the handles again. Finally, someone came to the door. A robust black woman pushed it open, whispering: "Sir, we're closed for the night."

"I know," Fats said. "I just need a place to sleep."

"I'm sorry, but we're not taking any more beds."

"Please," he said securing his hand around the door panel. She looked at his hand.

"Sir, we're full." She tried closing the door. He pulled it back to keep it open.

"It's not my fault," he lied. "The bus was late."

"I'm sorry to hear that. If you want a bed, you have to make it before nine."

The door slipped from his fingers and shut. The woman disappeared back into the darkness.

He turned around, angry.

Why didn't you catch the bus earlier?

"Fuck!" he shouted, leaving the church. He had yelled so loud that neighbors looked out of their apartment windows. There was no possible way for him to make it on time to the downtown shelter. And he didn't want to spend the money he'd stolen on another motel room. He wandered around for an hour, trying to figure out what to do, then decided to head to the diner.

He brought his bags in with him and sat down at a booth, sliding deep into the corner. He looked out the window, thinking about how stupid his life was.

Rita sped over ready to take his order. "Hello, what can I—oh!" she exclaimed, looking genuinely surprised.

"Just get me a cup of coffee," Fats muttered.

"Sure." She stood there smiling for a second, then trudged off.

Soon she was back with a mug and a long, silver coffeepot. She poured him a cup, then hovered over him. Lingering.

"So," she said. "Have you found another job yet?"

Her eyes were brown and button-like, pressed into her dough-white face. She stood with the coffee pot, blinking at him.

He cleared his throat. "I apologize," he said with great effort. He dropped his head and stared into the coffee mug as if he could find strength in there. He briefly met her eyes again. "It wasn't right for me to yell or curse at you." He looked away.

"It's okay," she said. "I understand you were upset."

He glanced at her. "I'm um . . . I'm just going through hard times right now."

She set the coffee pot down and eagerly took a seat at the table. "So what's going on?" she asked folding her hands. "Do you need a place to stay?"

He looked into his coffee again.

"If you need a place, you can stay with me," she said. "Until you get on your feet, you know."

He cupped the hot mug and peered at her, wondering why she was so interested in him. Was she lonely? Did she care? Or was she trying to be nosy? His inner voice suggested that she may even *like* him. He shook his head.

"No?" she said. "Okay, I understand."

"No, that's not why I'm shaking my head," he said. "Why are you trying to help me?" He knew all along she would, but why? Was she trying to pry into his life to humiliate him, like Dad?

"You just seem like a nice guy," she said. "I don't mind. And I have plenty of space."

He looked down at his coffee again.

She got up, took his hand, and squeezed it gently.

He blew at his coffee, feeling awkward at her affectionate gesture.

"Just think about it," she said. She let go of his hand, grabbed the coffee pot, and started for the kitchen.

"Rita," he called.

She stopped and faced him.

He signaled for her to come closer, and she did.

"I uh, I do need a place to stay," he whispered.

She smiled at him.

Feeling better, he added, "Do you guys have anything extra back there?"

"I'll have Javier make you something," she said. She strode off, announced the order through the pass-through, and returned to assist other customers.

Fats was asleep when they made it to Rita's house.

"Here we are!" she said, shutting off the car motor.

He sat up slowly, wiping sleep out of his eyes. It was dark, but he saw they were under a carport, alongside a manufactured home.

Rita reached behind her for her purse, then got out without warning. Fats grabbed his bags from the floorboard, climbed out, and followed her to an aluminum screen door. He looked over his shoulder at the neighborhood. She lived in a cul-de-sac with manicured shrubbery. A clean, quiet community. She fiddled with her keys and then unlocked the door.

"Welcome to my home!" she said, walking in. She turned on the lights.

He entered and saw an indoor garden. Plants were in the living room and kitchen. Some hung from the ceiling, near the windows, with leafy stems that grew to the floor. Others were on plant stands and plant shelves. The large display looked like the inside of a greenhouse.

He touched the leaf of a plant and rubbed it between his fingers. It felt waxy.

"That's a zebra plant," she said. "Do you like it?"

He nodded to be polite but stayed silent. He had taken her for a cat lover, not a green thumb. He followed her around the house, observing pictures on either side of the hallway. There were photos of a young black man. Fair-skinned with curly hair. Was that her son? Fats glanced at an embarrassing grade school picture. The boy was about ten years old in it, smiling hard and sporting a hi-top fade that was about a foot high on his head. Fats guessed from the eighties-style gear that he and the boy must now be around the same age. Fats walked along slowly, looking at more pictures. Her son had joined the U.S. Navy. Then Fats saw marriage photos of Rita coupled with a dark black man.

Fats stopped and fixated on an old family picture. Rita had been beautiful back in her day. She and her husband posed with their son. They were all smiling in Christmas outfits.

"Come on," Rita said, interrupting Fats.

He followed her to a door. "Here's your room," she said, opening it. He stepped in cautiously. It was freezer-cold in there. "This was Malcolm's room."

"Malcolm?" he asked, looking back at her.

"Malcolm was my son," she said, smiling.

Was?

"Well, I'm beat as a beaver. You get some rest now. I'm going to bed." She closed the door after her.

He looked at Malcolm's bed. The bedding was tucked in with precision. Fats looked across the room at Malcolm's dresser, arrayed with swimming trophies, military photos, and framed certificates. He approached the display and saw a small case containing a bronze medal with the bulging image of an anchor. On each corner of the medal was a star. He picked up the framed certificate behind the medal. *U.S. Navy and Marine Corps Achievement Medal,* the certificate read. He set it down, undressed, and settled into the stiff, cold bed.

Fats woke up around noon to urinate. He stood over the toilet, pushed out a bloody stream, and then spurted. He stopped, then dribbled, then spurted again. He dabbed himself with a wad of toilet paper, squeezed out a few more drops, then dabbed himself again. He tossed the red wad into the toilet, flushed it with the bloody urine, and then balled his hands to stop them from shaking.

What the hell is going on with me?

Rita knocked. He jumped, startled, then rinsed and dried his hands. What did she want already?

He started to answer the door when he felt cold wetness against his inner thigh and underwear. He checked inside his boxers and discovered a large, damp spot. He was still dribbling, even after he'd thoroughly wiped himself.

Maybe it was the wine. Yes, it was just the wine. He would slow down on the drinking. That should bring his urine color back to normal.

Rita knocked again.

"I'm coming," Fats said. "Shit."

He opened the door, still shaken.

"Well, good afternoon!" Rita looked at him smiling, then handed him a sheet of paper, oblivious to his growing concern.

He looked at the paper. There were duties and chores numbered from one to ten. He jerked his head up and said, "What's this?"

"Read it."

He barely started reading it when she began narrating it for him.

"First thing you need to do is make up your bed," she said. "Then clean the tub after you bathe. Water the plants and do the dishes, if there are any. But the dishes can wait until after you come home."

He almost balled up the paper. "What is this, Rita?"

"It's a to-do list."

"I don't need a to-do list," he grumbled, blinking at her. He folded the paper in half.

"You need structure and discipline," she said. "It's important to keep yourself busy and productive, especially when looking for work. Speaking of work, you ought to shave. No one's going to hire you looking like that."

The diner hired me, so what the fuck are you talking about?

"I'm grown," he said. "I don't need you instructing me."

"Get dressed," she said dismissively. "We have some errands to run. After that, we'll look for a job."

They pulled up to Walgreens and parked in front of a Redbox. "This is where I get my medication," she said. "The people here are nice, but they're always short-staffed."

"I'm not good with people."

"Well, what are you good with?" she asked, looking at him.

He shrugged and said, "I don't know."

"What type of work do you like to do?"

He sighed, then shook his head. "Anything that doesn't involve people."

"Well, that's helpful," she said with a frown. She paused, then took a deep breath. "Okay. Well, I'm going to run in here. I'll be right back."

Whatever.

He sat in the car, wishing the day was already over. He yawned, then wondered why he was so tired after waking up. He should have asked her to buy him something to drink. Water. Gatorade. Something. Why did they even leave without eating, and why was she so bossy? Did it have something to do with her son?

She returned minutes later. "They're hiring," she said, securing herself with her seatbelt. "You just have to go online and fill out an application. But I don't own a computer. Do you have a library card?"

"Yeah, but I don't wanna work with people."

"That's fine," she said. "It's just a start. Beggars can't be choosy, you know."

"I'm not begging."

"My goodness," she said, slapping her thighs. "It's just an expression. Lighten up. We're trying to find you a job."

"No, *you're* trying to find me a job. These people wouldn't hire me anyway. You probably gotta pass a background check."

Shit.

There was silence. Awkward silence. He realized he'd said too much, but maybe it'd gone over her head. After all, she was old, so maybe she didn't hear him.

"So you've been to prison?" she asked. "Is that what you're worried about . . . not passing a background check?"

If he said yes, he'd be homeless again. He should've kept his mouth shut or kept talking as liars often do when they've made some slip. Now, it was too late. "I'm just saying—I don't work well with customers."

"Sure," Rita said. She started the car and drove off the lot. "You know what you could do is work for a temp agency. They have a lot of warehouse work."

"I've worked temp before."

"Great!" she said. "So let's head down to Labor Ready and fill out an application. That way, you can start tomorrow!"

"I don't have any money," he snapped, lying. "How am I gonna pay for food? How am I even gonna get there? I don't have a car. I don't have any clothes. I don't have nothing."

She pursed her lips, then grasped his knee and shook it. "Don't worry about all that. You do want to work, don't you?"

"I wanna eat," he said. "That's what I wanna do. I'm hungry and I'm thirsty as hell. You got me riding around here, starving and shit. Can we get something to eat, please? Damn."

"Sure, Fasir. What would you like to eat?" she asked, focused on her driving.

He peered at her, breathing in and out like a tired gorilla, not liking her tone of voice, feeling patronized.

She glanced at him, smiling. The car veered and went over a rumble strip. She quickly adjusted the wheel and focused on the road again.

They eased into a McDonald's parking lot and joined the queue. The line moved slowly. Fats looked behind them, anticipating a motorist to come and box them in, but no one did.

"This line is too long," he griped. "Let's go in."

"Okay," said Rita. She reversed and found a parking spot. Fats stepped out feeling lightheaded and stopped. He steadied himself alongside the car.

"Are you okay?" he heard Rita asking. Then suddenly, everything went black.

When he regained consciousness, he saw Rita sitting across from him, reading a magazine. Things were fuzzy, and his arm was sore. He looked at the crook of his right elbow and saw a mess of white tape with a clear, thin tube running out of him. He followed the tube up to the IV bag hanging beside him on the hook of an aluminum pole next to a monitor with spikes and numbers. He felt sticky tape and hard plastic pinching his left thigh and his nakedness under the thin gown he was wearing. He slipped his hand under the bedclothes and discovered a thin tube had been inserted into his urethra. He moved his hand and swallowed dryly. Afraid, he tried sitting up.

Rita looked up from the magazine, tossed it aside, and hurried over to him.

"What's going on?" he asked, confused. His throat was dry, and his voice was hoarse.

"Wait a minute," Rita said, assisting him. He stopped, realizing he was too weak to move.

She then hurried to the sink to get him a cup of water. She gave it to him.

He put the cup to his lips, trembling, spilling water as he drank.

He handed the flimsy cup back to her. She quickly refilled it and returned.

He bottomed the second cup and looked up wearily. "What happened?"

"Just relax," Rita said. "I'll get the nurse for you." She took the cup from him, put it back by the sink, and then hurried out. Soon, she returned with a nurse.

"How are you feeling, Mr. Mansur?" the nurse asked.

"What's going on?" Fats asked.

"Sir, just try to relax," the nurse said.

"I'm trying to," Fats said.

"The doctor will be with us shortly. How are you feeling?"

"Fine, I guess." But he was confused and frightened and irritated. No one would give him any answers to why he was in a hospital. And why couldn't he remember?

Minutes later, a white-coat-wearing doctor came in. He was tall, dark, and looked to be of Indian descent.

"Fasir Mansur, I'm Dr. Singh. How are you feeling?"

"I'm good," Fats said. "Now, can you tell me what's going on?"

"Well, you're at Valley Medical Center," the doctor said. "You passed out at McDonald's. Do you remember?"

Fats tried to squeeze the pieces together. "No."

"Well, you took a nasty fall," the doctor said. "Seems your blood sugar level was pretty high."

"My blood sugar?"

What the hell is he talking about?

"You went into a diabetic coma," the doctor said. "You have type two diabetes."

Fats's eyes moved back and forth.

"You're what we call a brittle diabetic. Your levels are going up and down, so it may take us a few days to stabilize you. When's the last time you had a physical exam?"

"I don't know," Fats said, thinking never.

"What's your height and weight?"

Fats answered. The doctor moved over to the computer in the corner of the room and began making entries.

"Do you have any allergies?"

"No."

"What prescription or non-prescription drugs do you take?"

"None," Fats said, agitated.

The doctor continued typing. "Do you smoke?"

"No, man."

"Alcohol?"

"Yes," Fats answered, annoyed.

"How much do you drink when you engage?"

Fats didn't answer.

"Four or five drinks, maybe?"

Fats blinked for yes.

"How often? Once a month, twice a week, daily?"

"Every day," Fats said.

The doctor made a note. "Have you been noticing any changes in your body? Any symptoms before today?"

Symptoms? Why are you asking so many questions?

Fats shrugged and said, "I don't know."

Rita intervened and said, "Fasir, he's trying to help you."

With all these questions? I can't even think.

"It's okay," the doctor told Rita, walking back over to Fats, "I imagine this is scary for you. I understand."

Fats sighed, then decided to answer the question. "I've been tired, but I'm always tired."

The doctor nodded. "Anything else?"

Fats thought for a while. "I piss a lot, but that's because of the alcohol."

"So frequent urination and fatigue. And how long have you been having these symptoms?"

Fats sighed again. "I don't know, man. Over a year, I guess."

The doctor nodded with a frown. "Untreated, this could have been fatal." He sounded serious.

Fats dropped his gaze, thinking about his blood-colored urine.

"What is it?" the doctor asked. "Remember, we're here to help."

Fats looked over at Rita, then back at the doctor.

The doctor shifted in a way that said he was ready to listen. He put his hand around Fats's wrist, taking his pulse.

Fats licked his dry lips, then spoke. "Sometimes I see blood, but it's probably just the wine."

"Blood? In your urine?"

"I don't know," Fats said. "It could be, I guess."

"And frequent urination?"

Fats nodded sadly.

"Tell me about the urination flow."

"Flow?" Fats asked.

"Is it normal, or does it come out in spurts?"

Fats shifted uncomfortably. "A lot of times, it comes out in spurts, then leaks out when I think I'm done, but what does that have to do with anything?"

The doctor sighed. "I think we should run a few more tests."

"Why?" Fats asked, alarmed. "What's wrong?"

"We want to be sure we're not missing anything," the doctor said. "I'm going to order some blood work."

In the morning, Dr. Singh returned. He walked over to Fats's bedside. Fats muted the TV and straightened, then shrank back, feeling the man was too close to him.

"How are you feeling today?" the doctor asked.

Fats blinked. "Better, I guess."

"Good." The doctor clipped a device onto Fats's finger and glanced at the monitor beside him. "Looks like we're starting to get you stabilized."

Dr. Singh removed the device.

Fats looked over at Rita, who was still sitting across the room, looking tired. A male nurse had just taken his vitals ten minutes ago. So why was the doctor here? To serve him the bad news? Fats wished Rita was sitting next to him.

Dr. Singh looked at him squarely and said: "The tests we took show that your PSA level is abnormally high."

Fats swallowed and looked at the doctor wide-eyed. "PSA level?"

"Your prostate gland. The level for your age should range from zero to two. Your PSA level is at ten."

"So—so what are you saying?" Fats asked, not understanding the jargon.

"There's a possibility, I'm afraid, that you might have prostate cancer. We need to run a biopsy—"

Fats slammed his head back into the pillow. The doctor continued, but Fats wasn't listening. Tears crawled down his face into his ears.

When the doctor left, Rita quickly sat beside Fats and took his hand. He stared at the ceiling, saying nothing.

"Everything's going to be all right," Rita said. "I've been diabetic for years, and lots of people survive cancer."

It sounded like the dumbest thing a person could say, which made him angrier inside.

"I hate this fuckin' life," he muttered.

Rita gasped and said, "Why would you say that?"

Fats swallowed what felt like a brick. Was she oblivious? Did she live in Wonderland? "This life is a fuckin' joke, I swear."

"Stop it," Rita said. "Your life is not over yet."

He blinked out more tears. "You don't understand."

"I do understand," she said. "I understand that you have a drinking problem, you're depressed, and you feel like the world is against you. I understand you feel like life isn't fair. But that's life, Fasir! Life is challenging for everyone. We all have problems."

"Yeah? Does everyone get molested by their mother? Does everyone spend half their life being homeless?"

She sighed. "I'm sorry those things happened to you." She bowed her head, then raised it again. "Maybe you could join a support group of people who know what that's like."

He took his hand away from her. More tears poured from his eyes.

"You're not alone, Fasir, and you don't have to be." She squeezed his arm.

He turned away from her and buried half his face in the pillow. She didn't understand.

Eight

Duck sat in the hospital lobby with his head down, listening to Ms. Davis describe to the four officers what she had seen. He kept his eyes closed, covering his forehead and massaging his temples, thinking it was all a bad dream. Ms. Davis kept sniffling and weeping between sentences, trying hard to give her account. Duck wanted to help but felt unable to. The tears on his face had dried. Guilty words still hammered at his skull.

It's all your fault, Lucky Ducky! It's all your fault!

He groaned, wanting the voices to shut up and Ms. Davis to stop crying. He thought the officers had enough information and wanted to tell them to stop screwing around and to make an arrest. He wanted to know when he could go in and see Alexa. How bad was the assault? How bad was the damage?

He heard an officer respond to a call from dispatch, then heard him check with his colleagues to see if they had the matter before them under control. A male and female cop said yes. The policeman who had just responded to dispatch then left with another officer.

A moment later, a new voice emerged. A soft-spoken man had excused himself for interrupting Ms. Davis. Duck lifted his head and saw it was the doctor. Duck rose and hurried over to him. He had introduced himself as Doctor Nguyen and was beginning to update Alexa's mother on the status of her daughter.

"How is she?" Duck asked, butting in. "When can we see her? Is she going to be okay?"

Doctor Nguyen sighed, exchanging glances with Ms. Davis and Duck. "She's suffered some pretty significant burns," the doctor said. "First and second degree . . . on her face, neck, and chest. . . . As well as her hands. You two did well by quickly treating her with water. Unfortunately, she will still need reconstructive surgery, and she may be partially blind."

Ms. Davis put a hand to her mouth and yelped.

Duck turned away from her and the doctor, balling his fists, angry enough to punch a wall. He paced.

"I know this is hard," Doctor Nguyen said. "But we have a great team here at Regional. Our plastic surgeons are among the best in the Northwest. I, myself, have twelve years of experience treating burn patients. So Alexa *is* in good hands."

Duck stopped pacing and faced him.

The doctor went on. "Right now, she's in a medically induced coma. When she is ready, we'll do some skin grafting. I hope you understand."

Ms. Davis mumbled something to herself.

"I'm sorry?" said the doctor, not hearing.

"You," she said, eyeing Duck. "It should have been you!" She grabbed at his shirt and slapped him, knocking white blindness into his head. She hit him again and again, then tried to choke him, digging her fingernails into his neck.

The two officers rushed over to restrain her.

Duck stood with hot ringing in his ears. *You,* she had said. *It should have been you!* He lowered his head shamefully, feeling as though he deserved the beating or worse.

The officers guided Ms. Davis to a chair. The doctor had snuck off.

Ms. Davis cried into her hands.

The officers turned to Duck, looking restless.

"Are you ready to give your statement?" the male officer asked, removing his push-pen and blue memo pad from his left breast pocket. He clicked the end of the pen, raising his eyebrows as he looked at Duck.

Earlier, the officer had introduced himself as Officer Pratt, the other as Officer Owens. They had arrived with the other pair of officers an hour after one of the nurses had asked Ms. Davis if she would like the police to be called.

At her house, the cops had shown up in droves, but Alexa's mother had only provided a brief description of the assailant before they went on their manhunt, and she to her car. Duck had hurried to the car with her. By the time they got to the hospital, he was bombarded with voices, disabling his will to speak and ability to leave a statement. Now exhausted and desperate, he was ready to talk, whether the voices were there to condemn him or not.

He described everything he could remember, from the time he saw the goblin while waiting in the car, to the moment the ambulance arrived. He spoke with some resistance at first, recalling in his mind that he didn't know if the goblin was real or not. While speaking to the officers, it seemed to him that they knew, or in some way could detect his craziness. He kept seeing the green-faced goblin, his wide demonic figure, turning away and taking off.

"He was short and heavyset," Duck said shakily. "About five-feet-four. Maybe two hundred and sixty pounds."

Officer Pratt documented every word hastily, occasionally looking up from his memo pad into Duck's eyes as if reading them would confirm Duck's account.

"It was Fats!" Duck said suddenly. "Fasir Mansur, but he goes by Fats."

The officers looked at him strangely. "You said he was wearing a mask," Pratt said. "Did you happen to see his face?"

"No, but I know it was him."

I know it was him.

"I know it was him," Duck repeated. "He's shown up at her job. He's been calling and harassing her to the point she had to get a restraining order. I know it was this motherfucker!"

He broke into an angry sob, shuddering as he remembered Alexa telling him about the incident. He should have done something then. When he was well he could have done something then. Instead of her taking care of him, he should have been looking out for her.

Officer Owens stood with both of her hands hooked onto the inside of her bulletproof vest. Forearms out. Legs spread apart. Like a football player on the sidelines, watching. She broke her stance to touch Duck on the shoulder. "Sir, please try to calm down."

"Just fuckin' go after him!" Duck shouted, knocking her hand away. "I told you his name. You have all the information you need. Now go fuckin' arrest him!"

Officer Pratt closed his memo pad. Officer Owens reached down to the side of her utility belt and unfastened her pepper spray holder.

She's going to mace you.

"I'm sorry," said Duck. "I just . . . I just need you to arrest him, please."

Because if you don't, we're going to kill him.

Officer Pratt shoved the memo pad into his pocket, along with his push pen.

Nobody likes you. Did you see how she looked at you?

"Shut up," Duck growled clapping his head.

You're a weak man. You can't even protect your girlfriend.

"Shut up! Shut up! Shut up!" he jumped up and down and spat. "Leave me alone! Just leave me the fuck alone!"

Officer Owens withdrew her pepper spray and pointed it at Duck's face. Officer Pratt whipped out his Taser gun and aimed it at Duck's chest.

"Wait!" Ms. Davis cried. She got up and hurried over to them. "He was about to commit himself before this all happened. Please."

She eased in between the officers and Duck, grabbed him by the arms, and then walked him backward into a chair. She held his hands down to his lap and gave him a cold stare. "You need to calm down. Do you understand?"

He looked at her, then over her shoulder at the officers who were now holstering their weapons.

They turned calmly and left, to find Fats, Duck hoped.

Duck and Ms. Davis were allowed to visit Alexa the next morning. Duck walked in slowly, staring at Alexa's bandaged face. She was sedated and patched up all over. Duck sat down at her bedside. Ms. Davis quietly sat down on the opposite side of the bed. She examined her daughter, then expressed a few words of sorrow, shaking her head.

Alexa's head was swathed in gauze that blood had seeped through. Her lips were blistered. Clear tubes had been applied to her mouth and nostrils to administer food and medicine. More tubes ran from the crooks of her arms. Her left eye was closed. The right one was covered by a thick cotton patch that was carefully taped to it. Her neck, chest, and right shoulder were bandaged with white dressing. Duck looked down at her right arm. The gauze there sealed her hand like a mitten. He took her hand and held it, then brought it to his mouth and kissed it. Ms. Davis began praying. Duck bowed his head and joined her.

His eyes became teary as he tried to shake the image of Alexa's mummified face. He asked God to heal her, to bring her back to normal. She'd done nothing. Nothing at all to deserve this. She was nice and kind and spiritual, patient and understanding. Grandmother had told him that God could do anything. So God could heal Alexa. Duck prayed so hard that he forgot where he was until he raised his head and opened his eyes again.

During prayer, Alexa's friend Amy from daycare, and her husband, Stan, had slipped into the room. Duck stood immediately and offered his hand in thanks for their support, but Stan embraced him swiftly and held him tight.

"How are you holding up?" Stan asked after breaking the hug. He looked pale with shock.

Duck pursed his lips and shook his head slowly. He appreciated Stan's concern, but how did Stan *think* he was holding up? Duck lied and said he was good, then turned and glanced at Amy. She was consoling Ms. Davis, rubbing her shoulder and apologizing as if she had committed the crime herself. Amy's face was flushed with pink dread and horror, but no tears were in her eyes.

Stan said a few words of condolence, then offered his number, saying, "If you need anything, just give me a call." Duck saved the number in his phone. A moment later Duck's grandparents came in. He embraced them. They greeted Ms. Davis, and then quietly asked her about Alexa. The mother smiled sadly and said she was leaving everything in the hands of the Lord. They understood and said they would continue to pray for her daughter, then sat down gingerly on the cushioned bench on the far side of the room by the window. Soon after, a party of three entered behind them, members of Greater Glory, the Pentecostal church Ms. Davis attended. It was the pastor, his wife, and their teenage daughter. Soon there was an assembly in the room.

Duck sat down at the bedside facing the entrance. The mood was somber, and no one knew what to say. Ms. Davis had assured them that Alexa was going to be okay. God was good. Everyone nodded in agreement, but then their eyes seemed to fall on Duck.

He had been there but couldn't stop it. He buried his head in his hands and shuddered in a guilty sob. Soon others joined him, sniffling and weeping and blowing their noses. There was a stir. He sensed everyone shifting their attention to whoever had just entered the room. He looked up and saw it was his cousin. B nodded at people, then went over to Duck's grandparents and hugged them. They were B's grandparents too. He strode over to Duck afterward, slapped palms with him, and fist-bumped him, saying, "What's up?" Duck quickly noticed B reeked of cannabis. People moved away from the man.

A moment later everyone gathered in a semicircle around the bed. Hands linked together. Heads lowered and eyes shut.

"Lord," Ms. Davis said. "We pray that You give us the strength to forgive our enemies and those who offend us. We pray that our enemies repent and find salvation through Christ. May they inherit the New Earth and be saved. . . ." She sighed, sniffed, and then continued. "If it be Your will, Lord, we pray that You heal Alexa. May You fully restore her vision. May You deliver her from whatever pain she may be feeling. May you nourish her body, and bless these doctors with the strength and ability they need to operate on her successfully. . ."

"Yes, Lord," people said between her words. She went on a full minute and closed. Everyone said, "Amen," and then touched Alexa, whispering blessings over her.

The crowd began thinning by noon. Duck stayed with Alexa while Ms. Davis headed to the cafeteria. She said that she was hungry, but he suspected she just wanted to get away for a moment. Duck held Alexa's bandaged hand, trying to convince himself that everything was going to be okay.

B was standing in front of him, surfing through channels with his rear end in Duck's face. B was tall and slim and sagged his pants showing his boxers. Twenty-two years old with a long face and a fresh taper fade. Skin dark as an acorn. He was often mistaken as Somalian.

B settled for ESPN and turned the volume up, then complained that he still couldn't hear. He sauntered over to the opposite side of the bed and sat down, then leaned on the bedrail, talking over Alexa's body. "You see that game last night?"

Duck looked across at his cousin's dark face. B was high and didn't care. He completely disregarded Alexa lying there.

"My bad, you were here," B said. "OKC whupped on Dallas." B leaned back and fished for his phone, replied to a text, and then slipped the phone back into his pocket. "I heard you been hearing voices and shit. What's up with that?"

Duck looked at him again. "Who told you that, Grandmother?"

"My dad." B stuck a stick of gum into his mouth and chewed. "Said your mom starting hallucinating when she was about twenty-five. I think I remember that. You taking meds?" Their parents were siblings. B's dad was two years older than Duck's mom, but they were never close, not even as children.

Duck didn't feel like talking about his condition. Grandmother had told them enough. But he did want to answer the question of taking medication. "No, I'm not taking meds. I haven't even seen a doctor yet."

"I feel it." B stretched out his arms and back. "Cuz, this is some bullshit." He stood up and paced, then faced Duck again. "You trying to get on the sticks later? And what's up with your online? I tried to hit you up last week."

Duck didn't answer. B was referring to playing *NBA 2K*, but Duck's membership to play online hadn't been renewed since he had to quit working. Besides that, he'd lost the desire and hadn't been able to play effectively since the changes in his psyche.

B went to the hospital room window and looked out for a minute, then turned, facing Duck again. "So what happened, cuz? Straight up."

Duck side-eyed him and thought, did he feel like telling him? The story had been repeated enough. Duck sighed, then told him what he had seen that night. Then he told him all about Fats, and why he didn't like him. During Duck's first week of training on the job, he had caught Fats staring at a group of adolescent girls walking by the lube shop. They couldn't have been older than fifteen. Duck also saw Fats in the lobby once, flipping through the pages of *Girls' Life*, a magazine intended for teen girls. (Dad had subscribed to various magazines and kept them in the lobby for customers.) Then Fats would show up to work late, reeking of alcohol. So Duck would belittle him, knowing he was a fat, drunken pervert. Duck then told B how Fats had been harassing Alexa and how she had to get a restraining order against him. And now *this*.

B's face contorted with disgust. He asked Duck what he was going to do about the assault, then threatened to kill Fats himself. "You know the police ain't gone do shit. Especially if you didn't see his face."

B thought of himself as a gangster because he sold drugs and hung out with the Crips he grew up with on South Kenyon Street. But in reality, he was just a drug dealer and a peacemaker. When he was in high school he sold marijuana to every student who smoked it and often broke up fights. Then he got robbed for over two pounds of weed. Now he always carried a gun for protection, but as far as Duck knew, he'd never fired a pistol, let alone killed anyone.

The nurse entered and checked Alexa's vitals, then began administering medicine. When she finished, she entered notes on the computer in the corner and then started to leave.

"Excuse me," Duck said. "Do you know how long she'll be like this?"

The nurse stopped and looked at him sympathetically. "It depends. A few weeks, maybe. But you should ask the doctor. Sorry." She frowned, then turned and walked out.

"Shit's foul," B said. "I'm telling you we can get this dude. I know this cat from the military that can get his hands on anything. I'm talkin' M-fours and SR-fifteens. Whatever you need, my nigga." He said this excitedly, slapping the back of his right hand into his left palm. Those were both high-caliber weapons. One a carbine, the other a rifle.

Duck's anger now became fear. The consequences of criminal actions suddenly became real to him. He began to consider the forgiveness Ms. Davis had prayed about. Alexa would need him, and in prison what good would he be? Then a small voice in his head suggested that if he planned things right, he could get away with it.

"I don't need a gun," he said snapping out of it. "I could kill him with my fists."

Ms. Davis cleared her throat as she entered. Duck turned, startled, then sighed, secretly relieved at her presence.

"You should probably head home to shower," she said. "I'll stay until you come back." They both had spent the night in the hospital waiting area. Duck *was* hungry and felt a slight need to rest.

"My car is at your house, remember?" he said.

B stood up from the window sill. "C'mon, cuz, I'll give you a ride," he said, zipping his coat.

They went through the parking lot to B's Chevy Suburban. B unlocked it using his key fob. Duck opened the passenger side door and immediately caught a whiff of potent cannabis. He wrinkled his nose, and then cautiously looked inside the truck. Three empty Cîroc bottles were on the floorboard, and the ashtray below the radio was stuffed with roaches.

B climbed in and looked at him. "You gonna get in or what?"

"You don't have any guns in here, do you?"

B laughed, then slipped the key into the ignition. "Man, get in the truck."

Duck climbed in slowly, reluctantly. He footed the bottles out of his way and fastened his seatbelt, then turned to survey the back.

"What you looking for, little people?" B snickered, then started the motor. Gangster rap music blared.

Duck whirled back around and turned the music down.

"What the fuck's wrong with you, touching my radio?" B said, looking at him. He turned the music back up, slightly.

"Just take me to my car," Duck said. "I don't wanna hear any music right now."

B side-glanced him, then sneered. "All right," he said. "But we gotta make a few stops."

"I don't wanna make any stops."

"Man, look at my gas," B said, pointing at his gas gauge. "You want me to ride around on E?"

Duck shook his head, thinking it was a bad idea to catch a ride with this dude. B reached over into the ashtray and fished out a stubbed-out blunt. He parked it into the corner of his mouth, lit it, took four or five puffs, and coughed hard. Duck powered down his window to breathe in the fresh air.

B took another pull, blew out a large cloud, and sucked it in, then blew it out at Duck. "Fuckin' nerd. Let me hurry up and drop your ass off."

They drove to a Chevron gas station and parked next to a burgundy Ford Taurus wagon in the parking lot, away from the pumps. A hooded man got out from the backseat and climbed into the back of B's truck. He closed the rear door, barely.

Duck wiped his hands on his lap. What was B doing? They were supposed to be getting gas.

B turned and reached behind himself, taking the man's hand. They swooped up a gang sign together.

B said, "This's my cousin, Duck." Then "Duck, this's my nigga, Gravedigga."

Gravedigga?

Duck turned mechanically to face the man and said, "What's up?"

Gravedigga's eyes were red with murder in them. A thin scar ran from his cheek to his upper lip, creating a deep cleft in his mustache, which caused his lip to curl. His hoodie was blue, and a blue bandana was tied around his neck. Duck turned away and watched him through his peripheral.

B looked in the rearview mirror, then at his side view, and then casually opened the lid to the armrest compartment. He took out a golf-ball-sized bag of white powder and handed it to Gravedigga as Gravedigga handed him a thick wad of money.

B counted the bills fast, stuffed the fold in his jeans pocket, then turned the music up. It was Mozzy, rapping about getting money and killing black men.

B fished in the ashtray for the rest of the blunt and lit it, took a draw, and then passed it to Gravedigga.

Gravedigga took a long pull and coughed convulsively, wiped slobber strings from his mouth, and then pulled on the blunt again.

B looked back at him and said, "Say, cuh. You know some nigga named—" He stopped and tapped Duck on the arm. "What's that fool's name?"

The previous song had ended, but another hard beat had kicked in. Every other word of the rap seemed to rhyme with "Nick."

Duck's mouth was dry, and his palms were sweaty. He wanted to get out but didn't know how to without being awkward. He thought of an excuse to leave and come back when the gangbanging was over. He *was* hungry and *did* need to use the restroom. B hit him again. "What's his name?"

"Fats," Duck said.

"Fats," B repeated. "You know some nigga named Fats?"

Gravedigga's face hardened thoughtfully. He frowned, then shook his head slowly and said, "Nah, cuh."

"This nigga, *Fats*, poured acid all over his girl's face. She in the hospital right now, all ragged up like the mummy and shit."

Gravedigga looked at them unimpressed, then put the blunt back to his lips and pulled. He coughed, then passed it back to B. It was almost gone. "That's some savage shit, cuh. What you gonna do about that?"

The truck was now clouded with white smoke. "I don't know," Duck said, irritated. "Nothing I can do." *But leave it to the authorities*, he thought.

Gravedigga scoffed, leaned back, and lifted his blue sweatshirt. He grabbed between his waistband and boxers and pulled out a MAC-10. How it fitted discreetly under his clothes, Duck couldn't fathom. Gravedigga leaned forward, flexing it carelessly. "You can murk him," he said. "Or I could do it for a couple of racks."

B reached under his seat and pulled out an even bigger weapon. "I knew you was ready, my nigga, but you ain't fuckin' with this PAP M-ninety-two."

Gravedigga put his gun away, took the AK-styled pistol, and examined it.

Duck opened the door.

"Where you going?" B asked, whirling a look at him.

"I gotta piss." Duck stepped out, went into the service station, and used the restroom. Then he went over to the

McDonald's side and ordered a burger. When he came out with his order, half a dozen cop cars had the Ford Taurus and the Suburban surrounded.

He turned away as if he didn't know them. Went down the street and called his grandparents. His heart was galloping.

Grandmother answered. Duck immediately asked for a ride, but Grandpa was at the senior center shooting pool. Duck tried Grandpa's cell phone but didn't get an answer. He tried again and got no answer, still. What if somebody saw him and associated him with B and Gravedigga?

Duck walked further down the street and sat down at a bus stop, antsy. He had gotten lucky. He tried Grandpa again, then hung up, frustrated. Then he remembered Stan's offer to call if he ever needed anything. Amy answered and said that Stan was in the middle of a Zoom meeting, then offered to give Duck the ride he said he wanted to ask Stan for.

Amy arrived ten minutes later. Duck hopped in, buckled his seatbelt, and thanked her.

"No worries," she said, pulling off.

"I just need you to drop me off at my car. It's at Alexa's mom's house."

"I know how to get there." Amy flashed a smile at him, then grasped his hand. "Anything I can do to help."

He pulled his hand away and looked out his window. They passed three or four city blocks in silence.

"I can't believe someone would do that to her," Amy said. "I hope they catch the guy."

Duck said nothing.

She cleared her throat softly. "Stan thinks it was somebody she knew—like a jealous ex-boyfriend or something. But I told him you guys have known each other since high school. You're the only guy she's ever been with. Right?" Duck saw through his peripheral that she was looking at him and waiting for a response.

"Watch the road," he said.

She faced the road and braked at a four-way stop. She waited her turn and then drove ahead. "But you didn't see his face, so you don't know who it was. *Do you?*"

Duck kept quiet. He just wanted to get to his car, drive home, eat, and return to Alexa.

"Okay," Amy said. "I'll leave it alone. Sorry." She then hummed briefly, filling the silence.

Duck leaned against the passenger side door, looking at the trees, houses, apartments, and businesses they passed— one hand under his chin, the other resting on his thigh.

Amy stopped at a red light. "I know this is weird, but do you mind if I—" She reached over and touched the top of his hand and rubbed. "So smooth."

He moved his hand, feeling itchy and hot. He scratched his neck under his collar. He let the window down some and continued staring out of it.

"I'm sorry," she said. "I didn't mean to make you uncomfortable."

"I don't feel like talking right now. I just wanna be dropped off at my car."

"Okay." She nodded. "I understand."

Ten minutes later, she pulled up to it. He thanked her without looking at her and started to get out when she grabbed his forearm. He looked down at her hand. "Just a minute," she said.

He pulled his arm away from her and gave her a scalding look. "I need to get back to Alexa."

"But you just left her." She smirked. "She's not going anywhere."

He shook his head and then turned for the door. She grabbed his wrist. He snatched it back. "What the hell is wrong with you, Amy?"

"I'm sorry," she said. "Is there anything else I can do for you?"

He climbed out of the car without answering, hurried home, ate, and packed up a sandwich for later. He took a few books with him to the hospital. Books Alexa had suggested he read. When he arrived Ms. Davis was asleep in the chair across the room. It was evening.

He sighed, then quietly sat down beside Alexa. He opened the book by Maya Angelou, and riffled through the pages until he found "Alone." It was a favorite of Alexa's. He cleared his throat and read:

"Lying, thinking
Last night,
How to find my soul a home
Where water is not thirsty
And bread loaf is not stone
I came up with one thing
And I don't believe I'm wrong
That nobody,
But nobody
Can make it out here alone . . ."

He read "Still I Rise," then used his phone to listen to Pandora, playing some of Alexa's favorite artists, and then fell asleep.

Three days later Duck was visiting when the doctor came in with a nurse.

"How are we doing today?" the doctor asked, rather friendly. His hands tucked in the pockets of his white coat, his small face round and cheery.

Ms. Davis leaned forward and whispered a quick prayer. Duck said they were doing fine, then twisted in his seat, wondering what the doctor was going to tell them. Was Alexa going to have surgery? Was she going to be transferred?

"Well," said Doctor Nguyen. "Today we're going to change Alexa's dressings, check on her wounds, and see how the healing is progressing. We just need you two to step out. It should take no more than an hour. We'll notify you once we're finished."

Duck and Alexa's mom left promptly, went down to the cafeteria and ate, then returned to sit in the hallway.

The doctor came out an hour later. The two stood up. Ms. Davis, rubbing her hands together nervously. Duck, staring wide-eyed at the doctor. The physician smiled at them, then cleared his throat. "Well, Alexa is healing a lot faster than we expected. Her wounds are looking very healthy, and—" He paused. "We've decided to bring her out of the coma."

Ms. Davis gasped.

"Now, it may take her a while to wake up," the doctor said.

"How long?" Duck asked.

The doctor looked at him. "Twelve to seventy-two hours."

Ms. Davis whispered, "Thank you, Jesus."

Duck nodded agreeably. Prayer had worked.

"Alexa is very lucky to have you two," the doctor continued. "But I have to warn you, she may be a little confused or agitated, or even aggressive when she wakes up. And if she speaks, she may sound a little raspy—because of the feeding tube and disuse of her voice. But we'll see about all that tomorrow, okay? In the meantime, why don't you both go home and get some rest? When she's awake, we'll give you a call."

Duck was unable to sleep that night. He lay in bed wondering if Alexa would still be in pain when they woke her. Would she remember what happened? And if she did, would she be mad at him? What would he say to her? Would she even be able to see him? The doctor hadn't said anything about her eyes.

Duck worried himself into the next day. It was quarter to three in the afternoon when Ms. Davis finally called. Duck rushed to the hospital and met her in the hallway on the floor that Alexa was on. Doctor Nguyen approached them.

"So," he said, almost whispering, "she is awake. And she can see."

Ms. Davis cupped her mouth and gasped.

"But her vision is limited. She can only see straight ahead of her . . . not so much peripherally. Things outside of her direct line of sight are dark . . . or blurry. I just want you to be aware of that."

Ms. Davis nodded and said, "Okay."

There was some relief. Still, Duck felt like he was kicking himself out of a night terror.

The doctor then invited them into Alexa's room. Duck followed closely behind Ms. Davis. Alexa had been re-bandaged, and her right eye was no longer patched. She turned her head toward them, slowly.

"You can see!" Ms. Davis cried thankfully. "Oh, thank you, Jesus! Thank you, Jesus! You can see!" She sat down by Alexa and took her mitted hand, crying tears of relief and happiness.

Duck sat down on the opposite side of the bed, where Ms. Davis normally sat. He clasped Alexa's left hand with his right, crying himself.

She could see. In less than a week she could see! But she still had to endure the pain of healing.

The doctor asked to speak to Ms. Davis in private. She rose and slowly followed him out of the room.

Alexa then faced the ceiling. Duck looked at her, gently squeezing her hand. Her left eye was clotted and bleary. Her mouth, slightly open, poked out of a white mask.

What was the right thing to say to her? The woman you loved, but let down, now lying in a hospital bed. Burnt and scarred and wrapped up like a mummy. *I love you? I'm sorry? I can't wait until you heal and get better?*

He spent nearly a week imagining conversations with her. Now he was drawing a blank. He opened his mouth and made a guttural stammer.

Alexa slowly turned her head to look at him. *This is your fault*, her bleary eyes seemed to say.

"I'm sorry," he said. "It should have been me."

She faced the ceiling again, saying nothing. A moment later a tear escaped her eye. She sniffed, then turned her back to him.

He lowered his head and gritted his teeth. He closed his eyes and saw his hands around his enemy's neck, squeezing until his enemy's eyes bulged into dullness. Duck physically felt his thumbs press down into flesh, then into a rigid tube of cartilage. He felt the windpipe collapse in his hands and snap.

He shook the vision and stood, wiping the tears from his face. He took Alexa's hand again. Her flesh was cold, and she was crying hard and trembling.

"Everything's going to be okay," he mumbled. He gently patted her hand, trying to think of something better to say to her. Trying to fight back the tears surfacing on the rims of his eyelids. "You have a good doctor . . . And we've been praying for you. . . . That's why you can see."

"My face," she said suddenly. The words were like a fast-jabbing bayonet to the stomach. He felt weak. Gutted. "He took away my face!"

Duck dropped his head and stopped patting her hand.

Alexa sniffed, moaned, and then sniffed again.

Silence filled the space of the room.

Ms. Davis and Doctor Nguyen re-entered—Ms. Davis sitting, the doctor standing.

The doctor cleared his throat and then explained that they were going to put Alexa back into a medically induced coma to begin her reconstructive surgery.

"Tomorrow we will remove skin from your back and buttocks, which we'll use to graft and attach to the damaged areas of your face," he said. "We will start this procedure tomorrow at six a.m."

Ten other surgeries followed within the next six weeks. And on January seventh, Alexa's face was to be revealed.

When the day came, Duck's heart raced as he watched her. She sat upright in the hospital bed, staring into the mirror the doctor had handed her, exploring her face with her forefinger. Ms. Davis stood beside her, hands folded up to her chin, whispering praises to Jesus.

Alexa set the mirror down and stood, dragging herself and the IV pole to the restroom where the lighting was brighter and the mirror was bigger. Duck followed. They all followed.

Alexa leaned over the sink and looked deeply into the mirror, probing her new face. Her skin color was visibly two-toned. Brown blotches covered her cheeks with surrounding patterns of light tan. Lines appeared, plastic and stiff on her forehead. The cartilage in her nose appeared shrunken. Her eyebrows had vanished. Alexa turned slowly, looking at the dissolved cartilage that used to be her ear. An enormous patch of hair was missing above it.

There was no movement among them, only silence.

Alexa reached over her shoulder and peeled back the tunic, exposing her right breast. A thick, mud-colored web was splayed across it. The same horror covered her right arm.

"I . . . I think they did a good job," Duck said.

Alexa covered her face and wept. Duck rushed over to embrace her. Her fragile body shuddered inside his chest. He rubbed her back. "It's okay," he whispered into her ear.

She shrieked painfully and trembled harder. He clenched his teeth and thought of murder again. An evil chuckle then echoed inside his head.

His head.

N i n e

Ten a.m. Sunday. Duck pulled up as Ms. Davis was leaving her house. She came down her porch stairs stiffly, wearing purple heels and a black trench coat over a tight purple dress. She was headed to church for the first time in a month since Alexa had been home.

Duck killed the motor, got out, and went up the walkway. Ms. Davis mumbled that the door was unlocked as they passed each other in the cold. She hated him, he thought. But then sometimes when he visited, she would cook for him and speak to him cordially. Today was just one of those days she felt the stress of being a mother, he assumed.

He went in and saw Amy on the couch with Alexa. Alexa had her blouse unbuttoned, exposing her scarred breast, and Amy was tapping ointment across the scar. She looked up at him.

Duck greeted them and hung up his coat, then walked over and kissed Alexa. Her lips were stiff and cold. He ignored that and went to the bathroom to wash his hands, not wanting any germs on his fingers causing any infection, even if the wounds were closed. He hoped Amy had done the same before she started putting the ointment on.

He returned to the living room and sat down on the other side of Alexa, then reached into the small, blue container of Silvadene on the coffee table. He scooped out a smidgen of the creamy antibiotic.

Amy got up and excused herself to the bathroom. She was wearing a dusty pink work dress with pink pumps. The dress was tight on her body. Today was the second day she had helped with putting the ointment on. She did it yesterday too, showing up early, and taking over Duck's job. She'd been visiting Alexa every day after work, bringing over burn care and skin care products. And she and Stan had paid the remaining balance of the medical bills. Last week Amy told Alexa she could come back to work whenever she was ready. The kids missed her. But Alexa hadn't responded.

She'd been so depressed that Duck had neglected to get treatment for himself. And he had had three episodes since the attack. One psychotic break caused him to stay home for a week, following Alexa's second operation. When he finally was healthy enough to visit her in the hospital again, she accused him of leaving her and coming back only because he felt guilty for doing so. She wanted him to go home. To move forward because that's what he wanted to do anyway, she had told him. He told her about the episode, and she told him to get help. He needed to worry about himself, not her, she said.

Now he looked at her marbled face, then at the scar on her chest. It was still flaky and inflamed around the edges. He wished she'd stop scratching it.

"How are you feeling?" he asked, rubbing the medicine in with his fingertips.

Two seconds of hard silence passed. He looked at her for an answer. She was staring ahead at nothing, and her right eye watered.

"Fine," she muttered.

He looked at her chest and continued to rub. The texture of wet scar tissue stimulated the ends of his fingers. He fixated on the scar. It was webbed and thick. Dark brown around the edges, ending at the base of her neck. He rubbed feeling conflicted, at odds with the idea that the scar was some form of art.

She sighed and looked at him. "Why are you doing my chest again? Amy did it already."

"I know," he said, glancing at her. "I just wanna make sure it's done right." He focused back on the scar. "And try not to scratch it," he added. "It looks irritated."

"I'm trying."

"Have you taken your pain medication?"

"Yes."

He dipped his fingers in for another scoop. "Hold still." She stiffened and closed her eyes. He tapped around her leathery face, then circled her puffy cheeks. Slowly and carefully. She pursed her lips and exhaled through her nose.

He finished and then worked on her arm. Amy returned from the bathroom.

He screwed the lid back on the container as Amy sat down next to Alexa again. Alexa buttoned her blouse, then rose to go to her room. He got up to follow.

"Don't," she said, facing him. "I'm going back to bed." She turned and then trudged away as he stood there, dumb.

The door banged shut.

"She'll be fine," Amy said. "Just give her some space."

Give her some space?

Alexa had already hidden the full-length mirror in her room and had covered the one above her dresser with a blanket. She refused to leave the house, and last night, before going home, he counted out the OxyContin that was left. Alexa was instructed to take one every four to six hours. By his count, she was taking at least two at a time. She didn't need space, she needed support. She needed comfort.

Clammy fingers grabbed Duck's hand and tugged.

"Sit," said Amy.

He sat down on the couch. Amy crossed her long legs and commented on the snow outside the window. It was mid-February, and snow had just begun falling.

"Oh God, I hope it doesn't stick!" Amy said.

Her words became distant, as Duck started revisiting the acid attack in his mind. Alexa screaming. Him chasing the culprit. Alexa screaming. Him returning. The smell of acid on her smoldering flesh. How it cooked under his nose as he carried her away to safety. How Ms. Davis was behind him, yelling that Alexa needed water on her. How he failed to protect Alexa.

It would have never happened if I walked out of the house with her. He blamed himself again. Hated himself again.

"This shit is fucked," he said.

Amy stopped her babbling and peered at him. "This is hard for her, too," she said, seizing his hands. "This is hard for all of us."

For a second he believed she was being sincere. Her thumbs slid over the back of his hands and rubbed. She scooted closer. In her tight, mini-work dress. Closer. With her long, white, shiny legs.

He yanked his hands away and rose. "I have to go check on her."

He charged into the bedroom to find Alexa balled up under the covers.

He took off his shoes, lifted the bedding, and lay down beside her under it.

He reached over and touched her face, then leaned forward and kissed her. She stayed quiet. He then tickled the bottoms of her feet with his toes. She used to like that. But instead of giggling she whined, jerking her feet away from his. He moved closer still, found her face again, and slowly kissed her lips. She squirmed away, burying her chin in her neck.

He drew back, feeling empty and frozen and hopeless. How could he make her happy again?

After a while, she scooted toward him, then asked suddenly, quietly, painfully, "You don't think I'm ugly now?"

The words fell on him like a cinder block. "No. I love you, no matter what, Alexa." He was hurt by her asking such a question. "It's your spirit that makes you beautiful, and nobody can take that away from you. Nobody."

There was a knock.

He poked his head out from under the covers and shouted, "What?"

Amy spoke from the other side of the door and said that she was leaving before the snow stuck.

Good, he thought. A few seconds passed before she clonked off. He put his head back under the covers.

Alexa shrieked, grabbing her forearm.

"I thought you said you took your pain medication."

"I did."

"Well, maybe it isn't strong enough. I need to start massaging your arm more." He took her hand and rubbed the web of burned flesh that covered a third of her arm, then got out of bed to get the olive oil she kept on the dresser. Her mom had said since olive oil was used to anoint the sick, it must be good for treating wounds.

Duck sat down on the side of the bed and poured a spoonful of oil into his palm. He massaged the top of Alexa's hand, wrist, and forearm.

She relaxed with her eyes closed. He worked his hands up and down in slow methodical strokes, watching her. Her lips parted. For the first time in weeks, she looked peaceful. Truly peaceful. Without thinking he leaned over and kissed her. She let out a soft, passionate moan.

Soon after that, they were undressing. He stood, removing his pants. She sat down on the bed, unbuttoning her blouse. When she was done, she curled up under the covers with her back to him. He came over and joined her. He kissed the back of her shoulder, then slid one arm under her slender body. He slowly cupped her breasts, feeling the reptilian flesh on his fingertips. She squirmed uncomfortably.

"You okay?" he asked. She whispered yes. He kissed her shoulder again, feeling her erect nipples tickle the inside of his hands.

She turned to face him. Cold fingers touched his face, reading his skin. He met her soft lips and kissed them, breathing into her mouth as she breathed into his. He sucked her breasts, then eased on top of her and guided himself in.

She let out a deep gasp, clutched the sheets, and arched her back. He held her close and buried his face in between her shoulder and neck. He slid in deeper, moaning, as she did. He felt her slender arms holding him tight. Felt her sharp nails clawing his back.

He threw himself in. Harder. Faster. Her thighs parted wider as she became wetter. She moaned louder, then cried out. He slowed, grinding, curving himself in. Twisting. Down and up. Twisting. Down and up. Then in a frenzy, he hooked her legs over his shoulder and slammed inside of her, hard.

He pinned her arms down and raised himself, slamming his hips in. With love and anger. Over and over. She writhed beneath him and screamed, showering his pelvis. He held onto the bed for leverage.

Clenching his teeth, he threw in one last, powerful stroke. A whip of fire licked up his spine as he arched his back and howled like an animal, his hot loins erupting. It felt like his soul was pouring out of him.

He fell on top of her, laughing. They pillow-talked for an hour, giggling and cuddling like honeymooners lazing in bed after great lovemaking. Finally, he got up to shower.

When he opened the door, Amy was walking away.

"What the fuck are you still doing here?" he asked, angry.

She spun around. Her blue eyes were huge. "I'm so sorry!" she cried. "I thought you still needed some help." Her gaze fell downward.

He shrank back, realizing he was still in his boxers.

Alexa stepped out in a robe. "What's going on?"

"Nothing," Duck said.

"I'm sorry," Amy said to Alexa. "I thought I'd wait for the snow to stop."

Duck turned, disgusted, and went back into the room to get dressed. Alexa came in a few seconds later.

"I thought she left," she said, sitting next to him on the bed.

"So did I." He pulled on his shoes.

Alexa looked at him and asked, "Are you upset?"

He didn't answer.

She put a hand on his thigh. "You shouldn't be mad at her, Carlos. She just wants to help."

He scoffed, baffled that Alexa could be that naive. That blind. That trusting. He stood up and stormed out of the room to discover that Amy still hadn't left. She was in the living room, peeking out the window by the front door, looking out at the white storm.

She turned smiling. "It's coming down so hard."

"Do you need me to walk you out?"

"No. I still hadn't planned on leaving yet."

He grabbed her arm, opened the door, and forced her out.

"Wait a minute," she said facing him. She looked over his shoulder, then back at him. "You're a good man, but you deserve better. For God's sake, just look at her!" He shoved her with one arm. She slid down the snowy steps, grunting and half-falling.

She groaned and gasped for air at the bottom, then sat up and shrieked, holding her skinned knee.

Duck raced down the steps and picked up Amy's shoes, then lifted her by the arm. She pulled away and yelled, "You're going to jail, motherfucker! You're going to jail!"

He looked around to see if anyone had heard her. No one had, that he could see. He slammed the shoes into her chest, grabbed her arm again, and spoke firmly into her ear. "Don't ever come around here again." He released her and started for the stairs.

"You're going to jail, motherfucker! You're going to jail!"

"Go home to your husband."

"Fuck you! I'm a woman, and you assaulted me!"

He went inside and met Alexa at the doorway. She was wide-eyed, hugging herself in her robe, looking frightened. When he had left to see Amy out, Alexa was still in the bedroom. Now she was here, staring at him. How much had she seen?

"What was that?" she asked.

"Nothing."

He tried passing her, but she stepped in front of him, wanting an answer.

"Don't tell me nothing," she said. "What just happened?"

His heart was thumping with fear. He shook his head, then went around her, and plopped down on the sofa.

She sat down beside him, searching his face.

"That lady is not your friend," he said.

"Did you hit her?"

"You might want to find another job."

"Oh my God, you're not answering the question. Tell me what happened."

"I pushed her," he said, ashamed.

Alexa gasped. "Why?" She scooted away from him. "I have to call the police."

"The police?" He rose from the sofa. "That bitch has been flirting with me for months, and you wanna call the police for her?"

She looked at him, stunned.

"You think she's your friend when all she wants to do is fuck me! She doesn't give a fuck about you. When I come out of the room, she's outside the door listening . . . staring down at my dick and shit! She's a fuckin' whore, Alexa. A whore." He stopped, breathing heavily.

She looked away, then turned to him. "How come you never told me?"

"I don't know. It just didn't seem important."

"It didn't seem important?" Her face wrinkled. "That's not important to you?"

"It was the timing, Alexa, I'm sorry. And half the time I thought I was trippin'." He stood there with his hands at his sides.

She sighed, then looked away from him. After a minute she looked at him again. "How long has she been doing this?"

"I don't know." He shrugged. "It doesn't matter because I never did anything with her."

"Did she try anything while I was in the hospital?"

He side-glanced her without answering.

"Okay." She nodded. "So do you like her?"

"What? No!"

She stared at him, then let out a deep breath. "It's okay if you want to leave me. You can go find another woman. I'll understand."

The comment stung him like a thousand hornets. He thought he proved he loved her already.

"That's not what I want to do, Alexa."

"Are you sure you're still attracted to me?"

"Yes." He stared her in the eyes.

She frowned and looked away.

There was silence. A very long period of silence.

After a while, she got up and went to her room. A moment later he could hear her crying.

He went to check on her, but the door was locked. He knocked and called her name and asked for her to open, but she wouldn't.

He slowly walked to the living room and looked out the window for an hour. The cops never came. Only the snow did.

Ten

"Thank you," said the group leader. "Anyone else care to share?" No one in the group responded. "Okay, with that we're going to close with the Serenity Prayer."

Fats looked down, fidgeting in his seat.

"Yes. Fasir, did you want to share?"

His neighbor nudged him. "Go ahead, brother."

Fats cleared his throat and scratched his left palm.

"You got it," another person urged.

Fats had been coming to AA meetings for a month now and never shared. He looked up at the group of men and women seated around him. Their faces blinking, sober and waiting.

He stood slowly, rubbing his hands. "My name is Fasir, and I'm an alcoholic." They all nodded, understanding. He cleared his throat again, feeling pressured as they all stared. "Um . . . thank you for allowing me to share." He sat down and scratched the back of his neck.

"Thank you, Fasir," the group leader said. Fats's neighbor leaned toward him and touched him, whispering a few words of support. The group leader started the Serenity Prayer. Every head bowed with his and recited: "God, grant me the serenity to accept the things I cannot change; courage to change the things I can; and wisdom to know the difference."

The meeting ended. Friends gathered and talked. Fats went outside to where Rita was waiting and got in the car.

"How was it?" she asked, putting away *Our Daily Bread*. He gazed out his window, thinking the meeting was okay. He just felt uncomfortable sitting there for two hours, not knowing when or if he would wet his Depends. He had his prostate gland removed five weeks ago. Now he was incontinent and impotent. The two conditions drove him to binge drink for a week, after which she stopped giving him money and gave him the option to sober up or leave. He chose the former, then found himself being dropped off at an AA meeting, which he'd been attending for the past four weeks.

"It was all right," he said, watching group members leave. He debated with himself on whether or not he should tell her, and then added, "I shared."

"That's great!" she exclaimed, palming his knee. "You're making progress." He looked down at the hand invading his personal space. It quickly moved back to the steering wheel.

"Can we go now?" he asked, blinking, being more careful with his tone. Last week he had frightened her by yelling. She had been pestering him to clean up while he was trying to watch the game. He snapped, jumping to his feet, got in her face, and gave her a hard stare that sent her back into the kitchen where she hummed and cleaned nervously. The humming irritated him and he asked her to stop it. She did, then walked around carefully for two days, saying nothing. During those two days he thought she might give him the boot, but she didn't. He forced himself to apologize later—not because he was sorry—he just didn't want to be homeless again.

They drove home.

He plopped down on the couch and clicked on the TV. Rita stood in front of it, pulling items out from a small paper bag.

"I got you something," she said, placing a little green-and-white box on the coffee table.

"What is that?"

"I've been doing some research," she said, pulling out more things. "Turkey-tail mushroom pills and turmeric root help prevent cancer."

"How's that supposed to help me?" he spat. "I'm already in a fuckin' diaper."

She gasped and said, "Well, you're not dead."

"May as well be," he mumbled. He thought about being impotent. His lip curled at the thought. It was as if God had taken his manhood and kicked it down a flight of stairs, and was laughing about it.

"You are so negative," she said, switching her purse over to her right shoulder. "You have no faith in anything at all."

He groaned. Here he was, a grown man in a diaper. Confined to Depends and a limp dick. And she wanted to talk about faith and miracle pills.

"You ought to thank God for His mercy," she added. "Geez."

"Mercy? You call this mercy? Pissing myself and having a useless dick?"

She placed her hands on her hips. "You have a follow-up in a few months," she said. "The least you can do is *try* to be healthy. My goodness. Faith without works is dead!"

"I don't wanna hear this shit," he mumbled. "If God wants me to have cancer, then I'm a have cancer. Fuck it."

Her mouth fell open.

"You're in the way," he said, motioning his hand for her to move.

Her cell phone began ringing. She fished in her purse and answered, sounding surprised, then smiled at Fats, holding the phone against her shoulder. She took the phone call to her room and returned minutes later, still wearing her coat.

"I'm going to step out for a minute," she said.

He brushed her off, then realized her departure would give him a chance to run off and grab a beer. He would go into her bedroom and steal a few dollars in change from the Mason jar she kept on her cluttered dresser. "Drive safe," he said, as she closed the door.

Rita walked into the Starbucks and glanced around. It was crowded with people working on laptops, holding meetings, or reading. She headed for the counter and reached in her purse for her phone to call the private investigator. He answered and said he was seated at the far end of the store by the massive window overseeing the main street. She spotted him and waved, then got in line.

She got her coffee and joined him, setting her sleeved cup down on the small table. She looked the man in the eye, then scooted closer in the wooden chair. He looked serious.

"Thanks for meeting with me on such short notice," he said. He opened a folder and fumbled through papers. "Let's get down to business." He looked down and read.

"In nineteen-ninety-seven, he was arrested for voyeurism. Charges were dropped. The following year he was caught with a neighbor's daughter. Arrested for child rape in the third degree. She was fourteen. He was eighteen. Sentenced to a year in prison."

He turned the documents around and showed her. Her hands quivered as she handled the papers. She read over the contents, then looked at the investigator.

"He was released in nineteen-ninety-nine," the man continued. "In two-thousand-and-five, he was convicted of child rape in the third degree again. This time the girl was fifteen. He was twenty-five. The parents found out and pressed charges. He did two years on a thirty-four-month sentence. Other than that, he's got a bunch of DUIs, and recently . . . some harassment concerns here." The PI turned the papers around and slid them over to Rita. She pored over them with her mouth agape.

"If this guy is living with you, I suggest you call the cops and have him escorted out immediately," he said. "And maybe even get a restraining order." He rose from his seat. "I'm going to go now. Good luck."

He nodded and left.

Rita sat for twelve minutes, numb. What was she to do? She had a monster in her house. And to think she had felt sorry for him, thinking she saw something familiar in him. But he was nothing like her son. No. This man was a pedophile. A predator. A rapist!

She drove home afraid, believing he somehow knew about the investigation and was at home waiting for her so he could strangle her and do what he did to those poor girls when she was dead. He was probably a thief, too. Lord knows how many things he'd stolen from her. And to think she never bothered to put away any of her jewelry or cash savings!

She parked a block away from the house, locked herself inside her car, and waited for the authorities to arrive. She flinched at every car that cruised by, expecting to see Fats inside one of the vehicles, staring at her.

She turned at every sound, anticipating seeing him at one of her windows, yelling and screaming and yanking on her door to get it open.

What if I had a daughter? He would have preyed on her, or raped her while she was asleep! He could have raped me! She clutched herself in horror, then double-checked her locks. Soon after, she spotted the police in her rearview mirror, approaching. She hurried out to flag the cop down.

Rita walked inside the house with a tall, veteran cop by her side. Fats sat up and muted the television.

"We need to talk," she said shakily.

"What's up?" Fats asked, turning off the TV.

She gazed down, rubbing her hands.

He glanced at the tall, burly officer, who was in his cop stance, scanning the living room.

"Why didn't you tell me you were in prison?" Rita asked.

"I told you I did time," Fats said. "You acted like you didn't care." He had a buzz from the Four Loko he'd drunk with shots of Listerine and was trying to control his slur.

"No, I asked you about it, and you never answered."

"It was over twenty years ago, so why does it even matter?"

"It matters because you took advantage of someone," she said. "And you were dishonest when I gave you a chance to tell me the truth."

"This is bullshit," Fats mumbled. "You just wanna fuck with me."

"I'm sorry, but you have to leave," she said. "I don't feel safe with you here."

"You know I just had this surgery."

"I'm sorry, Fasir."

He scratched the back of his neck. "You're a hypocrite," he muttered. "You pretend like you're nice, but you're just like everyone else."

The officer turned the volume down on his radio. "Come on, buddy. Let's go."

Fats didn't move. Memories of his mother filled his mind. His crackhead, child-molesting mother, who Dad left him to live with until she died from a brain aneurysm at the age of thirty-five. Fats recalled the many things she did to him. How she left him alone with male strangers. How she had sex in the open when he was a child. How she'd pull on his dick whenever he tried to sleep, saying it would make him bigger. And he was just an infant! He rubbed his sweaty palms down his thighs.

"She molested me," he muttered. The alcohol was working, cooking his blood. "My fuckin' mother!" He looked up. "And none of you mothafuckas care!"

The officer clutched the butt of his service weapon. "Sir, you need to calm down," he said, lifting his free hand.

Fats stood, seething, fuming. Breathing heavily.

"She molested me!" he yelled, kicking over the table. It crashed on its back and tumbled toward the policeman's feet. Why couldn't anyone understand?

The officer snatched the speaker mic on his shoulder. "I have a distress situation! I need backup right away! I need it now!"

Fats grabbed his head and paced from one end of the couch to the other.

The policeman called for backup again. Soon the living room was crowded with officers. Every cop touched their weapon and closed in on Fats. He was arrested and taken to jail but released a few hours later.

He walked the streets of Kent-Des Moines until he found a corner store where he could buy cheap beer with the rest of the change he'd stolen earlier from Rita. He bought two tall cans, popped the top of one of them, and walked. He drank gradually at first and then finished in three tremendous gulps. He tossed the empty can, then started on the second beer. He finished the Steel Reserve 211, then caught the 150 bus to Tukwila, where there was a public library he remembered he could sleep in. Having to pee badly, he got off on South 144th Street and Macadam Rd South, three or four stops before his original destination. He turned the corner, and on that block, he found a porta-potty where a commercial building was under construction.

He used the Honey Bucket quickly, then turned around in the tight box to sanitize his hands. He suddenly remembered what someone had said at an AA meeting.

Fats broke open the hand sanitizer dispenser and tore out the near-empty, crinkled, green-labeled bag. He bit a hole through the corner of it and started sucking the alcohol gel. He gagged and almost vomited but regained himself, squeezing the bag, and swallowed the last of its contents. The cold, bitter fluid burned his throat.

He stumbled out and strode ahead onto a bridge. It had a divided lane for cars, and a sidewalk for pedestrians on either side of it. Below the bridge was I-5 South, and at the end of the bridge was a stop sign. Walking on the narrow sidewalk, he decided to look below at the speeding traffic.

He leaned over the rail and peered down. Cars raced beneath him on the freeway. He wondered where all the people were going, then spat down at the traffic, only to have his spittle blowback onto his face.

He wiped his face.

Fuck these people.

They were probably all married and had good-paying jobs and friends who cared for them. None of them ever had any problems. Not his at least. They weren't diseased.

They weren't homeless. None of them had any felonies or knew what it was like to be molested. With his hands on the rail, he imagined jumping and ending his life. A news helicopter would arrive and hover above, showing his splattered body live on the evening news. People would remember the event. But no one would be at his funeral. Not even Dad.

Fats heard laughter and turned to a group of boys headed in his direction. Four teenagers, hit each other with their backpacks, hooting and running from one another. Fats cleared his throat, and when they got close enough he asked, "Hey, one of y'all got a pen . . . and a piece of paper?"

The kids stopped. The tallest among them pulled out a notebook, tore out a sheet of paper, and told Fats to keep the Bic. The boys walked off, playing with each other in the street.

Fats scrawled out a note.

MAYBE NEXT TIME, it read.

He folded it and stuffed it in his pocket, looked down at the traffic, and straddled the railing. Rita, like everyone else, wanted him to fail. She waited until after his surgery to bring up his past. What did it matter that he liked girls that were younger than him? In this country . . . in this world even, men loved other men and women loved other women, so why couldn't a man and a young girl love each other just the same? If he was a pervert, his mom was to blame.

He turned so that he sat on the barrier, facing the freeway, holding onto the rail very tightly. His Depends were like a cushion against the metal. He looked down at the traffic and felt woozy. He lifted his head and closed his eyes. Nobody would miss him. Nobody. He opened his eyes again. Tears blurred his vision. He blinked to let the tears run down his face.

Why am I even here? This life is so fuckin' pointless.

Crying, he turned carefully and faced the street corner to give the jump more thought. A second later a car braked at the stop sign. Fats looked at the driver and the driver looked at him.

Fats lowered his eyes and clenched the metal railing.

The driver let down the passenger side window. "Hey, brother," he called out. "Everything all right?"

Tears were streaming down Fats's cheeks.

The driver shut off the motor and got out with his keys.

Fats glanced at him, then wiped his face.

"Say, brother, what you are doing?" the man asked, approaching. He spoke loud and strode over big. He wore a thick beard, and there were gold tassels around the hem of his blue T-shirt. Fats then noticed a child was in the back of the car. Strapped to a car seat, the infant was wailing.

The man turned, then returned his gaze to Fats. "That's my daughter," the man said. "You got any kids?"

Fats lowered his head and said, "No."

"Ah, brother, you gotta have kids."

He felt like the man was jeering at him and said, "I can't have any fuckin' kids." He turned and looked down at the freeway again.

"I got three if you want one. Two boys and her."

Fats hardened his eyes and pursed his lips.

The man, standing beside him now, grabbed onto the rail, looked down below, and then at Fats. "So you over here meditating? Is that it?"

Fats sniffed. The man was clever, trying to soften the mood with his wit. "I'm just tired."

"What you tired of, brother?"

"I'm tired of all this *shit*." Fats shuddered, sobbing. "I'm tired of always trying . . . and not getting anywhere. I'm tired of being homeless. I'm tired of people *shittin' on me!*"

"I feel your pain, brother. But self-pity is unproductive. I know that sounds cold, but believe me, it is. Every day you wake up, you have a chance to start all over again. And that's the beauty of life. If you do what you're thinking about doing, you won't have any more chances. You understand?"

Fats sniffed again, then carefully scooted a few inches away from the man. Fats swung his foot out, then thought of kicking off his shoe, just to see how it would fall, to see if it would cause an accident.

The man inched closer and said, "Remember we survived slavery and oppression. That alone makes you special. Your ancestors didn't give up and neither should you."

Fats raised his head then. A strong hand grabbed his shoulder. He looked at the hand. The man then took him by the arm and helped him down carefully, then embraced him. Solid was the hug.

The man released him and stepped back to examine him.

"What's your name, brother?" the man asked.

"Fasir."

"Fasir? All praises, brother. My name is Noah."

Eleven

"Lift your hands," the prison guard commanded. Twelve inmates stood naked, obeying. The lean, clean-shaven guard stood flanked by two other officers, six feet of space between them. The tall, husky guard on the left stroked his handlebar mustache, examining the inmates. The guard on the right, potbellied and bearded, picked at his teeth with a toothpick.

"Open your mouth," the lean guard continued. "Lift your tongue. Bend your left ear for me. Bend your right ear for me. Lift your sack. Now turn around. Lift your left foot and wiggle your toes. Lift your right foot and wiggle your toes. Bend over and grab your cheeks . . . and spread 'em. Now give me two good coughs."

The twelve men coughed.

"Good. Now get dressed."

The men got dressed. Duck got in line with the rest of the inmates, wearing orange coveralls and brown, rubber sandals three sizes too big for him. He took a bedroll and his prison identification card with a six-by-nine sheet of paper from the guard with the handlebar mustache. The paper said Duck was going to Eight Wing, C-Tier, Cell Two. He clipped the green ID onto his collar, then stood with the group on the right, as instructed.

A moment later, he and four inmates followed the lean officer out of the cement building into the cold and misty rain. Duck was at the front of the line.

He squeezed the bedding under his arm as he looked at the stone prison ahead. He pulled on the leg of his jumpsuit, trying not to trip as he repeatedly stepped on the back of its hem. He looked left to see a poker-faced prison guard in the gun tower watching them, holding a rifle.

A long buzzer sounded when they reached the prison door. The lean guard yanked the door open.

Duck entered with his heart beating out of his chest. There was a metal detector to pass through and a line of five officers to his right. The officers were wearing black, patrol gloves, tugging on them and flexing their hands.

"Step through," an officer commanded. Duck went through the metal detector, holding the bedding.

"Step aside," the officer said.

Duck stepped aside.

"What's your name?" the officer asked, snatching the ID from Duck's collar.

"Carlos Duckworth."

The officer looked at the ID, then handed it back. "Inmate Duckworth, do you know where you're going?"

"Yes, sir. C2."

Washington State Penitentiary. Eight Wing. C2. This would be home for the next few years, at least, Duck reflected. Two weeks after he pushed Amy down the stairs, he'd gotten a visit from the Renton police. He was sitting on the couch with Alexa, massaging her scars, when they came. Ms. Davis answered the door. Two officers stood at the doorway, asking for him.

They'd brought him down to the station for questioning. He wasn't surprised to see Amy there but felt confused when he saw one of the kids from the childcare center, accompanied by her parents, who were guarding the child closely. Duck followed the officers to a windowless room.

A large, black detective in plain clothes came in as Duck was seated. The detective, holding a folder, pulled up a chair to the round wooden table and sat down. "How are you doing, Mr. Duckworth?"

"I'm good," Duck said. "I just wanna know why I'm here." The incident with Amy was two weeks ago. Why would she be pressing charges so late?

The detective leaned forward and squared the folder in front of him. "We brought you in to ask you some questions about Lizzy."

Lizzy was the little girl from the daycare in the precinct with her parents. Duck instantly remembered the last time he saw her at the childcare center. It was when he went to visit Alexa and ended up reading to the children. He recalled how the little girl liked to play with his hair.

"You might've seen her out there with her parents," the detective continued. "You do know her, don't you?"

"Yeah," Duck answered, irritated. "She goes to the daycare my girlfriend used to work at. What is this about?"

"What is this about?" the detective asked wild-eyed. "This is about you molesting her!"

"What!"

The detective opened the folder, read a date, and said that on that day Duck was left alone with the children, and today it was reported that he fondled one of them. The detective said that Amy had been noticing Lizzy's strange behavior. Lizzy had been touching her genitalia and was shy about going to pee, reported Amy. And when questioned by Amy, Lizzy finally said that Duck had touched her. Amy asked where. Lizzy said, "Here," pointing to her private parts. Amy asked, "Here?"— pointing to her own. The little girl nodded. Amy then told Lizzy's parents when they came to pick her up, afraid all the while that she and her husband might get sued for negligence. That was the story.

"I didn't touch that girl!" Duck yelled. The detective went on. They argued for ten minutes before an officer entered the room. The officer bent over and whispered something into the detective's ear. Duck sat back and stared at the white walls, fuming.

The detective peered at Duck. Duck then peered at him. The detective nodded, and before Duck could think, the officer was placing him in handcuffs. When he was escorted out of the room, Lizzy's parents were there, shielding their daughter. The mother crying. The father called Duck a *son of a bitch*, breaking away from his family, yelling in Duck's ear as the cops were taking him down the hallway. Two officers rushed to restrain the man, just as he swung for a sucker punch that barely missed Duck's head.

When Duck got to jail, he was provided a top bunk, the last available bunk in the tank. He walked in, nodding at the inmates who were staring at him, then quietly set up his bedding. He'd never been arrested and wondered if the inmates would be able to tell. He tried to act normal like he'd been there before. During booking, he remembered stories B had told him about jail. Guys played dominoes and spades, drank prison-made wine called "pruno," smoked weed rolled up in Bible paper, and ate delicacies made from junk food.

But jail didn't look like a clubhouse to Duck. He lay on his bunk, pretending to stare at the ceiling, while stealing glances, listening to, and observing the felons. Most of them were drug addicts and gang members, or woman-beaters. Some of them stalked the tank in monologue, others paced around in silence. Groups of them cliqued up, played pinochle, and watched reruns of Cops on court television, which struck Duck as odd.

He spent the first night alert, not sleeping at all. He didn't eat the next day either. The portions of food were minuscule and looked like scraps you'd feed to a dog. Rice and raisins mixed was breakfast. A peanut butter and jelly sandwich with apple slices was lunch. Beans and a wiener was dinner.

He made quick pals giving his meals away. Then the half-dozen black men there tried to make friends with him, asking what he was in for, where he was from, and if he knew such and such from various neighborhoods.

Duck lied and said he was in there on domestic violence charges since that seemed to be the common crime of his peers. Plus it was nearer the truth than any other fib he could think of. He couldn't say he was a drug dealer because he didn't know anything about drugs. He didn't know too many gangbangers either. He talked about his cousin B, and one of the inmates from the south end of Seattle said he knew who B was. That validation saved Duck for a little more than a week.

Then, after his arraignment, he got into his first altercation. Other inmates being arraigned had overheard Duck's charges when they were read by the prosecutor. They learned he had been arrested for fondling a child. Once Duck was back in the thirty-man tank, he showered and returned to his bunk, only to be jumped and beat up badly.

Alexa visited that weekend. He entered the booth, picked up the black receiver, and sat down on the metal stool behind thick glass. She didn't look like she was glad to see him. But then again, he was locked up, accused of a horrendous crime, and had a shiner and a swollen nose.

She sat down and picked up the receiver. "How are you?"

He scoffed. "This is some bullshit, Alexa. A fucking nightmare. I don't understand why this is happening. Why am I here?"

She stared at his face. "Are you all right?"

"I'm good." He thought about the meeting with his lawyer. "Listen, Imma need you to do me a favor. This thing is serious."

She looked unmoved.

He hadn't asked about her yet. "Wait. I'm sorry. How are you?" The scars on her face looked the same. They weren't going to disappear. Not anytime soon.

"I'm fine, Carlos. What did you need?"

She was starting to sound cold, like her mom.

"You're still beautiful, you know." He felt he needed to remind her. And it was true.

She averted her eyes. "Stop it, Carlos. I know what you're doing. Just ask me whatever it is you want to ask me because I have something to say myself."

What did she have to tell him? Was she getting more surgery? Was she pregnant? He couldn't handle her being pregnant with him being locked up. That would drive him crazier than he already was. He had to get out.

"I may have to go to trial. If they don't dismiss these charges, Imma need you to testify. You were there when I pushed Amy down the stairs. And you know about her advances towards me. Your testimony would help."

She dropped her eyes. "I don't know." Then looked at him again. "Like I said, I have to tell you something."

Jesus. "What is it, Alexa?"

"Amy's been coming over. Visiting still. Helping me."

"What? Why are you hanging out with her? She's trying to ruin my life. What the fuck?"

"May I finish? She told me you're the one who's been hitting on her. All that time alone in the living room with her, all those visits at the daycare, pretending to see me, you were flirting with her."

He laughed. "You can't possibly believe that, Alexa. You know that's not true. Why would I jeopardize our relationship for a broad like her? For any woman for that matter? I love you, Alexa. You know that." He scoffed. "How is she getting inside your head? You're smarter than this. Fuck? So what—you believe I molested that little girl, too?"

She lowered her eyes, not answering.

"Oh, wow, Alexa. This is unbelievable. I don't have anybody right now but you. And you're here telling me that you don't trust me! That you believe this lying, conniving bitch, over me? The man you fell in love with. Do you—do you even love me anymore?"

She met his eyes again. "Look, I don't know what to believe. I think—whatever happens—you should work on yourself." She stood. "I wish you the best, Carlos."

"Are you leaving me?"

She set the receiver down. Then turned to leave.

"Alexa!" He banged on the glass. "Hey! Are you leaving me?"

She was gone. The guards took him back to population.

The court proceedings took forever. Dates were often rescheduled, and the voices inside Duck's head kept telling him he was a molester.

Since Alexa wouldn't help him, he would testify himself.

Duck had already consulted with his attorney about the idea, but she was reluctant to use it as a defense, advising him that his testimony would be incriminating if he admitted to assaulting Amy. But after exhausting other options, his lawyer decided it was their best defense. Amy desired Duck, but couldn't have him. Being physically rejected was her breaking point. Upset and seeking revenge, she created a fantastic story and put it into the head of a child. It was a reach, the lawyer said, but something.

Then, weeks later, she insisted he take the plea bargain. The odds were stacked against him. Even Alexa doubted him. Lizzy's claim was supported by a psychologist, family, and friends, plus Amy and Stan. Lizzy was four years old! How could she even know what she was talking about? Why couldn't they prove these things had been told to her? That she had been coerced and Amy was the devil?

Duck refused the plea bargain. He took it to trial, and Amy got on the stand. Her testimony made him look like a monster. She was trained to notice behavioral signs in sexually abused children. She said it was hard, but after a while she got Lizzy to open up to her. She described in graphic detail what Lizzy had "reported." Amy sobbed on the stand and blamed herself for leaving the children with a trusted friend, a friend who didn't work at the daycare. And now a child was scarred for life because of her mistake.

Then she was cross-examined. The issue of her being pushed down the stairs was decidedly left out by Duck's lawyer. But Amy denied pursuing Duck or seeking revenge for any reason. She said she initially only admired him for his interest in the children.

The plan backfired, and Duck's testimony would end in disaster. Impatient and on edge, he blurted out to the court that Amy was a liar and made the whole thing up and was mad that he rejected her and had pushed her down a flight of stairs. His lawyer ended the questioning promptly, and Duck was removed from the stand.

Again his public defender insisted he take the lesser charges of assault in the fourth degree with sexual motivation and communication with a minor for immoral purposes. He would spend a year in jail and have twelve months of unsupervised probation along with treatment. Still, he would have to register as a sex offender.

It was the best deal the prosecutor was willing to offer. If Lizzy were called to testify, it would be the end of Duck, his lawyer said. Child molestation in the first degree. Almost six years max. But he was *not* a pedophile, and he was determined to prove his innocence.

The nine moons he'd spent in jail going through trial was a nightmare. He fought inmates regularly. And then there were the demons inside his head.

Refusing to eat, he was eventually screened by medical and given medication for depression. That helped to calm him somewhat. But he lost the trial and was sentenced to sixty months. Now here he was, moving from jail to prison, preparing to fight all over again.

The officer pointed straight ahead. "Up the stairs . . . second tier."

Carlos.

Duck turned around to see who called him, but no one was there but the guards, instructing the other inmates on where to go. He ignored the voice and continued onward.

He could hear the criminals chattering. The grim cells seemed to be ten stories high. A thick billow of cigarette smoke hovered before them. Inmates yelled crazily, shaking the caged doors. It sounded like a colosseum of lunatics in an uproar. The metallic clanging increased as he passed by. Prisoners began whistling to get his attention, reaching out like zombies behind the iron bars. Banging. Yelling. Shouting. He avoided eye contact and hurried up the steel stairway, almost tripping in the oversized sandals. Murderers and rapists, thieves, and drug addicts continued to shout out for him.

He stood in front of C2 looking inside the cell at the silver toilet and sink in the back. Five feet above it was a clear, 13" TV sitting on top of a mount bolted into the concrete wall. There were four bunks, two on either side of the dungeon. He noticed the inmate on the top right bunk lying face up, reading a book. The cell door moved with a slight lift, opening itself slowly.

Duck stepped in. The cell door slammed shut behind him.

The inmate reading stopped to look at him. The top bunk on the left was empty. Duck tossed the bedding onto it and said, "What's up?" to the two inmates awake in the cell.

The inmate on the lower right bunk continued sleeping. The reader was around Duck's age. The inmate on the lower left bunk was old enough to be their grandfather.

"What's up, cuz?" the reader said to Duck, sitting up to face him.

He was a Crip. *He might know my cousin,* Duck thought. C-Dub was tattooed on the criminal's throat in big, blue, calligraphy letters. Duck guessed that was his name. Was he from Henderson? Holly?

"What you in here fo' ?" C-Dub asked.

"Damn, no names or nothing?" Duck answered.

C-Dub repeated the question.

Duck's heart was racing now. He knew there were no secrets in prison and that he would have to fight again already.

Fuck it, he thought. "First-degree child molestation."

C-Dub jumped down from his bunk.

"Look, man, I don't want any problems," Duck said. "I'm not a fuckin' child molester. I'm telling you, this broad set me up."

"I don't give a fuck about none of that shit, cuz," C-Dub yelled at him, making a strange gesture with his hand—an inverted peace sign with his thumb in the middle. Walking fingers.

Hoover Crip.

C-Dub thumped gang signs against his chest and continued yelling, then rushed forward raising his fist.

Duck jabbed at his chin. C-Dub stumbled back from the blow. Duck closed in quickly and clutched the back of C-Dub's head, yanking it down into his flying knee. Nasal bones crunched on Duck's kneecap. C-Dub's body weakened beneath him. Duck continued to slam his knee in over and over, crushing soft lips and nose cartilage to the sound of grunts and moans.

"That's enough! That's enough!" the old man in the lower bunk cried.

Duck stopped. C-Dub fell to the floor. He looked like a raccoon that didn't see the car. Blood ran from his nostrils. His eyes rolled back and flickered. He let out a scary groan, and his arms were stiff and locked.

"Well, you better hope you didn't kill him," the old man said, sitting on the edge of his bunk.

Duck grabbed his head and paced. His chest tightened from the stress, and his eyes filled with panic. He just got here and was already going to the hole.

"Where you learn that karate from?" the old man asked, following Duck with his eyes and reaching under his bunk for his trunk.

He began offering toiletries. "You need some soap?" He held out a box of Irish Spring. "I got deodorant, toothpaste, whatever you need. They call me Toothpaste, by the way, because I got a life sentence for stealing some toothpaste. Third strike, you know."

Duck knelt beside C-Dub and tried to shake him awake.

Toothpaste prattled on, telling the story. He and his friend had burglarized an unattended tractor-trailer parked at a motel. It was late. They had no money and needed to get high. He broke inside the tractor-trailer while his friend sat in the van to watch for cops. They loaded the van with boxes, running back and forth, and were just about done when suddenly they were surrounded by cops. Turns out they'd stolen over seven-hundred dollars' worth of Colgate-Palmolive products. Under the habitual offender law, a person convicted of two or more violent crimes or serious felonies receives a mandatory life sentence. A theft of that size is considered a serious felony. That gave him his third strike.

"We gone call you Tyson," Toothpaste said. "Rock 'Em, Sock 'Em Robot and shit."

The gates on the tier started to open. Duck shot up, wide-eyed and frantic. "What's going on?" he asked, thinking the guards were coming for him.

"C-tier! Chow time, mainline, pill line," a voice over an intercom announced.

"Chow time," Toothpaste repeated. The sleeping inmate on the right lower bunk popped up. Convicts flooded the tier and were moving like cattle. Duck returned his attention to C-Dub, who, semi-conscious, sat up to push him off. Duck went to the metal toilet and came back with a wad of toilet paper for C-Dub's nose.

Pushed off again, Duck held the tissue in his hand. He apologized for the fight, then squeezed into traffic, hustled down the steel steps, and darted through the metal detector.

"Stand for search," an officer commanded. Duck stopped, then stepped aside, thinking he'd been caught. He winged out his arms and spread out his legs. Bowing his head, he noticed drops of blood printed down the leg of his orange suit.

The guard kicked at his feet. "Spread your legs."

Duck felt the guard's breath on his neck. Duck spread out his legs further, then glanced over his shoulder at the man's badge. *Officer Meyer,* he noted.

The guard leaned into his ear and said, "Spread-your-fuck-ing-legs."

Duck stretched out his groin. Any further, he'd be doing the splits. Officer Meyer began the pat search.

Duck felt soft hands slip around his neck, then trickle down to his shoulders, and gently grasp his right arm. He shuddered at every sickening touch. The search continued. The guard clapped down Duck's torso and patted his waist, then knelt and swept a feathery hand up Duck's inner thigh.

Duck whirled around, facing the guard.

"Stand for search!" Meyer shouted, springing up.

"You ain't gotta be touching me like that!" Duck fumed, peering down at the officer, sickened by his effeminate graze.

Meyer returned the stare, looking up with his beady little crab eyes, smirking. Three COs surrounded Duck as Meyer grabbed Duck's arm, forcing him around to restrain him. Duck felt the cold metal handcuffs tighten at every click. Meyer and his goons hauled him off to the sergeant's office, where Duck was slammed down on a chair he had to make himself straight on. The three officers towered over him, staring at him.

The sergeant sat behind a cluttered desk pinching tobacco out of a green-and-black container. He stuffed the muddy wad inside his bottom lip, while Officer Meyer told him all about Duck's misbehavior.

The sergeant spat into a Folgers can on the edge of his desk and grunted. He searched for his reading glasses and put them on, then sifted through the stack of files in front of him. He opened one and read, then looked up, grimacing.

"Mr. Duckworth," he said, squinting through his spectacles. He sighed, then snatched them off. "Let's get something clear. What we say here goes. When we say eat, you eat. When we say shower, you shower. When we say stand your ass for search, *you stand your ass for search!*"

Duck said nothing. The sergeant snarled, then referred to the file again. "You like children, I see."

Duck cocked his head and blinked, annoyed.

"Well, nobody admires that shit around here," the sergeant said. "You're going to straighten up, or by the end of the month you'll be known as Carla. . . . I'll make sure of that."

Duck looked down at his feet, then shook his head.

"Get his child-raping ass out of here!"

Meyer shoved him out the door.

Duck followed a few inmates to the prison cafeteria. Convicts were seated everywhere.

He started past the row of prison guards.

"Stand for search!"

He stopped and turned with his arms out, sighing.

"State your number," the CO commanded.

"Seven, five, nine—seven, four, five."

The officer started the pat search.

Duck felt heavy hands slapping up his ribs, then squeezing down his right arm.

"All right, go eat," the guard ordered once he was done.

Duck got in the long line, thinking about the inmate he beat up, about all the pat searches, and now the terrific sight of the chow hall. It was full of convicts, men with life sentences for crimes like murder, kidnapping, and necrophilia. Men who had been there since the seventies. Men with three strikes. Men with tattoos and scars on their faces.

He looked to his left at the four tables in the middle occupied by a group of skinheads, their white T-shirts tucked tight into their state-issued jeans. Their pale bodies were inked with blue prison art. One had a spider web tattooed on his elbow. Another had a large swastika on the side of his bald head. The initials A.B., for Aryan Brotherhood, were thickly printed on the back of his wide neck. Most of the skinheads had sleeves: illustrations of Hitler, lightning bolts, and eagles, covering their arms.

Can't sit with them, Duck thought.

He looked at the Natives, then at the Hispanics, who, he later learned, sat divided according to gang affiliation. At the structured segregation, he marveled.

He took the plastic tray that was handed to him, frowned at the single, stickless corn dog, then moved down the line to have pineapple-filled Jell-O and steamed carrots plopped onto his tray by prison workers behind glass, wearing hairnets and white, kitchen uniforms.

Duck turned slowly, looking at all the black men that were eating. *Somewhere in there, but where?*

He saw a table with one empty seat and approached it. The three men seated stared at him.

"What's up, G?" one of them said.

"Is it coo' if I sit here?"

"You a Disciple?"

Duck shook his head and said, "No."

"Then keep it movin', pimp."

Duck sighed and glanced around, then noticed a table with two empty seats. He proceeded nervously. A black man wearing thick, prison glasses sat with a sleazy-looking white fellow. Both wore wooden crucifixes around their necks and were overweight and balding. They eyed him curiously, seemingly weird, but welcoming. Duck started toward them.

"Is that my cutty?" a familiar voice called out.

Duck looked left and saw B sitting with two other convicts. Duck hurried over and set his tray down as B stood up and embraced him, pounding his fist on his back. They broke up quickly, remembering they were in prison. Duck sat down, smiling.

"This my cousin, Duck," B announced. The two inmates nodded, showing little interest.

B had grown out his hair and had it braided in cornrows. Duck stared at it, wondering who did it for him. *Maybe his celly?* Duck hoped whoever did it wasn't a prison punk. Seeing a man braid another man's hair was still something he hadn't gotten used to. He shrugged it off, then engaged in small talk, first by asking B about how much time he had. B said he had been sentenced to fifty-six months for possession of a firearm and narcotics, with intent to deliver. But he was expecting to be out in a few years, with the good time he'd been credited.

A moment later the two inmates they were sitting with, got up and left.

"Listen, cuz," B said once the inmates were gone. "These tables are for Crips, so you can't sit here." He looked around, then nodded in the direction of the odd couple. "You can probably sit with them. And I won't be able to protect you, either. I know about the charge."

Duck started to say he didn't need his protection, but B interrupted.

"You ain't gotta explain . . . I know you didn't do that shit. But cats in here ain't tryna hear that. Plus . . . my nigga Digga thinks you ratted on us."

Duck sighed, recalling the event in his mind.

"What happened?" B asked. "You get out the car, and the next thing we know . . . we surrounded by the po-lice."

Duck remembered the scar on Gravedigga's face, the knotted bag of cocaine, and getting out of the truck when B and Gravedigga started pulling out guns just before the police arrived. From their point of view, he *would* look like a snitch.

"I just went to the store, B. That's it. You got your police report, right? Is my name ever mentioned? Does it say I called the police? Besides that, Gravedigga got out of a car with three other people in it. Remember? Who's to say one of them didn't snitch? You guys were blasting music and blowing weed and showing off guns in broad daylight and shit. Anybody could have seen you and called the police. So what are you talking about?"

B nodded. "You're right, man. That's what I keep tellin' Digga." He looked down, scratching his plastic fork across his empty tray. "So how much time they give you?"

"Five years. Three years and four months with good time, but I've already lost three months of that." Duck told him about the fights and the one he just had with C-Dub, who B knew as a Crip. Then Duck told him how he was set up by Amy, and how he had to register as a level-three sex offender once he was out. Level-two and level-three sex offenders are required to register for life. His crime was a Class A felony; therefore he had one strike. Two more, and he'd be in prison until death (not that he planned on breaking any laws). Also, under the Habitual Offenders Act, he could be sentenced to life imprisonment if he were ever convicted of the same crime again.

"Why didn't you appeal it?" B asked.

The idea had never occurred to Duck, so he thought about it for a second, then nodded, thinking he would do just that. He finished his Jell-O.

A guard approached the table and told B to leave if he was done. B got up and left.

Duck scarfed down the rest of his food as the next wave of inmates came in. He didn't want to be confronted by one of the Crips, so he got up, tossed his tray through a pass-through, and left the chow hall.

He entered the wing and walked through the metal detector. Officer Meyer stopped him and said to come with him. Duck followed him to the sergeant's office, where Meyer tossed Duck a pair of state-issued jeans and a beige button-up. Startled, he received them and then searched inside the pair of pants for the size.

"These are size thirty-four," he said, looking at the two men. "I wear thirty-eight in waist and thirty-eight in length."

The men chuckled.

"Where you think you at, the Men's Warehouse?" The sergeant scoffed. "We ain't fitting you for a suit."

"Back to C2," Meyer ordered.

Duck went to C2 with the clothes. When he got there, Toothpaste and C-Dub were deeply engaged in a chess game. They sat across from each other on wooden stools. The game board sat on top of a white, overturned bucket.

Toothpaste glanced at Duck, then focused back on the game. C-Dub's left eye was puffy. His lips and nose were swollen and red, his under lip, shredded. He was visibly straining not to look in Duck's direction.

Duck walked around Toothpaste to the back of the cell and dropped the folded clothes at the foot of the silver toilet, then rigged up a sheet from one bedpost to another. Now he was shielded. Behind the sheet, he tried on the jeans. The tight denim wouldn't get past his butt. He took them off in a hurry and put on his jumpsuit.

Pulling back the curtain, he slung the jeans onto his cot. "These pants are too tight," he said. "Like some damn skinny jeans."

Toothpaste laughed. "They fuckin' with you, youngster."

Every gate on the tier suddenly racked back. "Yard time!" a voice over the intercom announced. Inmates hurried out from their cells like children for recess. Duck slipped out behind his cellmates into the rush of human traffic. He flip-flopped down the stairs and then marched through the metal detector.

"Stand for search," Meyer ordered.

Duck stopped dead in his tracks, sighing. *Why does this guy keep fucking with me?*

"Stand for search, I said."

Duck shut his eyes, and then opened them. He stared ahead and exhaled.

"Stand for search, chimo! I'm not going to tell you again!"

He wanted to knock the man's head off. Better yet, choke him.

"That's it!" Meyer cried, approaching him from the shoulder.

Duck spun around with his fist and socked him. The CO fell hard. The three guards that were with him tackled Duck in a hurry. They took violent shots at his face and the back of his head, roughing him up on the ground before putting him in handcuffs. They hauled him up and slammed his head against the wall, kneeing him in the stomach and groin, cursing him.

Maybe this was best. Maybe he'd spend his entire time in the hole. That way he wouldn't have to worry about inmates and guards harassing him.

Twelve

Duck lay on his side, wearing a V-neck T-shirt and orange coveralls, the top half peeled down and tied at his waist. His cell was no bigger than a studio apartment bathroom. A metal sink-toilet combination unit was by the head of his bed. At the foot was a concrete stool and desk.

"Hey, Two," someone yelled from down the cellblock. "I got something coming to you."

Shhhhhhht.

That something was pushed down the tier. A stuffed legal envelope, likely to be tied to a string pulled from the prisoner's jumpsuit. Inmates called this activity fishing: Passing contraband from one cell to another in a manner similar to casting a fishing line.

The packed envelope landed in front of Duck's door.

The inmate in the cell to his left said: "Hey, neighbor, slide that down as far as you can. It's going to Two."

Cool, something to do. Duck rose from his bed, took two steps, and got to his knees, then lay flat on his stomach. He saw the envelope across the floor beneath the door panel. An orange string was tied tight around the envelope, twisted for reinforcement and strength. Duck reached through the inch of space between the door panel and floor, stretched out his hand more, then felt the corner of the envelope on the tip of his middle finger. By the touch he could tell the envelope was stuffed with pictures. The inmate's girlfriend or wife. Nude. Being rented out for vittles. Duck tried fingering the envelope closer to him.

As he did, the heavy gate at the head of the tier clanged open behind a set of rattling skeleton keys.

"Shit."

The envelope was quickly pulled back by the inmate. Duck bounced to his feet, hoping the guards didn't see his hand. Squeaky, rubbery footsteps started down the tier. Two sets of them. Two guards. One with the rattling set of skeleton keys.

"You must want that confiscated, huh, LaFell?" a guard yelled.

No response from the inmate. Nothing but guilty silence on the tier. And the command of respect. You could feel the COs approaching.

Duck had been in the hole for a week and was scheduled to have his hearing today. Maybe they were coming for him. He stood at the solid cell door, listening to their footfalls.

Their steps got closer and closer and then stopped at his door.

"Inmate Duckworth," a guard said at the narrow window.

"Yeah."

"Turn around to cuff up. You have a hearing."

Duck turned around and unraveled the coverall sleeves that were tied at his waist. He pulled the top half of his pumpkin suit up and stuck his arms in its sleeves. Wearing the jumpsuit properly, he quickly zipped up the front and stepped away from the cell door. The cuff port opened. He stepped back a pace and stuck his hands and wrists through the small opening. He heard the clicking of the manacles and felt the cold, metal restraints being tightened around his bones.

He stepped away from the door again. It slowly began to roll itself open. It was loud, like a big heavy machine. It banged to a stop. Duck felt his left arm being grabbed by one of the guards. Duck turned, and they all started to walk. The officer squeezing Duck's left arm wore thick mutton chops—sideburns that connected to his mustache, covering his jawline and cheeks. His dimpled chin showed, for that part of his face lacked facial hair. He chewed tobacco, as evidenced by the lump in his underlip. Duck imagined him in camouflaged rain gear, hiding in bushes, aiming a rifle at an innocent, unsuspecting creature. A pheasant perhaps. Or a rabbit. Something small and cute, destroyed by this large, overpowering white man.

The officer on Duck's right was slightly less aggressive. He was thick-bodied and clean-shaven. Ruddy cheeks. Natural blonde curly hair. He was maybe half the age of his colleague. He held Duck by his jumpsuit sleeve, guiding him along gently.

They escorted him past the gate, made a left, walked about a hundred feet, and made a right into the lieutenant's office. Duck took a seat when instructed. He sat down at the lieutenant's desk, meeting his penetrating gaze. The lieutenant wore about thirty years of correctional experience on his brown sagging face. His eyes were dark and merciless. And steady. His mouth was closed tight, like a fist, and his hands were folded over the desk. All business, like Grandpa, Duck thought.

Duck felt then that the hearing wasn't going to go too well. Which was okay, he thought. He had assaulted an officer after all. A staff member and peer to this serious-looking lieutenant. Duck had received the notice of infraction a few days ago. He had read the report and shook his head at what was said by the witnessing officers.

Everything they wrote was shamefully true, but Officer Meyer himself made Duck sound like a vicious beast.

Duck had slid the report over to his neighbor to get an opinion as to how serious the infraction was, plus to get an idea as to how much time he would have to spend in the hole. The neighbor, an older brother with fifteen years of prison experience, was housed in the cell on Duck's right. The brother called himself Corleone, after the Godfather, a fictional mobster Duck had never heard of. But everyone on the tier called Corleone by his cell number, which was nine. Nine had been in solitary confinement for three weeks already, for fighting an inmate over a seat in the chow hall.

On Duck's first day in isolation, Corleone had asked Duck if he would like to play a game of chess. Duck asked how they were going to play, for they had no chess pieces or chessboard. Corleone then explained to Duck that he would have to draw a chessboard on a sheet of paper, or on the white painted slab called a desk in his cell, and then they would call out their chess moves and record them. They played for two days, and then Duck lost interest. That's when he received his notice of infraction.

Corleone read the report, then suddenly announced to the tier, "Hey, ya'll, this mothafucka knocked out Meyer!"

"Who did?"

"This mothafucka in ten."

"Who's in ten?"

"This mothafucka named Carlos."

"Ten, you knocked out Meyer?"

"Yeah," Duck answered humbly.

"Good, man. That mothafucka always fuckin' with people."

Corleone then slid the infraction report back to Duck with a note written on the back saying: "Smile. This is a thirty-day thing."

Duck expected the penalty to be worse. Maybe Corleone had said that because he once had assaulted an officer himself. Whatever the case, Duck took his word for it. After all, the man was a career criminal.

"Close the door," the lieutenant said to his colleagues.

The guard with the mutton chops shut the door quietly. Why did they need the door closed? Duck wondered. No one was around but them. It wasn't like they were going to be interrupted.

Duck looked across his shoulders. Both guards were at either side of him now, standing close to him. He scooted up. He knew very well how officers would beat up inmates to avenge their coworkers like they'd already done to him. Now, were they going to do it again already? The officers themselves were a brotherhood. A fraternity of sorts. Some, he heard, were even Masons. Were they going to kill him?

The lieutenant picked up his copy of the initial report and read it loudly. Then, meeting Duck's eyes, the lieutenant asked, "What do you have to say?"

Duck leaned forward in the handcuffs. The pressure of his weight in the seating position was causing discomfort in his elbows and shoulders. "Um. I apologize." He spoke sincerely, even though he still felt Officer Meyer had been harassing him. "I was wrong, and it shouldn't've happened."

"You gave him a concussion."

Duck twisted his lips, trying to hide his smirk. The lieutenant's voice rose when he got angry, like Grandpa's.

"You think this is funny?"

"No, sir." Duck adjusted his body and tried to look serious.

The lieutenant squinted at him. "I'm sanctioning you to thirty days, and placing you on administration segregation."

Administrative segregation? Duck cocked his head and blinked, not understanding.

"I'm also taking thirty days of your good time. You've lost—" The lieutenant glanced down, referring to the documents in front of him. "Four months so far. While on ad seg you're expected to be infraction-free. Any major infraction you get while on ad seg will get you an extra thirty days added onto the six-month program. Plus loss of good time. You got that?"

"Six months?"

"You should be sanctioned to a year. This is a staff assault! The officer should be pressing criminal charges! If you want to earn any of your good time back I suggest you keep your nose clean when you get back to general population. When you get there, start programming."

"Wait, but I thought you said I had thirty days?"

The lieutenant didn't answer. He picked up a thin stack of papers beside him on the desk and held them out toward the guard with the mutton chops. "That's it," the lieutenant said. "We're done here."

The guard with the mutton chops walked over and took the papers. Duck was then escorted back to his cell. He tried asking the guards what exactly he was sanctioned to, but the ruddy-faced gent only answered that Duck was going IMU.

IMU?

He stepped inside his cell, still confused. The door wheeled itself shut. He shuffled backward to the cuff port once it was opened. The biting handcuffs were removed.

He turned around and rubbed his wrists. The guard with the mutton chops handed Duck the infraction report and sanction through the cuff port, then slammed the wicket closed, locking it. Tight. Duck sat down on his bunk with the papers, skimming through them. The guards left the tier, shutting the gate after them.

"What'd they say, Ten?" Corleone asked behind his cell door.

Duck continued reading, sifting through all the memorandums, administrative segregation referrals, and serious infraction reports. There were a lot of them. Copies of the same documents from the same officers and lieutenant. The ad seg referral mentioned Duck's conviction and past fights he had in prison, suggesting he was a threat to other inmates and prison staff.

"Ten?" Corleone called again. "Ten? . . . Ah, this mothafucka's trippin'. Ten, you all right? What'd they do to you, Ten?"

Duck opened his mouth and finally said, "They put me on ad seg."

"Ad seg? Shit. You 'bout to go to IMU, then."

Duck stood up and walked over to the door and said, "What is that?"

"Intensive management unit. That's where they put all the serial killers and shit. Yeah, man. You gone be over there with Gary Ridgway."

Gary Ridgway?

The inmate in the cell on Duck's left said, "They have pods out there."

"What's that, Eleven?" Corleone asked.

"They have pods, I said. The cells aren't in a straight row like here. They have units shaped like a horseshoe, with lower and upper tiers. But yeah, it's better over there.

You get a radio after your first thirty days, and a TV sixty days after that. But you can't have both. And you get to go to rec for an hour. There's nothing to do but push-ups and shit, but at least you get to get some fresh air, and make phone calls, you know. Yeah, brother. You'll be in here for about a month, then they'll send you out there."

"Hell, yeah," Corleone said to Eleven. Then to Duck, "Damn. I didn't think they was gone put you on ad seg."

"How long is your program?" Eleven asked.

"Six months," Duck said.

"Shit. You're lucky you didn't get a year."

"That's what the lieutenant said."

"Eleven," someone called out. "Stop talking to them jigs."

"Fuck you!" Corleone yelled.

"Fuck me?" the voice said. "Fuck with me on mainline, boy. I'll fuck both of you motherfuckers up."

"How can you be an Aryan with brown eyes?" Corleone asked. "Don't make me expose you, Fourteen. You had a black girlfriend on the streets."

"Fuck you, nigger. I didn't have a . . ."

Crap, here they go again.

Duck walked away to his cot, pushed it up against the narrow wall, and sat upright, crossing his legs. Other inmates had joined the squabble, shouting at one another, calling each other racial slurs, and misogynistic and homophobic epithets. It went on for eight minutes. Annoyed, Duck got up and tore out two sheets of toilet paper. He rolled one up and wet it at the sink, then molded it into a small wad. He stuffed it into his ear canal and then did the same with the other sheet of TP.

The noise was muted. Muffled. *Six months in the hole,* he thought. What was he going to do? What else could he do but work out and think. He returned to his cot and thought about what the lieutenant had said about programming once Duck got back to general population. What classes did they even offer in prison? And what could you possibly do for work, besides work in the kitchen? And did he have six months or seven? The lieutenant wasn't clear on that. He had sanctioned Duck to thirty days in segregation but also said that Duck was on a six-month program. Duck wanted to get answers from his neighbors, but he could hear inmates still arguing, yelling threats at each other. He would wait until after dinner. By then everyone would be quiet.

Dinner came. Soupy pork and beans on a thick, plastic food tray. There were five compartments. Dry cornbread was in one of them. Mixed vegetables in another. Corn chips in the top center. Apricot for dessert. Gobble, gobble. Duck scarfed everything down using his Spork. They only had five minutes to eat.

The tier was silent. The guards had come and picked up the food trays. Everyone was waiting for mail now.

Duck came up to his door and leaned against it, looking at his papers. "Hey, Eleven," Duck called quietly.

A second or two passed. Time long enough for his neighbor to walk up to his own door.

"What's up, brother?" Eleven answered just as quietly.

"I'm confused about this sanction. Did they give me six months or seven?"

"Six," Eleven answered. "Like I said, they'll send you out to IMU after you do your thirty days in here. But they'll run that time concurrently, meaning it'll be a part of your six-month program."

"Oh. All right, man. Thanks."

"No worries, brother."

"Hey," Duck said. "One more thing. What kind of classes do they have in population?"

"Ha! You don't know? What'd you do, get in trouble fresh off the chain?"

Duck didn't answer.

"Uh, let's see. Last time I was here they had barber school. But that usually had a pretty long waiting list. There was art, English, and keyboarding. Business management. Basic math and accounting. You can prepare for your GED."

"Huh. What about work?"

"Shit, you can be a shower porter, tier porter, work in the kitchen, or the garment factory. They also have a program that allows you to work with dogs."

"Dogs?"

"Yeah. You train service dogs, but that too usually has a long waiting list. You get a lot more opportunities in medium custody, brother. Or the camps. The camps—shit, man—you're practically free. Here, you don't have shit."

"What about IMU?"

"What about it?"

"You said you can have a radio or a TV, but what about books?"

Eleven laughed and said, "Wishful thinking, brother. No books. The only thing they let you read in there is the Bible. That's it."

"Damn. Well, all right, man. Thanks again."

"Anytime, brother. My name is Patrick, by the way."

"Patrick," Duck repeated to himself. "They call me Duck."

"Duck? Nice to meet you, Duck."

"Yep."

Duck set the papers down on the table and shuffled back to his cot. Considering the situation, Patrick was okay. Duck lay uncomfortably with his hands behind his head, thinking out his six-month stay. He could work himself up to doing a thousand push-ups and sit-ups a day so that by the time he made it back to population he'd be strong enough to defend himself if he ever had to again. He could play games of chess if he had an interested neighbor. He didn't know how big the yard was in IMU, but he could jog to build up his stamina. He set his mind on thirty minutes a day. That was the standard recommendation, he recalled hearing somewhere. But he would have to jog in socks, or prison sandals, for in the hole you weren't allowed to have shoes. He wondered if the yard had gravel. He wondered if the lieutenant would let him out of the hole early if he maintained good behavior. But then again, a part of Duck didn't mind isolation. So far, he hadn't had any troubles. Not with inmates or prison staff. He rolled over and propped his pillow to take a nap.

An hour had passed.

Corleone must've fallen asleep for he'd been silent. Now would be a good time to play a game of chess. Duck rose from his cot and stretched, cracked his neck, then got down to the floor, doing a set of fifty push-ups. He stood up with his hands on his waist, panting mildly; thinking about Alexa. He wondered what she was doing. How she was doing. Hopefully, she was feeling better about herself. Hopefully, she was back working.

He wondered if she was sleeping with anyone, and selfishly hoped that she wasn't. He recalled the last time he made love to her. She had cried out, pushing him off suddenly, then turned her back, shuddering. He thought he had done something wrong. Was he too rough? Had he hurt her? He sat up to comfort her, but she had brushed his hand away, telling him to not touch her. She was sensitive and needed a moment. During that moment he thought her actions had something to do with the Incident. He let her recover, then kissed her when she finally turned around and faced him. She said she had had a crying orgasm. He remembered how that made him feel big inside. He even stood in the mirror afterward. Naked, flexing his muscles.

He finished ten sets of fifty push-ups within the hour. Fatigued, he drank four or five cups of water dispensed from the metal sink. He put the cup away in a spot between the wall and the edge of his cot, then stood with his hands on hips, catching his breath still.

Bored now, he went to his door. "Corleone," he called out softly. "You asleep? I'm trying to get in a game of chess."

No response. Every day around this time Corleone would be out cold. Duck began to wonder if his neighbor was on some sort of medication. But Duck had never seen a nurse or officer supply Corleone any drugs. Maybe the guards were poisoning him, mixing barbiturates into his dinner. Maybe the guards were poisoning Duck himself.

"You bored over there?" Patrick asked.

"Yeah, man. Shit."

"Here," Patrick said. "I'll give you something to read. Something my wife sent me." He took a minute, then slid the heavy envelope over. Duck reached onto the cellblock and grabbed it. It was full of copied pages from a spiritual book.

He read for forty minutes, then slid the reading material back to Patrick.

Patrick pulled the envelope back into his cell. "So . . . what'd you think?"

It wasn't exactly Duck's cup of tea. It was mixed with Bible verses and subjective viewpoints and interpretations. The author believed the devil was a real thing that could influence you, and you had to battle against him, the same way that Jesus did. These seemed like superstitious ideas. "It was coo'. Just some self-help, motivational stuff."

"You didn't like it. Well, it was just something to read."

"I mean, there were some good points, like how having a bad attitude can prevent you from having a happier life and all of that. Who wrote it anyway?" Duck asked to be polite.

"Ah, it's out of this book by Joyce Meyer."

"*Joyce Meyer?*"

"Yeah, brother, why you say it like that? Joyce Meyer's pretty good. She gets deep into the spiritual and the battles of the mind. You've got to have a balance, you know. The spirit, the mind, and the flesh. You've got to study all three, and master them."

"Right."

"I'm serious. Your mind is a battlefield, and you've got to protect it, and most times you have to protect it from the devil. Whenever people get mad and threaten you and call you names, you have to remember you can't control them. You can only control yourself. You're responsible for your thoughts and behavior, not theirs. And really, that's the best way to motivate people, to inspire people. By being a living example. By being mindful of your thoughts and actions, and not giving in to evil."

"Huh. That's pretty deep there, Dr. Phil."

"Joyce Meyer, brother. I'm telling you."

"Yeah? I'mma have to check her out."

"Do that."

Sly comments were made on the tier. Normally whites didn't converse with blacks in the penitentiary. So Duck had to ask. "Say, man, why you being so cool?"

Patrick chuckled, then said, "We're in the twenty-first century, brother, c'mon. Besides that, I'm from Detroit. My best friend was black."

"Oh, yeah?"

"Yeah. Virgil Miller from Forest Park. He always wore these crazy braids. Reminded me of that rapper Coolio." Patrick chuckled.

Coolio? Damn, this guy must be old.

"And Virgil he had these great, massive hands. He could cover a whole basketball with one of them. Good god, his hands were gigantic!"

"Fruitcake!" More epithets were hurled by hateful inmates.

"Okay," Duck said to himself, feeling awkward. He then tried to speak more quietly, bringing his voice down even lower. "So you're not scared of these dudes?"

"That motherfucker better be scared," someone yelled.

Patrick laughed, then said: "I have a life sentence for murder. The only thing I fear is God." Threats were yelled at him in the background. "I'm here on a transfer, so I'm not worried about these dudes. If something does happen to me, I can rest peacefully knowing I was true to myself. Shit, half these motherfuckers become Aryans because they're scared."

Duck nodded as if his neighbor could see him.

The gate at the head of the tier was unlocked and opened. Duck turned his attention to the sound and could hear the creep of steady footsteps.

The patrolling guard made his rounds and was now leaving the tier.

Shower time would be next.

"Hey!" someone shouted. "What the fuck's up with our mail?"

The guard didn't answer. Just kept moving right along in meek silence.

"Hey, you fucking pig," another inmate yelled. "You hear us talking to you?"

"Where the fuck is our mail? Hey! You fuckers skipped us yesterday.

"Hey!"

The guard closed and locked the gate behind him.

Inmates began banging on their doors, yelling and shouting, donkey kicking the thick metal. No guards brought out mail. Soon toilets were being flushed. One after another. Repeatedly and simultaneously, creating one loud continuous roar. Ten minutes after that the tier was flooded. Water came out of nearly every cell. The inmates had stuffed their toilets with bedding, clogging the receptacles. Ten minutes after that the goon squad arrived. Ten men deep. Specially trained. Fully armored in matte black riot gear. They wore thick, sturdy helmets with face shields. Protection vests with chest plates and shoulder pads. Tactical knee pads. Shin guards. They held clear, circular riot shields and long, black rubber batons.

They lined up and stood in front of the cells, banging their clubs against plastic.

Clunk. Clunk. Clunk.

"Back away from your cell doors," an officer demanded.

"Fuck you, bitch! Where's our mail?"

Clunk. Clunk. Clunk.

"Uncover your windows, now!"

"Fuck off, piiiigs!"

The guards then gathered in a triangle formation, sloshing through water.

Duck pressed up against his door, trying to see through the crack.

Nothing.

They were out of his line of sight now, but he knew they were marching toward the end of the tier, crowding in front of an inmate's cell door, getting ready to attack. A command was shouted out by a guard, and then—an inmate's door began to let itself open.

Almost immediately the inmate began screaming.

Duck's heart was drumming. The convict that had been yelling obscenities at the officers now sounded terrified. What were they doing to him?

And then the inmate was silent.

Shit.

There was talk amongst the guards and more yelling on the tier. Then—Duck saw two of the COs dragging the sleeping convict. They were hauling him up the flooded cellblock, pulling him along by his restrained arms, which were handcuffed behind him. He was slumped over, his head drooping down, almost touching his lap. And his back was to the officers, who were now drawing him past Duck.

He kept watching, trying to see down the tier.

Still, inmates were shouting threats at the guards.

"Hey, don't worry, Erikson, you're next," an officer said to one of the prisoners.

Duck could hear things being thrown out of the unconscious inmate's cell.

"Hey, Jones, we just want our mail," an inmate said.

"You get your mail when we bring you mail, motherfucker. You want to tear shit up? C'mon, now. Let's tear some shit up."

"Jones?"

"Open thirteen."

"Jones!"

The door to cell thirteen began to open.

"Jones, wait!" Duck heard a crackling electric sound and the inmate shrieking. He fought back. His body thudded against the walls.

Then there was silence.

"Jesus Christ!" a guard said. "The fucker shat himself." There was laughter amongst the guards and some high-fiving.

Duck turned around and looked about his cell. Sat down. Stood up. Paced. Yelling still filled the tier.

He lay on his cot, looking up at the ceiling. The fluorescent lights buzzed. The vent above and behind him blew out hot air.

The vent!

He rose and stared at it. It was covered by a small metal plate with dozens of pinholes. Radio frequencies were being sent through the vent. To control him. To make him think thoughts that weren't his. Frequencies sent from the Pentagon, authorized by the President. Duck needed to protect himself. Protect his thoughts. So he could think. So he could focus.

He turned and looked about his cell again. What could he use to protect himself? There was nothing available to block frequencies. No steel. No foil. No copper. Then he remembered the small carton of milk he saved from breakfast.

He reached under his cot, grabbed the carton, opened it up, and drank its lukewarm contents. He rinsed out the carton and flattened it into a rectangle.

Yes. He'd construct himself a helmet, using toothpaste to glue the milk cartons together. The plastic coating and paperboard would protect his brainwaves from being contaminated. He'd start the project tomorrow.

Thirteen

The hard water made his body itch. He had no lip balm, lotion, or deodorant. He licked his chapped lips but his mouth quickly absorbed the moisture. He nibbled a piece of peeled skin from his lower lip and played with it on the tip of his tongue. The dead skin was like a morsel, making him salivate.

He spat it out and called for the guards. "Hey! I'm ready to go back to my cell."

Duck had been waiting outside the single shower stall, behind a barred cell door that had been locked. The guards must've forgotten about him, for he'd been there for over half an hour. He felt as dry as a scarecrow. Shower towel around his neck. Damp facecloth and the small complimentary bar of soap in his hand.

Two minutes after he called for the officers, they appeared, trotting down the tier with their handcuffs.

"What took you so long?" Duck asked. "I have to get back to my cell."

"Turn around to cuff up," a CO ordered.

Duck did so promptly. They unlocked the gate and took him back to his cell. The door was open. His bedding was disassembled, and thrown on the floor with his cot, and it looked like all of his saved food items had been taken. His cell had been ransacked. Raided.

He groaned in despair and then was shoved inside. The door slowly rolled itself shut behind him.

After being un-handcuffed he stepped away from the door. The wicket closed and locked.

He went over to the bed frame and discovered they had taken the extra tube of toothpaste he'd gotten from

Corleone, who had been released back into general population. They'd also taken the butter pats, and Duck's extra bar of soap.

"Hey!" Duck yelled at the guards.

He tore through the balled sheets of bedding on the floor, lifted the cot, and searched by the toilet.

"Hey! What did you guys do with my helmet? Hey!"

He hadn't even finished making it yet. He was about halfway done, needing at least fifteen more milk cartons. Now he had to start all over. He went up to his door and banged on it hard, looking out through the glass slat for the guards, who were walking the inmate in cell eleven out to shower.

"Hey!" Duck yelled again.

The COs stopped and met him at the window, holding onto the inmate's arms. "Something wrong, Duckworth?"

"Yes, you guys stole my helmet!"

"It's considered contraband and you know that. Now, are you going to be a problem?" The guard stared, waiting for an answer, grasping the microphone clipped onto his shirt pocket, ready to make the call.

"No, sir." Duck lowered his eyes and head, then turned away, not wanting any part of the stun baton.

He collapsed on his disheveled bunk. How was he going to protect his brain now? He should've taken the helmet with him to the shower. Hid it under his orange suit, or had it carefully wrapped in his body towel. But they knew. They knew he was trying to stop the waves from affecting him. That's why they raided his cell. They had gotten orders from the Pentagon. Duck had to be more careful, for the guards were now picking up on his thoughts.

A cell search report was on the table. He got up and looked at it. They had written him up. Three separate infractions. None of them major. Yesterday they confiscated pictures from an inmate because the photos didn't have his DOC number written on the back. They were pictures of his young son and daughter. The inmate had just gotten them in the mail two days before. Livid, he filed a grievance report against the officers who had searched his cell.

Maybe Duck would file a grievance as well. Since the guards raided his cell he had nothing that could block the radioactive messages.

He put his cell back together, then plopped down on his cot. He lay with his arms folded across his chest. If he could evaporate he'd float himself out of there. Through the door, right past the guards. Then he'd materialize himself and soar into the sky. He'd join the clouds and ride them, reclining with his hands behind his head and his legs crossed. Smooth sailing . . .

The inmate in cell nine began beating on his table and rapping again. He was entertaining, but he always seemed to do it at the wrong time. Like now. Duck sighed and turned over. After shower would be lights out (with the lights on). So some inmates were resting already.

"Hey, motherfucker! People are trying to sleep!" someone yelled.

The rapper said: "Well, go to sleep then, bitch. I don't give a shit. You can have a dream about suckin' my dick."

A few inmates chuckled. Others moaned.

The rapper laughed himself and said, "Hey, Ten. Bust a freestyle." The inmate beat on the wall, making sound effects with his mouth.

"I don't rap," Duck said over the beat.

"All right. Well, check this out." The inmate rapped passionately for five minutes. Fast with anger. "Hell, yeah," he said afterward. "You feel that?"

"You sound like Eminem."

"Eminem?! Mothafucka, you got me fuuucked up! You think 'cause I'm white I sound like Eminem? I sound like me! Danny-Ru from East Side Piru. I got my own style and shit. I don't sound like Eminem, MGK, or none of them cats. On Blood, homie. Hey, Marcus, you hear this mothafucka talkin' about I sound like Eminem?"

"You Marshall Mathers, homie."

"Man, fuck y'all. I'm 'bout to kick back and work on my shit."

A week after the revolt, Patrick had been transferred back to his mother institution, Stafford Creek, while Corleone had been released into general population. Four of the inmates responsible for the flooding were moved to other parts of the hole, their cells quickly occupied by other threatening prisoners. Two other inmates had been released, and those two cells remained vacant. The inmate in cell eleven never spoke to Duck or anybody for that matter. And the few Aryans on the tier never said a word to Danny-Ru about his association with the blacks. Probably because the Aryans were now outnumbered. Or maybe Danny-Ru just wasn't their type of recruit. He belonged to a street gang. Attacking him in population alone could potentially cause a gang war between the Aryans and Bloods. Maybe to the Aryans, he was a lost cause. A pariah, undesirable and disowned by his kind.

The next morning, the rapper slid his empty milk carton over to Duck, flattened, as Duck had been asking.

Duck grabbed it and stood up.

"Anything else?" his new neighbor asked.

"Nah. Just let me keep getting that, and your butter. And your toothpaste before they send you back to population. . . . I mean, if you get out before they send me to IMU. Oh, yeah. I forgot. Stop eating your dinner, too."

"Why would I stop eating my dinner, blood?"

"Because they poison it. They put something in it to make you sleep. That's what they did to the last guy that was over there."

"Word? So you don't eat your dinner?"

"Yeah, but they don't poison mines. Only the chicken."

Danny-Ru laughed. "Okay, then let me get your chicken from now on. And your powdered drinks. You know they put saltpeter in 'em. So we don't get horny and shit. But check this out, homie. I'm 'bout to kick back and work on these raps. A'ight." He pounded on the wall twice.

Duck opened the milk carton and saw that Danny-Ru had slipped the two butter pats inside, both protected by paperboard and parchment paper. Duck immediately pulled them out and removed the paper from one of them. He dipped his finger and applied a small amount to his lips. Cool butter filled the cracks in his skin. But that sensation would last about five minutes before his lips became chapped again. He hid the butter chips under his cot with the other two he got that morning.

When the guards came to pick up the food trays, Duck asked the nicer officer for a tube of toothpaste, saying he had run out. The unsuspecting officer brought Duck the toothpaste.

In two weeks, Duck had the helmet made. He had divided the cartons up into playing card pieces, carefully gluing them together, sparingly using dots of toothpaste to hold the paperboard in place.

He stood in the dull, metal scratched-up plate called a mirror, checking himself out, seeing how he looked with the helmet. It fit perfectly over his thick hair. It was boxy but stylish, canceled out some noise, and, most importantly, shielded his mind from cosmic messages.

A guard banged on the door and shouted, "Inmate Duckworth, what the hell is that on your head?!"

Duck spun around alarmed, and touched the helmet to take it off, but decided to leave it on instead.

"It's an anti-wave voice deflector," he said defiantly.

"A what? Take that shit off and back up to the cuff port. You're being transferred."

Duck didn't move. They were going to take all his stuff again. His food items and everything he'd collected. His toiletries. His condiments. His travel-sized bottles of shampoo for his increasingly dry scalp and hair. His Sporks. His helmet!

He mumbled these concerns to himself, flushed the toilet for no reason, and then danced.

"Jesus Christ," the guard said to his colleague. "Is this guy on meds? Inmate Duckworth, turn around and back up to the cuff port! I'm not going to tell you again."

Duck whirled around and faced the guards and said, "No! You are not going to take my helmet!"

The guards laughed. "He thinks he's freakin' Magneto or something," one of them said.

"All right," said the other. But his partner stopped him, pulled him to the side, and had a quiet conversation with him.

Yeah, figure it out. Because you're not taking my helmet.

After a minute the mean guard returned to the window and said, "Okay, Inmate Duckworth. You can keep the hat."

"And my stuff? What about all my stuff?"

"Yep. You can keep your stuff, too. We'll pack everything up nicely for you. You're going to IMU."

Bzzzzzzz. The mean guard pulled the heavy door open. They entered the secure building, the metal door slamming shut behind them, leaving an echo. Duck, in transport chains, looked up and around with fresh eyes. IMU was just like Patrick described. A pod shaped like a horseshoe with a lower and upper tier. A long, wide flight of stairs led to the top. Some of the cells were close together, then widely spaced apart by ten feet.

Duck imagined communication and fishing would be harder. You'd never get anything to or from anyone on the neighboring tier. The unit was quiet, and he could sense there hadn't been any rowdiness in the place for months. He wondered if Gary Ridgway was here. The Green River Killer. Would they be neighbors?

Duck was led up the stairs on that thought. His feet were shackled. The chains clinked. He took slow, careful steps, glancing around at the cells above. Inmates' faces were plastered to every narrow window, seeing who he, the new prisoner, was.

"Here we are." A guard approached the cell. Duck stood stiff, facing the door. After a second it began to let itself open. He shuffled inside. His wrists tethered to the belly chain around his waist. With the three of them, it was tight in there. The guard on Duck's right tossed the infraction reports onto the table next to him. The guard on the left began taking the helmet off Duck's head.

"Hey!" Duck twisted his body away from the guard.

"Inmate Duckworth, calm down!"

Duck wailed, then leaped, trying to weave his head back inside the helmet. He missed badly and was forced to his knees, then to the ground with his face against the cold cement.

Their heavy bodies kneeling on him now. He growled, wiggling like a worm under magnified sunlight.

"Inmate Duckworth, stop it!" The guards panted and grunted. "This is contraband! You can't have this!"

Duck squirmed and fought uselessly. "Give me back my helmet!"

"Lord have mercy. Do I need to call in a code two?"

"No!" Duck paused. Code two was for SERT to arrive and assist them. The special emergency response team. Known to the inmates as the goon squad. "No code two. I just want my helmet, please."

"You're not getting this thing, Duckworth, so let it go. Now, we're going to stand you up. Are you going to be a problem?"

Duck sniffed and said, "No, sir."

"Jesus." The guard exhaled.

They stood Duck up, unchained his feet, and backed out of the cell. Once un-cuffed Duck made his way to the narrow window at the foot of the dungeon. Patrick hadn't mentioned that. The glass slat was no wider than a two-by-four and about the same length. Duck looked out of it, amazed to see twenty Holsteins slowly feeding on endless land. The cows were beautiful. And so was the land.

He and Alexa went to the zoo once. It was a rare hot day in the summer. Not raining in Seattle, Washington. Cloudless. Ninety-five frigging degrees. People were crying over the heat. Including Alexa. She had two or three Slurpees that day, and wore cut-off jean shorts with a yellow bikini top, showing off her navel, soft skin, and model breasts. He wore a wife beater, exhibiting his toned, teenaged muscles, and Ray-Ban sunglasses on his sweaty face.

He grinned at the memory. He remembered the giraffes and the smell of dung and the big and bad, huffing gorilla that pounded his chest and made the crowd gasp in awe. He remembered the slow-moving massive hippo and the terrarium full of hissing cockroaches, and how Alexa shivered and turned into his body at the sight of them. That made him laugh just now, and feel slightly unusual. And even mad.

Now, here he was in IMU, on administrative segregation. Four two-tier pods containing twenty-one cells. Nearly every one of them holding a killer, who stood thinking, gazing through a small window like his.

Duck turned to the round, silver seat and square desk bolted into the white stone wall across from his bunk. Went over and made his cot with the clean bedding. He had none of the belongings the guards had promised him, only his paperwork, some stationary items provided for him, and the new toiletries that would barely last him a week.

He returned to the window, thinking about writing Alexa. On the table were ten complimentary sheets of lined paper, two self-addressed stamped envelopes, and a golf pencil with no eraser. All courtesy of Washington State Penitentiary. He kept the letter short, apologizing, telling her how much he missed her, wishing her health, wishing she'd respond as he did in every letter.

He told her he loved her, and that when he got out he was going to get a job and buy them a house with a two-car garage, marry her, and start a family with her. He ended the letter, staining it with tears of anguish, hoping she'd write something in return. Then he remembered what she had said to him when he was in the county jail, on the black phone with the silver cord, behind the thick glass.

"I don't know what to believe," she had told him. Words that had made him feel cold. Distant. Angry. Despicable.

How could she not believe him? Time provided no answer for him, still.

On the hard stool, he sat with discomfort. An intense itching crawled inside of him. The burning sensation made him hop off of the seat.

He tried to walk it off, then lay on his stomach, side, and back to relax. The inflammation seemed to grow by the minute. It had been bothering him for weeks.

He got up and pressed the buzzer. The guard squawked, "What?"

Duck told him what was wrong and the guard told him to put in a kite. It took three days to be seen.

At the infirmary, Duck was given a month's supply of suppositories and was asked if there was anything else. Was there? Anything else. Sitting uncomfortably, he looked across at a mirror at himself. He hadn't combed his hair properly in over a month. On his face were whiskers, sprouted along his jawline and chin. A few strands had grown out of his cheeks. He looked dangerous. Like a criminal. Like a hobo. Like someone who ought to be on meds. The hairs of his mustache had grown over his top lip. And in places, his curly natural looked ratty.

He remembered seeing his mom this way; disheveled, and it scared him, seeing he was becoming like her. How long had he been looking like this? He dropped his head and shook it to remember who he was. He was Carlos Duckworth, a good man who didn't deserve to be in prison. But he would appeal and prove his innocence. He was smart. He was a loyal boyfriend and someday would make a great husband and father. He was strong. He was honest.

He was also the son of a schizophrenic.

"I need meds," he said, slowly lifting his eyes. "Something is wrong with me. I keep hearing voices but you guys took my helmet!" He looked over at the two officers standing on either side of him, both of whom had nothing to do with the legal confiscation of the property.

"It could be stress," the doctor said calmly. "A lot of inmates get stressed in your position. However, I am not a psychiatrist." He reached over for a yellow sticky pad and pen. "But I will make note of this and schedule you for an appointment. How's that sound?"

Duck nodded, satisfied.

The appointment was made and in a week Duck saw a psychiatrist who referred to his records. Upon seeing he had been prescribed antidepressants in jail, she followed the same trend, prescribing the same meds, saying Duck was just depressed. In a month the medication did make a difference. He was no longer depressed and agitated.

He'd been issued a radio by then and had written Grandmother, who'd sent him money to buy the limited amount of stationary items and toiletries he was allowed to have. The only book he was allowed was the Bible. He settled on the book of Proverbs and read a chapter from it every day. He worked out daily as well. He listened to sports talk and Public Radio and to a science fiction program that talked about aliens on Earth and other conspiracy theories. Sometimes they told creepy stories at night, but he stopped listening to them and eventually found a contemporary radio station that made him forget all about his nightmares.

By the time he got tired of their playlist, he was issued a 13" TV. It was small but he couldn't believe he was afforded this luxury. No wonder it was always quiet in the pod. TVs were pacifiers to stop the crying, to calm the rebellious.

Channel surfing, he found a Christian network where Joyce Meyer was speaking, preaching to an audience of five thousand. A megachurch they called it.

"Before honor is humility." Duck stood in front of the TV. "There's nothing more dangerous than pride." He stayed still, listening to her sermon. Five minutes in he began taking notes.

According to her, you have to humble yourself, before and after being rewarded for your work. He saw why Patrick was a fan of hers. She was direct and simple. Still, Duck thought she was a fraud.

He changed the channel and stopped at CNBC. They were interviewing an elderly white man named Warren Buffet. He talked about the economy and business. Duck wrote the man's name down. Beside the man was Bill Gates. From the summation of the interview, Duck guessed that they were friends. Gates also spoke about the economy. Duck wrote his name down as well.

Two months later, Duck stood at the back of his cell, peering out the skinny window, watching twenty Holsteins slowly feed on endless land. Behind them was sunrise and the purple hue that the sky now gave. He looked forward to this peace every morning, rising at dawn to meditate, marveling at life outside of prison.

He turned to the round, silver seat and square desk bolted into the white stone wall across from his bunk. Went over and made a tally mark on the yellow paper he used as a calendar with the short pencil he was allowed to have. Today made one hundred and eighty marks.

He returned to the window, staring. Alexa still hadn't written him once. But he did get a letter from B. He was in medium custody now. The food there was a lot better, and there was less tension amongst the inmates, he wrote. He had a job in the garment factory making fifty-five cents an hour. Duck doubted his own custody level would be lowered at his first classification review. But hopefully, he'd be out of prison by the time his second was due.

A door slammed open at the mouth of the pod. Soon, the squeaky footsteps that could be heard on the floor began marching up the metal flight of stairs. Judging by the sound of the footfalls, four guards coming. Two large and tall. Two short and stocky.

The squeaky boots stopped at his cell.

"Inmate Duckworth, time to roll up!"

Duck turned, facing the guard behind the glass slat.

The cuff port opened.

Duck stared ahead, dumb.

"You wanna stay here or go back to population?"

Duck hurried over and submitted his hands through the small opening, then stepped away once he was handcuffed. The loud steel door began wheeling itself open, ending in a deafening bang. Was this real, or was he hallucinating?

They stuffed his belongings into a brown paper bag and escorted him out of the pod.

We're freeeeeee!

Duck giggled.

The CO on his right squeezed his arm.

"You off your meds, Duckworth?" the guard on the left asked. "That's right. It's too early. You haven't even had breakfast yet."

Duck had grown to like that officer. He usually accompanied the nurse who brought the meds over to Duck in the morning. There were days when Duck would hear voices whisper to him, and he'd respond, talking and laughing as though he were in a full-fledged conversation. It helped pass the time and entertained him. But sometimes the guard would catch him, and ask if he was all right.

Duck lost his smile, recalling scripture. *Do not boast about tomorrow; for you do not know what a day may bring forth.*

"Well, remember," the guard said. "Mind your own business, and follow orders, and you should be fine."

Right.

Duck stared ahead as they walked. He'd been the only black prisoner in the pod, so he hadn't spoken to anyone but the guards for five of the six months. Some officers wanted to make sure you never came back to prison. Others wanted to break you, or they hated you because in their eyes you were a stain on society. Still, others expected you to be a repeat offender and even made bets on how fast some inmates would be back.

Being out in the open space made him feel weird. The walkways seemed enormous.

The first thing he needed to do was work on his appeal. See about school and work, and find books on investing. He thought about Officer Meyer, how he and the sergeant had tried to force him to wear jeans that were too small for him. He hoped he wouldn't have that same problem again. Sometimes he wished he had gone to Monroe, where there was a Special Offenders Unit and Treatment Program for inmates with mental health issues and sex crimes, but initially, he refused to go because he was no rapist or child molester. He had lost the privilege anyway due to the many fights he'd had in the Shelton, Washington corrections center, the transition hub of Washington state prisons.

They passed an exit. At that point, the guards un-cuffed him and handed him his bag of belongings.

He followed the guards outside into the morning sun. Nearly blinded by the natural light, he blocked the rays with his hand, squinting. The distance to the cell block seemed infinite.

They moved along. He gazed at the gun tower to his left, watching the guard with the assault rifle.

They reached the entrance to eight wing. The door buzzed loudly as one of the prison guards yanked it open. Duck entered feeling that chilling wave of darkness wash over him again. He handed his bag to an officer, passed through the metal detector, stood for search, and was frisked.

"Back to C2," an officer said. He gave Duck a bedroll. He took a deep breath, retrieved his bag from the guard who had checked it, and walked up the stairs. He stood in front of the cell with his arms full, waiting for the cage to be opened all over again.

He entered.

Toothpaste stood up. "Heyyy! Rock 'Em Sock 'Em Robot! Where the hell you been?"

"IMU." Duck tossed his bag and bedding onto the top bunk, annoyed already.

"Well, I figured that. Goddamn! They got weights in there? You looking pretty swole under that jumpsuit. You must've been curling your mattress. C-Dub, look at this boy. You really don't wanna fuck with him now. Ewwww weeee!"

"Don't touch me!" Duck said.

"Okay," said Toothpaste. "I ain't on no funny shit now."

Duck moved his bag to the floor and started making his bunk.

"We just got off of lockdown, you know."

"Uh-huh." Duck spread out the sheet and began tying the ends under the cot.

Toothpaste came closer to him, lowering his voice. "Some crazy white boy who thought he was a rapper."

Duck stopped what he was doing and looked at Toothpaste.

"Yeah," Toothpaste continued. "He was a Blood, from Piru, I guess. One of them gangs. Anyway—two of them Aryans caught him slippin' in the kitchen where they was working together. One of 'em had that WP tattooed big on his throat. Anyway—they got the boy while he was in one of his rap spells. 'Boom-bap-bapidy-boop.' They jooged him seventeen times, I heard. But the boy tough. I think he Irish."

"He lived?"

"Hell yeah, that son-of-a-bitch lived. Must got seventeen angels watching over him. Them Pirus wasn't happy about it though. I guess the Aryans figured they had 'em outnumbered and that the Bloods wasn't gone do nothing. But they did a surprise attack and fought back like the tribe of three hundred. Except it was maybe like five of them against twenty Aryans in the Big Yard. One of them son-of-a-bitches died too. Shanked right in the heart. I guess that Blood knew what he was doing, or he got lucky. Shit. And one them got killed by the guard in the gun tower because the nigga wouldn't stop fightin'."

"Damn."

"I know. So we were on lockdown for a month. I guess the guards were expecting a race riot after that. It certainly smelled like one was coming. I tell ya."

"C-tier, mainline. Pill line." The gates on the tier slammed back. Inmates herded into a line and hurried out for breakfast.

Duck quickly finished making his cot, and then headed out as well. Every prisoner seemed to be walking on eggshells. He walked over to pill-line and waited his turn with the rest of the zombies, met the lady at the protected booth, bowed into the squawk box, and said, "Inmate Duckworth. Seven, five, nine, seven, four, five."

The lady searched, then gave up. "We don't have any medication under that name. Sorry."

"I just got out of IMU. I was on meds there."

"Oh. Well, in that case, you're going to have to fill out a kite to medical or use the kiosk to renew your prescription."

"Okay. Thanks." Duck wondered where the kiosk was, then decided to fill out a kite instead. He went to breakfast.

After breakfast, there was movement for those who had school in the morning. C-Dub left with a folder and a GED study guide. Toothpaste lay back on his cot, watching *Martin*. After the gate closed, Duck asked, "Toothpaste, how to sign up for classes?"

Toothpaste chuckled at the TV, slipped off his headphones, and looked across at Duck. "What you say, youngster?"

"How do I sign up for classes?"

"Damn, boy, you slow? You didn't see C-Dub standing at the cell door with his book? You could've asked him."

"Man, just answer the question."

"You go to the education department and talk to a counselor."

"All right. How do I sign up for work, and get a haircut, and a weight card?"

He sighed. "For jobs, you need a kite. Haircuts they give at the barber school. Weight room costs seven dollars per quarter just like anything else—music room, hobby craft. Fill out an application to the rec department and pay up. Now let me get back to my program."

Yard was called in the afternoon. Duck went to the law library and asked the helper clerk how to file an appeal. The prisoner, who was an assistant to the law librarian working with him behind the counter, told Duck it was probably too late. "Usually, you've got to file within thirty days after the trial court entered decision."

"So there's nothing I can do?"

"Sometimes there are special situations that let you move forward. There are always loopholes. But you're going to need the notice of appeal, the docketing statement, praecipe, and you have to pay for the deposit, which is like two hundred and fifty dollars. Or you could file a motion to proceed forma pauperis, which means you're broke."

"What's prae—" Duck couldn't pronounce the word.

"Praecipe to the court reporter. It's a written request for court action."

"Oh. Why don't they just say that? And what about all that other stuff you said?"

"A docketing statement is an overview of the case you're appealing. It tells the appellate court and all the other parties involved that you've taken the first steps to file your appeal. Here." The inmate grabbed all of the applicable forms and handed them over to Duck. "Everything you need is over there."

Duck turned to where the inmate had pointed, took a golf pencil and scratch paper, selected two law books at random, and sat down at a wide desk. The library was sprinkled with quiet prisoners working alone. They looked too busy to be bothered and he wanted to ask questions. Under what circumstances could he file late? What if he could prove he had a decline in mental health during the trial process? Would that make a difference? That situation alone seemed special enough. And didn't his lawyer misrepresent him? She never interviewed Alexa to verify his stories of sexual harassment from Amy. What would you call that? Incompetence?

He flipped through the pages of the law books, searching for cases similar to his.

He worked for two hours until yard was over. Once he passed through the metal detector he was told by a guard to report to property. There Duck picked up his court documents from the county jail, infraction reports from Shelton, and his state-issued clothing and shoes (in the sizes he had provided the staff member). He returned to his cell, got dressed in the blue jeans and white T-shirt, and smacked himself on the head for forgetting to check out a few books. Nor did he get a chance to work out. He was going to have to figure out a better schedule.

But every other day inmates were allowed to go to yard twice. Once in the afternoon, and again in the evening. So at six o'clock second yard was called right after dinner. He went to the library, asked the assistant there about a job, and was told they weren't hiring. Duck filled out a kite anyway. Then, getting the clerk's help, Duck found a biography on Warren Buffet called *The Snowball*. He added to it *Think and Grow Rich, The Millionaire Next Door, Rich Dad Poor Dad,* and a Jack Reacher novel entitled *Gone Tomorrow.* He intended to read one book a week, but *The Snowball* alone would take him a month. He carried the books down to the gym at gate-call and did a rigorous calisthenics workout to end the night.

Fourteen

"Yard time," a voice blared from the PA system.

Duck jumped down from his bunk, slipped into the line of convicts, went through the metal detector, stepped aside, and stretched out his arms, reciting his DOC number loudly. Meyer did a quick pat down, then let him go. Duck hurried along to the law library.

He studied for an hour before the second gate was announced. Gate calls gave inmates five minutes to move from the gym to the library—or from the library to the gym —from the gym to the yard, or back to their cells.

A few inmates came up to the law library and browsed around. Fewer inmates left. Duck got up for another book, then came back and sat down. He jotted the legal jargon, then gave himself a break, laying his pencil on the legal pad. Thumb under his chin, index finger on his temple, he sat sowing things together when he noticed the old man he'd been seeing for the past few days. The old man always came and went. He just grabbed different books, as if he had multiple projects, worked quickly, and left. He was speaking with another inmate, then turned as if he felt someone staring at him. Duck looked down at his notes and pretended to be studying. But it was too late. The old man was coming over now.

He sat down at the table.

"What you working on?" the old man asked, speaking through a gray goatee. He had coffee-stained teeth that crowded at the bottom, and a smooth-raspy voice that dragged when he talked. His mini-afro was the color of ash, and his eyes were plagued with brown, restless anguish. He placed his big, ugly, mud-colored hands onto the tabletop and folded them thoughtfully.

"Just my appeal," Duck said, guarding the papers.

The old man looked over at them and nodded. "Yeah, child molestation is a tough one."

Duck widened his eyes.

"Pretty easy to be convicted of. All you need is hearsay and a testimony." The old man flicked a smile. "Don't be surprised. Everybody knows everything about everyone around here. I'm Lincoln. Lincoln Carter." He offered his large hand.

Duck stared at it, wondering how long he'd been in prison, then took it, introducing himself. The man's grip was prison-strong. Like an ironworker's. His big fingers felt like tree bark, and his callouses were as rough as sea barnacles. Duck took his hand away, careful not to withdraw too quickly. He didn't want the old man to think he was afraid of him.

"How long you been working on this deal?" Lincoln asked.

Duck hesitated for a moment. *Is he a booty bandit? Nah. He has to be too old for that.* "Four days," Duck said. "What about you? What are you working on?"

Lincoln leaned back in his seat, placing his fingers behind his head. "I help people out with their cases. They pay me a small fee, and I help them get free."

Duck wondered why Lincoln wasn't free himself.

Lincoln reached over. "Let me see what you got here."

Duck jerked back as the convict seized the papers. Included in the stack were Duck's documents from the court.

Ten minutes passed before the old man looked up. "Yeah, I can help you with this."

"How long will it take?"

Lincoln stroked his goatee with his big hand. "Court of appeals . . . could take about six months . . . maybe a year."

"A year?"

"I tell you what," Lincoln said with a sudden burst of energy. "Give me a couple of days and I'll put your case together for you."

"I don't know," Duck said. Toothpaste had just schooled him on not accepting favors from convicts. "I don't have anything to pay you with, and I could just do it myself."

Lincoln cocked his head and smiled crookedly. "Yeah, you could do that. But if you screw things up in litigation, they'll deny you . . . and you *won't* get a second chance."

Duck blinked, thinking about what Lincoln had just said.

"Don't worry about paying anything right now. We'll work something out later."

"Later?"

"Yeah. It's what lawyers call pro bono, but what I call helping a friend." He stood with the papers. "I'll go over this stuff tonight and meet with you here tomorrow so we can talk about it." With that, the old man left.

Two weeks later they strolled the Big Yard discussing Duck's case. The afternoon sun beamed down on Duck's frame. It was so hot he could feel the heat cooking his skin. He peeled his damp shirt off and slung it over his shoulder, slick with sweat.

"So you should hear back from the courts within a month," Lincoln said, gazing ahead. It had taken him longer than the two days promised, but the notice of appeal was thorough, addressing all the matters they both deemed important: Duck's mental health during the trial process, hearsay, and Amy's sexual harassment. Lincoln had also focused on a term Duck had never heard of regarding a lawyer: "ineffective counsel." Overall the appeal felt solid.

Duck stopped at the dip bar across from a cement wall where four Mexicans were playing handball. It looked like they were getting good exercise, not like they would be stabbing each other soon.

Duck grabbed onto the dip bar. Lincoln waited. Duck lowered himself, pushed himself up, and then came down again. He repeated the process until he maxed out his energy, then stopped and continued walking with Lincoln.

The track was full of dirt and gravel, circling like a high school relay field. In the middle was grass where a half-dozen inmates lay half-naked, sunbathing. A long row of phones was attached to the stone wall left of the entrance. Half the phones were taken up by convicts.

Duck and Lincoln continued to walk.

Two skinheads nodded to Lincoln as they passed by. Lincoln nodded back in return.

"What was that?" Duck asked. This expression of mutual respect confused him. The skinheads never acknowledged anyone but themselves or the Natives, which also struck him as odd, considering the whole history between the two.

"Respect," Lincoln said in his smooth, raspy voice.

Duck said nothing for the moment. He thought as he listened to the crunch of gravel beneath their feet. No skinhead had ever greeted him. Not that he ever wanted them to. It was just the fact that they were supposed to be racist, yet here they were respectfully acknowledging a black man.

Lincoln had been locked up longer than Duck had been alive. For thirty-seven long years. Paroled not even once. Duck had recently heard that Lincoln was once a successful boxer, back when they allowed boxing in prison. Back when bikers rode motorcycles in the Big Yard at some festival. Back when the fashion was bellbottom jeans and platform shoes and big thick mustaches and tie-die shirts and afros. It was then that Lincoln had shot and killed two cops during a bank heist, and had been sentenced to double life, which, according to the judge and Lincoln's attorney, was a real mercy considering that Lincoln could have gotten the death penalty. He could have been hanged and buried somewhere on the property by now. But instead, he lived and now had respect from every officer and inmate, including, apparently, the members of the Aryan Brotherhood.

Lincoln knew of every narcotic that came into eight wing, what officers could be paid off, and which inmates had drug smuggling visitors. He had eyes everywhere, watching for him, and whenever the drugs were sold, he got a piece of the profits. He could have you killed or spared. Anyone. Including the guards. He once saved an officer's life, legend said. During a routine search, mistakenly approved by a sergeant, the rookie guard and another officer went in and took some contraband from Lincoln's cell. Members of the biker's club got word of it and planned an attack, but Lincoln had called them off before the murder was realized. Later, after things were cleared up, the rookie returned the girly magazines and apologized to Lincoln.

An hour after their walk in the yard, Duck was back in his cell. It was Wednesday and Toothpaste was going on about skipping chow. He did this two or three times a week, preferring to stay in to make prison nachos, quesadillas, or his special penitentiary burritos.

"They serving that mystery meat," Toothpaste said, sitting on his bunk. "You don't wanna mess with that mystery meat." Mystery meat was Salisbury steak. It was served with powdered mashed potatoes and gravy. Every time Duck tried it, it would upset his stomach.

Toothpaste reached under his bunk for his trunk and started pulling out commissary: a huge bag of Nacho Cheese Doritos, a summer sausage, cheese dip, three Top Ramen noodles (beef flavored), and a seven-ounce bag of dehydrated refried beans. He laid them all out beside him, then tossed the summer sausage to C-Dub, whose job it was to barbecue the meat.

C-Dub tore the package open with his teeth, then used a plastic knife stolen from the prison cafeteria to cut slits around the sausage. After that, he made what inmates called a doughnut, out of toilet paper. He wrapped TP around his hand until it was thick enough to sustain a fire, then folded the ends in, creating a hole where he was to drop a burning match. He hid behind the sheet to cook the sausage, sitting backward on the commode, using two pencils for skewers to twirl the meat around the flame.

Duck kept watch at the bars. He looked right, then left, smelling the barbecue. Smoke seemed to fill the cell. It should be going through the vent. He listened to the sausage crackle under the fire, then wondered how far the smell would travel, but didn't worry yet about any guards. Instead, he leaned against the cage, looking out left at the head of the tier. C2 was the second cell on the block. If a guard came up the stairs and entered the tier suddenly, they'd be caught. Duck switched shoulders to spy the other end, but because of the awkward narrowness, he couldn't see very far.

He stroked his chin, feeling like a real criminal now.

"All right, celly," Toothpaste called.

Turning, Duck saw Toothpaste patting a spot on his bunk for him to sit. For some reason Duck didn't understand, Toothpaste always wanted him to sit with him. Toothpaste was like a man with no family, fond of moments like this.

They had the spread laid out on a stool and began to eat. Duck stared at the concoction, remembering how he thought it looked like vomit the first time he saw it. Then he remembered tasting it and feeling crazy sitting there eating it with his cellmates. He wrote Alexa that night, telling her all about the experience.

He stood there, thinking about how he still hadn't heard from her.

"C'mon, celly, sit," Toothpaste said.

Duck sat down next to Toothpaste and scooped up refried beans and cheese and noodles and bits of summer sausage with an already soggy Dorito chip. C-Dub sat across from them on a small wooden stool, smacking loudly with chipmunk cheeks. The fourth cellmate had been transferred to a medium-custody prison the previous week.

Al Green played quietly in the background. "Love and happiness." Duck nodded to the pitch of the organ and the soft kick of the drum.

"You know what I miss?" C-Dub said with his mouth full.

"What?" asked Toothpaste, bobbing his head, tapping his foot, munching.

"Hot sauce."

"You gone put hot sauce on nachos?"

"No. I'm just saying I miss hot sauce. I'd pour that shit all over some chicken and jojos."

"So," Toothpaste said, turning to Duck. "You still fuckin' with that Lincoln, I see."

"He's helping me out with my appeal. I told you that." Duck looked at Toothpaste, tired of being harassed about Lincoln, and prison rules for that matter. A few days ago, Toothpaste condemned him for playing basketball, claiming he could get himself killed for blocking a jump shot. It could piss the wrong inmate off, Toothpaste had told him. Then yesterday, after chow, he told Duck to stop walking to mainline with his hands in his pockets.

How you gonna protect yourself, if someone was to run up on you? the old man asked. He then rushed Duck inside the cell, pretending to shank him. Duck appreciated the advice, but sometimes it felt more like nagging. He thought about the discussion he had earlier with Lincoln. The man was upbeat and certain they'd get a positive response from the courts.

"We just sent it out last night," Duck said.

"Last night, huh?" Toothpaste frowned, then stuffed his mouth with nachos. Speaking with his mouth full, he continued. "That's something you could've done yourself. I told you that. Have you even paid the man yet?" He paused to swallow. "You know ain't nothin' free."

"He said not to worry about it until later."

"Later?" Toothpaste slammed his bean-stained hands down on his lap. "Boy, you 'bout as dumb as you look. You never accept gifts in prison. I told you that. And you never let anybody do anything for you without paying them first." He slapped Duck in the back of the head.

C-Dub laughed and then stopped when Duck looked at him.

"The man said not to worry about it, so I'm not going to worry about it," Duck said. "I barely have anything to pay him with anyway. Why do you think I had to gamble?"

He was referring to the admonishment for playing spades that Toothpaste had given him the previous day.

Toothpaste was about to stuff his mouth again but threw the loaded Dorito chip back into the pile. "Boy, you young'uns just don't get it. These fools cheat in here. They got signs and signals and shit. Coughin' and winkin' and kickin' each other under the table." He kicked his leg out for emphasis. "They tap their hand a certain way to communicate what they got." He tapped his fingers against an invisible fan of cards. "But you go on ahead anyway, dummy! Now I gotta pay your debt before they decide to rape you! You lucky I like you, boy. But I ain't doin' that shit again. You need to get your ass a job working in the kitchen or something. What's wrong with you kids?"

Duck sighed, then shook his head. He was on a waiting list for every job he applied for and couldn't go to school until the next quarter. He re-explained this all to Toothpaste.

"Yeah, well, you need to do something."

A month later, the Court of Appeals responded stating that there were no errors, and therefore Duck had no grounds for an appeal. In addition to that, they stated the notice wasn't filed within the thirty-day time limit.

Duck sat down with Lincoln the next morning to discuss the news over breakfast. Agitated, Duck opened the tiny carton of milk and poured it over his cereal. "This is bullshit."

"Well, it was worth a shot," said Lincoln. "You don't have but a few years anyway."

"That's not the point," Duck griped. "The point is I wanted to prove my innocence."

Lincoln's face was stern. He cocked his head as he listened.

"How am I gonna get a job?" Duck asked. "Everywhere I live, I have to register as a sex offender." He pounded his fist on the table and then got quiet. Guards were looking at him. "I'm not a rapist. Or a child molester."

"Yeah, well . . . life goes on."

Life goes on? What kind of a bullshit comment is that?

Then again, he *was* talking to a lifer. Someone who had nothing to live for but Ramen noodles and cigarettes. Someone who had spent more than three decades in prison. *Life goes on. Right.*

But life *had* gone on and was moving at a steady pace. Alexa seemed to have vanished and B had gone to another prison. And here Duck was with strange convicts and no friends, and no one believed he was innocent. Life had to go on. But in what direction?

They finished eating and got up to go back to their cells.

Outside, Lincoln covered his mouth to hide his talking. "So listen, I'mma need that favor from you. But we'll talk about it later."

"Favor? What favor?"

"Later, I said."

They entered eight wing and then passed through the metal detector.

"Stand for search," said Officer Meyer. Duck stood for search. Officer Meyer patted him down and found the banana Duck had inside his coat pocket. "This is contraband," Meyer said confiscating it.

He then gave Duck a verbal warning.

Duck apologized for having the banana and continued to his cell, wondering what Lincoln meant by a favor. Yard was called a few hours later. They met up and walked around the track.

"I need you to take care of this problem for me," Lincoln whispered after they passed by a few inmates.

"Problem? What problem?"

"We've got this guy," Lincoln said. "You've seen him. He sweeps the tiers at night and sits in the office with the COs. Helps 'em sort out mail and stuff. Problem is . . . pictures been coming up missing. Lotta guys ain't gettin' pictures of their kids, you know. I'm a point him out to you in a second."

They walked about twenty paces. Gravel crunching beneath their feet.

"Don't look too hard," Lincoln said, approaching the blacktop where sweaty inmates were shooting hoops. "See that guy with the bald head?"

Duck glanced over at the two teams playing basketball, spotting the tier-porter amongst them. His brown head was big and sweaty. He was one of a few inmates who didn't run with a gang, or affiliate himself with any religious organization. He simply kept to himself and swept the tiers at night, never doing favors for anyone such as passing a message or pushing an item from one cell to another for inmates who owed one another or who were friends. What did Lincoln want with him?

The mysterious, bald man landed a jump shot and hustled back, playing defense. "Yeah, I see him."

"I'mma need you to take care of him," Lincoln said. "Cut his throat . . . do whatever you gotta do, but he needs to be dead by tomorrow."

"Whoa!" Duck said, halting. "What the fuck are you talking about?"

"Let's keep walking."

Duck took a hesitant step, then another.

"You owe me a favor, remember?"

"You said we would work something out."

"And that's what we're doing."

"No, I didn't agree to this," Duck said. "The appeal didn't even go through."

"A deal is a deal, young man."

"I'm not doing that shit," Duck said, almost yelling. "I'm out in a few years. Why the fuck would I kill somebody?"

Lincoln nodded at two passing inmates. "You need to calm down, young man. You wanna prove your innocence, now this is how you do it. *In here.* Who you think been holding the dogs back, huh?"

Duck muttered, "I'm not doing that shit."

"Is that your final answer?"

"Yeah, hell yeah, that's my final answer!"

"All right then, youngster."

Duck went back to his cell, angry.

Toothpaste was sitting on the edge of his cot, playing chess with C-Dub across from him, pondering his next move.

"What's going on, celly?" Toothpaste asked as Duck came in.

Duck shook his head and climbed onto his bunk.

Toothpaste looked up at him with genuine concern. "What's going on?"

"Nothing."

Toothpaste stood up, pausing the game. "It's Lincoln, isn't it? He asked you to do something, didn't he? I told you not to fuck with that mothafucka."

Duck turned over on his side, closing his ears to the scorn. He picked up his book and started reading.

"You better do what he says."

Duck turned over to face Toothpaste. "I ain't afraid of that dude."

"You ain't gotta be. But you better do what he says."

Duck rolled back over and read until dinner.

"Mainline, pill line!" The gates racked back. Inmates flooded the tiers. Duck got up and went to pill-line, then took his time walking to the chow hall, got his tray of food, saw that Lincoln saw him, and sat down at another table.

Lincoln got up with his tray and sat down with him. "You avoiding me now, youngster?"

Duck ignored him. He just picked up his brown plastic eating utensils and cut off portions of the Salisbury steak.

Lincoln sniffed and nodded like a mob boss deciding what to do with him. "You think about what I said? This your last chance."

Duck slammed down his plastic fork. "I don't give a fuck about you threatening me! I'm a man. I don't care how long you've been in prison."

Lincoln smirked crookedly, returning a sadistic gaze.

Duck felt his heart knocking at his chest. He made a conscious effort not to show any fear but blinked and swallowed nervously anyway. He'd made his decision and was going to stick with it. Now what was going to happen next?

Lincoln got up with his tray, smiling. "All right, young man." He winked at Duck before walking away.

Yeah, fuck you, too.

Duck finished eating. Seconds later, his stomach began bubbling. He hurried to his cell as fast as he could without being stopped by a guard.

He hid behind the sheet, flushing repeatedly.

"I told you about that mystery meat," Toothpaste said. "You must think you He-Man or something."

"Shut up, Paste." Duck wheezed, clutching his stomach.

The cell door started to open. He peeked over the sheet. Two white men appeared. Clean-shaven and bald.

Without words, they entered.

Toothpaste disappeared into his bunk. C-Dub turned with his book and faced the wall.

Duck quickly tried to wipe himself. The two Nazis snatched the sheet down and hooked him off the toilet, handling him like a pair of angry bouncers. Was this a dream? Fear surfaced. He screamed.

He hit the floor with his face and blacked out for a second, then regained consciousness feeling the pressure of someone sitting on the back of his exposed body. Strong hands under his chin yanked his head back. Duck was in a wrestling hold known as the camel clutch. His neck burned with ripping pain. He yelled out and grabbed at the hands pulling his head back. Urine left his body and pooled under his legs.

Please, no!

The man pulled harder.

"You owe Lincoln a favor," the man said. "But there are other ways you can pay up."

Duck could hear the other inmate behind him unzipping his pants.

"All right, all right, all right!" Duck screamed. "I'll do it! All right !"

"That's what we thought."

"Please, God," Duck cried, sobbing.

The skinhead let go and got up, then walked toward the opened cell door and stopped. He lifted his T-shirt, took out a shank, and tossed it, almost hitting Duck in the face with it. It stopped dead in a spin, near the small puddle of slobber and teardrops. "Tomorrow. . . . And clean this shit up."

The skinhead behind Duck laughed, zipped up his pants, and stepped over him.

The two Nazis walked out with the cell door closing behind them.

Duck pulled up his pants as he got up. Wiped his face. Fixed the sheet. Picked up the shank. He stuffed it under his cot, then got back behind the sheet to clean himself, feeling as though he *had* been raped.

He tried to sleep afterward but lay there thinking about why this was happening and how to stop it. Maybe he deserved it. Maybe he *was* a monster.

No. *They're the real monsters. They want you to be an animal. Like them. They want you to be a murderer.*

He thought of doing something that would land him in solitary confinement again. Maybe start a fire in the cell. Maybe attack another officer. He thought about reporting the incident, but worried about retaliation. A sex offender *and* a snitch? Someone would surely kill him.

Just how much conspiring was done in the prison? How could two skinheads walk into his cell and leave at a time when there was no movement? Did they pay the guard in the control booth? Was he in on it? How could they even make weapons? Where did the metal shank come from?

Why was killing this man so important? Why did the guards even let him sort out the mail? The man Lincoln had ordered Duck to kill was a *real* pedophile. A *real* child molester. Convicted of raping and killing children. *Children!*

Maybe he should kill him.

He tossed the blanket aside and sat up. Maybe if he did it the prison would respect him.

He then heard the barking of a large dog. A German shepherd, or a bull mastiff perhaps. He covered his ears, trying to ignore it for five minutes, and then five minutes more. He leaped down from his bunk and went up to the bars, yelling, "Shut up!" It was maybe midnight, or eleven, or two in the morning by then. Either way, a dog was barking, keeping him up.

Toothpaste was out of bed now, doing his own yelling.

Duck turned to face him.

He and C-Dub were both there telling Duck to chill out.

Duck seized the blanket from his cot and shoved it out of the bars, believing it controlled the barking. He turned back to his cellmates, pointing at it. "Make it stop. Make it stop!"

Inmates from other cells were yelling for him to shut up.

Toothpaste charged him suddenly and slapped him, then grabbed him by the arms. "Get a grip! Get a grip!"

Duck shook himself free and paced. His hands on top of his head. Heart racing. Breathing heavily. The prison walls were alive now, inching in closer and closer, squeezing in on his body. The cell began to quake, just like it did when he was in solitary confinement.

He threw down his hands and laughed hysterically.

Toothpaste touched his shoulder, prompting him to sit down on the bunk with him. "Get a grip," he kept saying. "Get a grip."

Duck chuckled upon hearing the words.

Toothpaste mumbled to himself before giving up.

The next morning Duck felt no better.

He went to pill-line, chow, and sat down staring at his waffles.

Lincoln appeared and plopped down with his tray. "So what's the plan?"

Duck peered at him, hating everything about him and his sly and arrogant squint. The man smirked, tapping his big ugly fingers on the table.

Duck thought about killing him instead. Someone like him deserved to die. He had no business living anyway.

But neither did the child molester.

Shower time, a voice said.

"Shower time," Duck said.

"Good." Lincoln nodded, got up with his tray, and congratulated Duck by clapping his shoulder. Shower time was no more than twelve hours away.

Duck stayed in his cell all day. When it came time, he stood in front of the cell door, waiting. He wrapped the shiv in a towel and cradled it close to his half-naked body. Finally, the gates opened. He marched down the stairs and into the shower room, where several inmates stripped out of their clothes and piled them on benches before scurrying out to secure a shower head.

He walked onto the wet tile, naked in his flip-flops, gazing about. The child molester hadn't come down yet. Duck found a shower head and started washing, holding the thickly wrapped shank close to his chest.

He showered for what seemed like an hour. Two tiers came and went before he finally saw the bald man enter with the next flood of convicts. The man trudged to the left of him, showering with his back turned, in the far corner. Duck faced the wall again and slowly unveiled the weapon, dropping the soaked towel that hid it. He turned, firmly holding the shank by its handle.

He surged forward, sloshing through the water. The bald man spun around alarmed. His eyes large with fright. His mouth screaming in womanly terror.

Cut his throat, Lucky Ducky! Cut his throat!

Duck raised the shank over his head and lunged. Tripping over his flip-flops, he fell onto the wet tile, tasting the defiled water. A large dog started barking again. He got up quickly, spitting. He turned about. The shiv still in his hand.

The black pedophile ran into the arms of a white mob.

Cut his throat, Lucky Ducky! Cut his throat!

The dog barking still. The men shoved the pedophile. The man ran awkwardly, trying not to slip while screaming for his life. Screaming for the guards.

Something inside forced Duck to chase him. And without self-control, he pursued him with a blank mind. Felons scrambled out of their way, shifting around the shower room naked.

Cut his throat, Lucky Ducky! Cut his throat!

He saw himself catching the pedophile and slitting his neck. Blood sprayed Duck's face, staining him with murder.

Murder!

"No, no, no, no, no!" He stopped and threw the blade as if it were crawling with a million spiders. He grabbed his head, turning away from the child-preying monster, wishing everything would just stop. He bobbed back and forth mumbling, and then screamed as a sharp pain ripped through his side.

He whirled around to see his attacker. The man stabbed him again, thrusting the shank into his gut.

In his mind, Duck begged him to stop and begged for someone to intervene, but no one did anything. They just watched. He realized it was all a plot—to pit them against each other. Two sex offenders. One accused and innocent. The other still thirsty for blood.

Duck gazed at his attacker. Was this the same man who ran away screaming seconds ago? The man raised the tool in answer, wearing the evil grimace of a merciless god.

Suddenly the goon squad came charging. Tactical boots splashed with the beat of their batons. The pedophile tossed the weapon. Duck fell and held himself, expecting to die.

Memories of Alexa flashed through his mind.

Fifteen

Fats, Noah, and his two sons stood on the corner of
Twenty-Fifth and Jackson, lined up outside of a church.

It was mid-afternoon and dozens of worshippers were
pouring out of the building, leaving from the Sunday
service, congregating on the sidewalk in an afterglow of
spiritual glee. Bald men with clean-shaven faces and loud
women in dresses showing cleavage were so possessed
with Christianity that they were blind to the Truth.

Fats shook his head, then remembered two years ago,
that he too was ignorant. With that, he became humble
again. He side-glanced Noah's fifteen-year-old son,
Malachi, who held up a cardboard sign listing the twelve
tribes of Israel.

In Calligraphy, it read: *Judah, Benjamin, Ephraim,*
Manasseh, Simeon, Zebulon, Gad, Rueben, Asher, Issachar,
Naphtali, and Levi, the Priests. Each tribe had a dash and
race attributed to it. Blacks for Judah, West Indians for
Benjamin, Puerto Ricans for Ephraim. Cubans for
Manasseh, Dominicans for Simeon, Guatemalans for
Zebulon. Native Americans for Gad, Seminoles for Reuben,
Columbians for Asher. Mexicans for Issachar, Argentinians
for Naphtali, and Haitians for Levi, the Priests.

Noah began to greet people as his eldest son, Josiah,
handed out tracts.

"Shalom. Did the pastor tell you that Jesus is black?

"Shalom, brother. Do you know that you're an Israelite?

"Shalom, sis. Can you tell me who you are according to
this list? I'll tell you who you are! You're an Israelite from
the tribe of Judah. But America has labeled you as *black*.

Black is a color in a Crayon box, *not* a nationality. Your nationality is of Israel."

Members ducked by in droves, avoiding eye contact as if Noah and the congregation were a sideshow of panhandling miscreants. But Noah continued, booming out charges at every churchgoer he encountered. Eventually, two or three persons stopped to read the tribal names or to look at the two images of Christ glued onto the cardboard A-frame sign set out on the sidewalk before them. One image was of an effeminate-looking white man with thin facial hair. The other was of a fiery-eyed bearded black man. Most people would scan the images and walk on, but a few would always stop for questions.

Fats had gotten used to this pattern. In the past few years, he learned his people were lost. They were hypnotized by lies and glamor and in consequence despised order and discipline. But he had learned the Truth. That God was a black man and that black people were chosen. But they were also cursed because they wouldn't abide by the Law. That's why black men killed each other. That's why black women went unmarried. That's why he had been sexually abused and neglected. That's why he had gotten cancer and diabetes. Because the Most High had chosen him and rebuked him, for He, the Most High, rebukes the one He loves, and tries them like gold through the fire. *To rid them of their impurities*, as it said in the Bible.

He prepared himself to read, quickly thumbing to a scripture he knew Noah was leading up to. By now a nice crowd had formed, hanging on to every word that Noah said.

Fats licked his dry lips and held his Bible up to his face.

"Give me Deuteronomy, chapter twenty-two, verse five," Noah commanded.

"Deuteronomy, chapter twenty-two, verse five," Fats shouted. "The woman shall *not* wear that which pertains unto a man, neither shall a man put on a woman's garment: for all that do so are an abomination unto the Lord thy God."

"According to the Bible," Noah said. "Women are supposed to wear dresses—with fringes and a border of blue. Our sisters are not supposed to be wearing pants, dressing up like men . . . and our men are not supposed to be dressing up like women like you see so many doing today."

A shapely woman in black leggings said, "The Bible says, come as you are. So it doesn't matter how you look or dress."

"Where in the Bible does it say that, sis?"

She stared blankly. Church members around her stirred.

"Nowhere in the Bible does it say 'come as you are,'" Noah said. "Nowhere. This is why we need to study. God gave us a dress code so we would remember the Law, and so we wouldn't be like the heathens. I'll give you an example, sis. The reason you know a police officer is a police officer is because he or she wears a uniform, correct? And when you see a police officer you know he or she enforces the law, and when you greet them you tend to do it with a degree of respect. Right? Because you know what that police officer represents. It works the same way with God's uniform. If you're wearing a saintly dress with fringes and a border of blue, people will respect you, because they know what you stand for. But you will also respect yourself because you will think twice about breaking God's laws when you're in that godly dress, just like an officer knows not to break man's law when he is in his police uniform."

People nodded. Hard questions followed.

Noah answered, proving every word with scripture.

Within an hour the crowd thinned into an audience of one.

Fats gave the man a flyer and told him to call if he wanted to congregate. Fats, Noah, and his sons then left and made it to Noah's house in Tacoma by two.

Fats followed Noah to the workout room. Noah had been personally training Fats for the past two years he'd been staying under his roof. They only rested on the Sabbath, which was Friday sundown to Saturday sundown. The two-story house had four bedrooms. Two upstairs, two downstairs, and a basement where nobody was allowed to go, except Noah and now Fats. The room they were in was left of the front door. It had been converted into a small gym complete with a dumbbell set, a squat rack with a pull-up bar, a multi-purpose weight bench, and a treadmill.

An hour later Fats stood with his hands on his hips, oozing sweat and panting as he watched Noah curl an EZ curl barbell with two forty-five-pound plates on either end of it. Noah lay on a bench when he was done, then took a hundred-pound dumbbell in each hand and pressed them upward.

"You don't get enough of this at work?" Fats asked. "Hauling all that goddamn furniture?" Noah had his own business, a moving company called Noah and Sons. He'd owned it for five years and had just finished paying off the loan on his twenty-six-foot moving truck and was thinking about expanding his business by buying another twenty-six-footer. Fats could put a crew together and work the Seattle area, while Noah and his sons continued growth just south in Tacoma. Fats liked the idea, as it gave him a sense of ownership. It also made him feel trusted. Two things he'd never felt before.

"You gotta stay healthy," Noah said, huffing. He rose from the bench, dropping the two-hundred-pound dumbbells. They landed like two rounds of thunder.

Fats sat down on the bench after him, seizing the twenty-five-pound dumbbells on either side of his body.

Noah's two-year-old daughter ran into the room, giggling.

"Out!" Noah said, pointing.

She darted out playfully as he followed behind to tell his wife to keep an eye on her.

Fats finished his set, then stepped out into the kitchen to get a glass of water. Noah joined him.

Fats drank his refreshment. "Two years sober," he said proudly.

Noah exhaled after downing his own drink, then clapped Fats on the shoulder. "All praises, brother. And *you've* lost a lot of weight. You see how the Most High works?"

Fats looked down past his stomach. For the first time in a long time, he was able to see his own feet.

All praises.

Thanks to Noah he was alive. Thanks to Noah he was healthy. Thanks to Noah he had a job, a car, and shelter. Thanks to Noah he knew who he was. An Israelite! He was special. He was not destined for failure but chosen. He was part of a kingdom. And thanks to the Most High, he was no longer an alcoholic.

All praises!

He looked at the empty glass in his hand, then filled it back up with faucet water.

After the workout, he sat down on the sofa reading his Bible, waiting for Noah, who finally appeared twenty minutes later. Tassels dangling from his shirt. A small black plastic case in his hand.

"Shalom, brother, you ready?"

Fats stood up closing his Bible. "I'm ready."

A half hour later they eased into a secluded parking lot and parked.

Noah shut off the motor. "You sure about this?" Fats asked, side-glancing him. "I'm not gonna get arrested coming out of here, right?"

"Nah, brother, you should be good. We just go in, sign some papers, and pick out a target. They're not going to do a background check, Yehuda."

Yehuda was Fats's Hebrew name. A title he chose naming himself after the tribe of Judah and Judah Maccabeus, a priest, who had led a revolt against his oppressors and won.

Fats got out and followed Noah inside the shooting range, hearing loud claps of gunfire as they entered. As a felon, it was unlawful for Fats to be around firearms.

Noah went to the counter next to the glass case displaying handguns. He showed his ID, then signed a paper clamped onto a clipboard. Fats did the same when Noah was done, mimicking everything—from Noah's calm, confident demeanor to how he laid down the pen after signing his name. The man behind the counter seemed to stare. The small eyes in his pink, round face looked about as friendly as the bullets he sold. Fats looked away at the display of handguns.

Noah pointed, picking out a target. The clerk turned to grab the poster: a human silhouette with white rings and scoring numbers in the center. He handed it to Noah, who then picked out two pairs of earmuffs and safety glasses and paid. Noah motioned with his head for Fats to follow him.

They turned a corner and came to an opening that had no door, then made a left. Fats trailed cautiously, flinching at every thunderous clap. Each shooter they passed fired a different weapon. A white man, dressed in army fatigue pants and a hunter's vest, fired a semi-automatic rifle. Two shooting stalls after him, a slender woman with a ponytail, wearing a black cap, fired a silver revolver.

Noah stopped at an open booth and handed Fats the earmuffs and protection goggles. Fats put on his share of the safety gear. Noah set down the gun case and proceeded to set up the paper target. He attached it to the target holder, then sent the silhouette drifting down the lane. He stopped at ten feet at first, then moved it down another five.

Noah unlocked the gun case, took out the .40 Caliber Sig Sauer, slipped in the magazine, and pulled back the slide. He got in his shooting stance. The gun jerked back with a bark. Noah fired again and again, then broke his stance, turning to Fats with the gun.

Fats felt a surge of energy warm his body.

"Now remember," Noah said. "Keep a firm grip and your stance aligned with the target. Make sure your sight is centered and leveled. Always focus on the front sight and not the rear. And pull the trigger smoothly. Don't jerk it. Now let's get those two shots off."

Fats held the gun, feeling colossal. Feeling flushed with exhilaration and power. Feeling the sharp and bumpy texture of metal against his sweaty palm. He put his left foot forward and extended his arms, keeping one elbow and knee bent slightly, concentrating on the sights, while also viewing his target. He focused, seeing only the white dot of the front sight and the blur of the silhouette, and then fired. He squeezed the trigger again.

"Stop," Noah said, touching Fats on the shoulder. Noah fingered the control lever toward him and smirked as the target came up. He studied the two holes in the black face of the poster, then sent it back, twenty-five yards down the lane. "Let's try it again. That might have been luck."

Fats fired twice and stopped.

"I aimed for the heart," he said.

Noah reeled the target back and examined it, scratching his head. "Good job, brother." He seemed surprised by the twin marks.

Fats smiled like a child impressing his father, knowing he'd done something special.

They practiced for an hour before realizing they should get back because class was about to start.

They sped home and rushed inside the house. Noah turned on the computer and snatched his serpentine trumpet —a polished, Yemenite shofar. Smooth and curvy with three different shades of brown twisted around its shiny body. He put it to his lips, tilted his head, and blew out his cheeks like Dizzy Gillespie. The sound was like that of a fog horn.

The boys rumbled down with haste, then grabbed folding chairs that clanked as they sat down next to each other. Noah's wife, Sarah, sat down behind them, holding Abigail, her and Noah's daughter, who wore a blue dress with fringes like her mother. The online class had already started. (Class was held every day of the week and taught by different leaders from various cities in the country. Only the Sabbath class was held by the elders.) Fats sat down on the couch with his Bible and notepad and prepared to take notes from the Sunday lesson.

Six months later, he stood alone on the corner of Twenty-Fifth and Jackson trying to pass out flyers.

"No thank you, but happy New Year," a woman said, passing by him.

"According to the Bible, the New Year begins in spring," he yelled after her.

A man on his phone strolled by. Fats chased him with a leaflet. The man pointed to his phone and kept walking. Fats blessed the man, then whirled to face the next pedestrian.

"Shalom, brother. We trying to wake our people up," Fats said, handing him the tract. The man looked at it walking, then balled it up and tossed it into the street with the others.

A woman ducked by, waving off the offer.

Fats sat down on the rail in front of the church feeling exhausted. No one wanted to hear the Truth. They all wanted to believe a lie. They all wanted to remain dead. Dead to wisdom. Dead to knowledge. Dead to understanding that they are to celebrate the High Holy Days of the Bible. Not Christmas. Not Thanksgiving. Not New Year's.

He looked up and saw that a tall young man was headed his way. Fats got off the rail and stood erect, remembering what Jesus did for Lazarus, remembering what Noah did for him. If Fats could only save one life, he could save millions.

"Say brother, let me ask you something."

The young man stopped. "What's up?"

"Can you tell me who you are according to this list?" Fats held out the flyer listing the twelve tribes of Israel.

The young man stepped closer, reading the list carefully. Finally, the young man pointed to the tribe of Judah.

"That's right," Fats said. "You're an Israelite from the tribe of Judah, not a so-called black man, or African American. *You* are a descendent of Jacob."

The young man wrinkled his face.

"Take the flyer, brother." The young man took the flyer. "My name is Yehuda and I represent the twelve tribes of Israel. We tryna to wake our people up and get 'em off the streets and into the word of God. This Bible is the *only* thing that can save us from the traps and snares of this world: pornography, alcoholism, violence, homelessness, drugs, molestation, and depression; all of these things are designed by the devil to keep you from the way of God." Fats pulled out his Bible and pointed to it. "This is the only thing that can save you. But you have to come back to the Lord and abide by His laws, statutes, and commandments. You have to repent to Yahweh." Fats paused to examine the man's countenance. "What's your name, brother?"

"Benjamin," the young man said, offering his hand. "But everyone calls me B."

"B? All praises, B. What you doing out here?"

"Looking for a job," B said. "I just got out of prison."

"Oh yeah? I can help you with that. My brother owns a moving company and we're looking to expand. Take down my number."

B saved the number in his phone. "This is what I'm talking about," he said, putting his phone away. "Brothers helping each other out."

"That's right."

"Well, look, I appreciate this, yo, but I gotta go."

"All right, brother. Shalom, and shalom means peace."

B bowed awkwardly, bringing his fist up to his chest and shaking it as if to say, "Right on," and then walked off.

Fats drove home to a small motel room he recently rented for seven hundred dollars a month in Tacoma. He settled in and then saw that he had a missed call. He called the number.

"Hey, brother, it's B," the voice said, answering. "I just had a few questions."

"Speak, brother."

"It shows here in this pamphlet that Jesus is black."

"That's right."

"Then it says . . . we are the Jews the Bible speaks of."

"That's right."

"Wait . . . So are you saying . . . the people in the Bible are black?"

"I'm not saying anything, brother. That's what the Bible says. That's what God says. Read the scriptures and see for yourself. We are the true Israelites. Read Deuteronomy, chapter twenty-eight. It's all there in plain English. It tells you about the curses we had to endure because of our wickedness. It tells you about us being enslaved . . . first physically and then mentally, and how we will cry for help, and how no one will help us."

"Black Israelites, huh?"

"No," Fats said. "Israelites. Calling us 'black Israelites' is like calling us fake. You are a true Israelite, brother. Your identity and your heritage have been stolen. You need to understand that."

"Yeah, I remember somebody telling me that in prison. But I don't know, man. That's kind of deep."

"It is deep, but if you read the scriptures you'll understand that it's the truth. Check this out." Fats already had his Bible in hand. He flipped over to Deuteronomy twenty-eight and read.

The lecture lasted until midnight, only ending because Fats had to get up early for work. B called throughout the week, never asking about the job, only about the Bible and scriptures.

Fats informed Noah of B's eagerness to learn. The three agreed to meet the following Friday evening at a neutral library location where B had reserved a study room.

They sat down at the table. Fats and Noah on one side. B on the other.

"Thanks for meeting me," B said.

"No problem," Noah said. "I see you brought your Bible."

"Yes, sir. Brother Yehuda suggested I bring one."

Fats looked at the blue hardback. "Is that that New English crap? I told you to bring a King James."

Noah touched his shoulder. "Calm down, brother. Excuse him," he said to B. "He gets like a firecracker sometimes."

"It's all good," B said. "I just got out of prison a few months ago, and there was this brother there telling us our history's in the Bible. But I didn't know what he was talking about. I thought he was crazy."

"Right," said Noah. "First of all, do you know who you are?" He pushed the list of tribes forward.

B examined them, then pointed to the first one listed. "Judah."

"Right, now let's go over to the book of Deuteronomy," Noah said. Then to Fats, "You know what I want."

Fats turned to chapter twenty-eight. Noah flipped to the scripture himself, then turned his Bible around. B leaned forward to see the highlighted area. Fats took a deep breath and read.

"Stop," Noah said when Fats was done.

B looked up confused. "It's like it's talking about us, but—"

"Israel lost its kingdom because we wanted to practice the customs of other nations and not the customs of our own," Noah said. "So God cursed us for that. He said we would be enslaved and scattered across the earth because we refused to abide by the Law. What other people have become a byword? What other people have been enslaved and scattered? What other people have had a yolk of iron placed upon their neck?"

B leaned back in thought.

"You're an Israelite," Fats said. "Do you understand that?"

"Man, I do," B said. "But how come you never hear about this in church?"

"Because," Fats said. "They teach the Bible the way they learned it from their oppressor."

"The Most High can use you," Noah said. "First thing you gotta do is repent, then grow out that beard."

B touched his face, stroking his bare cheeks and chin. "Man, I gotta tell my cousin about this."

"Your cousin?" Fats asked.

"Yeah. He's locked up right now, but he should be out soon."

"Everybody need to know about this Truth," Fats said. "Everybody."

"You should come join us next Sabbath," Noah said.

"Sabbath?"

"Yeah, we'll be celebrating New Moon," Fats said as he stood up and stretched. "I can talk all night, brothers, but

I'm tired." He yawned, then addressed B. "If you have any more questions, just give us a call."

B did. And within a month he accepted the faith.

Easter Sunday, the three men were together with Noah's sons. B, now fully converted, went by his birth name Benjamin, which was regarded as Hebrew. They stood outside of the church on Twenty-Fifth and Jackson. The five of them with fringes and borders of blue around the hem of their shirts. Church was letting out and the congregation was quickly filling the sidewalk. Fats turned to Benjamin, checking his position, then returned his attention to the church. Men in crisp suits and women in big hats talked and laughed loudly in groups.

Fats sucked his teeth, disgusted. The church members were all proud of their idol worshipping but were about to be humbled by the Truth. Noah and his sons stood right of Fats, while B flanked his left, keeping an eye out for trouble.

"The very first commandment demands that Israel do what?" Noah shouted. "Refrain from idol worshipping. This is the primary sin that has brought us down, and what are we doing today? We are celebrating a holiday, a pagan holiday, representing rabbits and fertility and attributing it to Christ. This is foolishness people. Ask yourself, would Jesus, the Messiah, be praising a bunny?"

The pastor forced his way through the church congregation. "You need to leave," he said. "You guys keep popping up here, week after week, month after month, causing problems. You need to leave, now."

"We're causing problems?" Noah asked. "We're trying to save our people while you're trying to destroy them. Give me Exodus, chapter twenty, verse three."

"The book of Exodus, chapter twenty, verse three," Fats shouted. "Thou shall have no other gods before me."

"Read it again."

"Thou shall have no other gods before me."

"Again."

"Thou shall have no other gods before *me!*"

"You hear that? So why are you misleading our people into worshipping a false god? Easter comes from the fertility goddess Ester. Give me first Samuel, chapter seven, verse three."

The pastor cocked his head and crossed his arms.

"The first book of Samuel, chapter seven, verse three . . . put away the strange gods and Ashtaroth from among you."

"Stop! Ashtaroth was a male deity named after the fertility goddess Ishtar. This is why you do Easter egg hunts. This has nothing to do with the resurrection of Christ."

The pastor shrank back a pace.

"Give me Jeremiah, chapter seven, verse eighteen."

Fats read.

"Stop," Noah yelled. "The queen of heaven is Ishtar, the fertility goddess. Continue."

"That they may provoke me to anger."

"And that's how you know what you're doing is a sin. You are provoking God to anger, with your idol worshipping. Give me Psalm ninety-six, verse five, in case they still don't understand."

"The book of—"

Fats stumbled backward, dropping his Bible. Jarred and disoriented, he fell to the ground searching for it, frantically crawling around like a blind man looking for his eyeglasses. He found his Bible, then held it up as though it were a delicate artifact, never minding that he'd been hit.

There was commotion. He looked up in time to see an angry man push through B and Noah, who both had failed to restrain the lunatic. The crazy man was now running at Fats. The man looked familiar, and in that brief moment of recognition Fats saw the man's foot swing back.

It landed hard in Fats's stomach. He gasped deeply, fumbling his Bible again.

"What are you doing?" Benjamin yelled, shoving Duck.

Duck stumbled into Noah, who had grabbed him by the arm. "Get off me," Duck shouted. He tried pulling away. But the grip was too powerful.

"What the hell is wrong with you?" B asked, standing in front of him.

"What's wrong with me?" Duck shouted. "What's wrong with *you*? That's Fats!"

B turned around and stared at Fats, who was scooting back on his hind part, watching them in fright. Noah's sons had knelt to help him up, but he was too busy trying to see what Duck was going to do next. B returned his attention to Duck. "Uh . . . I didn't know that was him." B looked at Fats again, then back at Duck. "Look, brother . . . you gotta let that go."

Duck broke away as Noah loosened his grip, walked around in a circle, and then charged at Fats again, to be knocked off his feet by Noah.

"That's enough, brother," Noah said, pulling him up.

Duck yanked his hand back and dusted himself off, then noticed the audience recording with their cell phones. He turned away from them.

Noah's hand landed on Duck's shoulder, squeezing firmly. Duck looked at the hand, then at the man. The man's face was round and bearded. His brown eyes were soft but tired, with decades of agitation burning in them.

"What's going on here?" the man asked. "Why are you attacking your brother?"

"That dude ain't my brother." He pulled away from the man's grip.

"They have a history," B said.

"Let him speak, Benjamin," Noah said.

Duck said nothing but paced.

Noah looked over his shoulder at Fats, then back at Duck. "All right, so you two have a history. We all have a history, brother."

Duck turned his head and spat.

Noah continued. "Now I don't know what happened between ya'll, but this man has repented, and now lives for the Most High. You understand?"

Duck sighed, walking back and forth, from one spot to another, shaking his head.

"In Israel, it's important that we forgive one another. Do you think you can forgive him . . . for whatever he did?"

Duck scoffed. Was this guy serious? He didn't know Fats at all.

"How can you expect God to forgive you if you don't forgive others?" Noah asked.

"I don't need forgiveness," Duck said. He met Noah's eyes, burning through them with a spirit of hatred, then stormed away.

B yelled, chasing after Duck, touching his arm.

Duck whirled to face him. "This is what you wanted me to see? This the bullshit you were writing me about?"

"Bro, I didn't know."

Duck turned away and walked faster.

"The brother helped change my life," B said, following. "Whoever he was then, he's not the same now."

Duck stopped and faced him again. "Did you forget what he did to Alexa? Did you forget what he did to her face?"

Sixteen

The probation office was quiet. Duck sat down in the hallway with three other parolees, waiting for his community placement officer. Duck arrived at 9:00 a.m. After this, he would see the sheriff, look for employment, and then stop by the library to see if he could find Alexa on social media. Tomorrow he would renew his driver's license, go to the bank to check his savings account, replace the battery in his car, and stop by the mental health clinic the psychiatrist in Walla Walla referred him to.

Two of the men began talking, breaking the silence. Duck wiped his hands on his knees, hoping the conversation didn't work its way up to him. The guy next to him fidgeted like he was getting ready to attempt some small talk. Soon he'd be asking Duck how long he'd been out of prison, where he did time, or what the conditions of his supervision were.

"Carlos Duckworth?" A man appeared at the end of the hallway, reading from an open manila folder. Duck shot to his feet and strode over to meet the man, who looked to be about his age. He was of medium build and average height. Blue eyes. Potato white skin. Clean-shaven with spiky hair that had been tapered into a Mohawk. He offered his hand and pumped twice and hard, introducing himself as Gordon Ryan, Duck's community placement officer.

"Nice to meet you," Duck said.

Gordon Ryan turned. "Follow me."

Duck did, observing the man's uniform. He wore black cargo pants and a tight navy polo. And on the back of his duty belt were a pair of encased handcuffs.

"Come in," Gordon Ryan said. "Have a seat."

Duck entered, glancing around the office.

"Have a seat." Gordon Ryan slapped the folder onto the desk. Duck sat down at the office desk between them. The man smoothed his shirt and enthroned himself. On his desk was a computer with the usual office clutter. "How was your Easter?"

Duck drew his hands back on the arms of the chair and clutched them. Did the CPO know about the fight?

"It was fine," Duck said. "My grandparents took me to see my mom, and we had dinner there."

Gordon Ryan leaned over the desk, folding his hands. "I'm glad to hear that. So no problems then?"

Did he know about the fight or not?

"No problems," Duck said rubbing his forehead.

The man nodded, then shifted his attention to the folder. He studied quietly, flipping page after page, while occasionally sipping his coffee.

Duck glanced around the office again. Behind Gordon Ryan was a large poster of a bald eagle. On either side of the poster were two quotes framed in gold. The one on the left was titled, "The Man in the Arena" by Theodore Roosevelt. The one on the right was a poem called, "If" by Rudyard Kipling. Duck read both, reflecting lightly on the one before moving on to the other. Immediately he understood why they were hung up on the wall. Gordon Ryan was conveying a message to parolees: that no matter what, you always have a choice, so feeling sorry for yourself is not an option.

Duck continued surveying the room for clues that would tell him more about the officer. There were no family photos on the man's desk, but there was a wedding band on his finger. Maybe he'd decided not to have pictures of his family around because of what he did for a living. He *did* supervise criminals. Criminals like murderers and thieves. Criminals like pedophiles and rapists.

Duck wiped his palms on his knees, thinking the man was reading his file now, prejudging him. Gordon Ryan turned a page, then reached for his coffee. He brought the mug to his lips, then set it back on the desktop. Duck suddenly had an urge to finish the hot beverage. He looked away at the wall and started re-reading the poem, "If." And after the poem "If," he re-read, "The Man in the Arena."

Gordon Ryan cleared his throat and closed the folder. "You were released Saturday—"

"Yes, sir," Duck said.

The CPO leaned forward, folding his hands over the desk. "That wasn't a question. Don't interrupt me again."

Duck nodded.

"Today is Monday," Gordon Ryan said. "You have three working days to register as a sex offender. The sheriff's office is open until one. It is closed on Tuesdays but opens again on Wednesdays at eight-thirty a.m. Failure to comply is a violation of your supervision. Do you understand?"

Duck nodded.

Gordon Ryan stared at him for about five seconds, then went on. "You are to be home by nine p.m. for the two years you are under my supervision. You are not to be around any children. If you decide to travel, you are to notify me and the sheriff twenty-one days before you leave. If you decide to change residence, you are to notify me and the sheriff before you move. If you become homeless, you are to report to the sheriff's office once a week. You cannot work or reside within two thousand feet of a school or daycare, or a church that has a daycare as long as you are under my supervision." (There is no residency restriction law in the state of Washington, but the prosecuting attorney, on behalf of Lizzy's parents, had asked the judge for harsher conditions.) "On Halloween, you are to post a notification on your door informing the public that inside resides a sex offender. And on that day you are not to leave your home, under any circumstances." He stopped. "Do you understand your conditions?"

Duck nodded, feeling as though he were about to vomit. "Two thousand feet seems like a lot."

The CPO cocked his head and said: "In my opinion, it's not enough. It's less than half a mile. You just make sure you keep your distance." He referred to the file again. "Says here you were diagnosed with depression while you were in jail, and then . . . bipolar disorder . . . shortly after you were stabbed in prison?"

"Yes, sir."

"Tell me about that."

After the stabbing Duck had been sent to the infirmary where he stayed for a week before being transferred to protective custody. There he ran into Eddie Blodgett, the peculiar individual he met at the support group meeting he'd attended with Mom, her boyfriend, and Alexa. Eddie had been arrested for indecent exposure. During a psychotic break, he had stripped himself naked and urinated at a school playground full of children.

Eddie was sentenced to two years, based on the point system and his long criminal record. Duck didn't recognize him at first, for the unit was full of strange men Duck tried to avoid. Most of the inmates were heavily medicated, or just odd. In the dayroom, one man cursed the television daily. Another staggered around, grabbing at the air like a child after soap bubbles.

The majority of inmates in protective custody were mentally ill, informants, sex offenders, or inmates who were too scared to be on mainline with the rest of the prison population. Eddie was arguing with one of them about who was the better runner, Bruce Jenner or Jesse Owens. The inmate he was debating with screamed that Jesse had four gold medals, while Eddie yelled that Bruce had more records. All this started with a commercial featuring the Kardashian women.

Eddie turned to Duck for an opinion. Duck ignored him, moving away to a seat near the ping-pong table, where he watched two inmates contend. Eddie followed and sat down next to him, then reintroduced himself, mentioning the support group meeting and Alexa, referring to her as the pretty girl Duck was with.

Duck remembered him and acknowledged their prior encounter and consequently was harassed with conversation for a week.

Duck rarely showered. He only took sponge baths in his cell on the days he felt his body itching. In protective custody, there was no shower room, only shower stalls. Despite this, Duck was afraid of getting stabbed again while showering, or that the voices could be triggered by the patter of water. Some of the convicts started complaining about his body odor. Others went to authority, who did nothing.

Soon Duck quit coming to dayroom altogether, thinking seclusion was better. He stopped going to yard and pill line for his antidepressants, not wanting to stand in the long, slow-moving queue. During chow, Eddie tried to convince him to get help, reminding him of the discourse they had at the group meeting. Duck refused passively by never responding.

Unbeknownst to him, Eddie had forged a medical kite in Duck's name, requesting he be seen by a psychiatrist for an updated evaluation. When the guards arrived at Duck's cell he fought them. He was taken to solitary confinement, then back to the infirmary where he was eventually diagnosed as bipolar.

He argued with the doctor, saying his mother was schizophrenic. Still, Duck was prescribed 400 milligrams of Seroquel, which he took daily. The medication did help him manage the voices. But it also made him sleep for over twelve hours a day, and gain about twenty pounds during the stint. But once he got better he started programming, going to school in protective custody, reading, and working in the unit's garment factory. Eventually, he earned all of his good time back.

He explained this all to Gordon Ryan.

"So you hear voices?" the officer asked.

Duck thought before answering. It made no sense to hide the truth. The man was already judging him. "Sometimes, but the meds help me control them better."

"I see. And do you ever have any thoughts about children?"

Duck clenched his teeth, flexing his jaw muscles. Offended, he started to curse at the man but took a deep breath instead. "No, sir," he said calmly. "I haven't had any thoughts about children." He paused, taking another deep breath. "I just want to find a psychiatrist . . . so I can continue taking my medication. My prison doctor gave me a list of clinics I can go to. She said therapy would help. And as you can see in my file—" He pointed to the folder. "—I haven't had any issues since I've been on medication."

"I see. And what are your overall plans?"

Duck shrugged. "To find a job, and fix my car so I can make it to work." His car was buried deep in his grandparents' garage. Dilapidated. Paint faded into stains of rust. The roof overgrown with moss and algae. And it wouldn't start, but he suspected it just needed a battery.

"We're going to hold off on work," Gordon Ryan said, palming the mouse and averting his attention to the desktop before him. "Right now I want you to focus on treatment." He clicked the mouse twice, then got up and went across to the printer and returned with two sheets of paper. "Here is the schedule for STOP, a victim awareness program for newly released sex offenders. You'll attend group sessions three days a week, for one year, and will receive a certificate upon completion. I also want you at Sex Addicts Anonymous, for the remaining two days of the week. I want you busy with treatment and therapy, for at least three months, before you start working. And I expect you to bring proof of your attendance, to show you are complying. You mentioned seeing a psychiatrist. That's great. Perhaps we can arrange for sexual deviancy evaluations. And before you start driving I want a note from your psychiatrist, saying that it's safe for you to drive. You mentioned something about the pills making you drowsy, correct? By law, you cannot be impaired as a driver."

Duck shifted in his seat. "How am I gonna transition without working?"

"You'll transition just fine," Gordon Ryan said. "As long as you comply. Here, take my card."

Duck stood up and took the card, reading the name: Gordon Ryan and underneath it in smaller letters, Community Placement Officer.

"Call or come in any time you have questions," Gordon Ryan said. "Other than that, I will see you next week. . . . And get started on those sessions."

One of the last books Duck read before being released from prison was *Secrets of Power Persuasion*. He needed to get on the man's good side. Duck looked at the poems on the wall again and cleared his throat. "I wanted to ask you about the poems."

"What about them?" the man asked.

"Well, what made you put 'em up there?"

The man cocked his head and crossed his arms over his chest, with a face showing interest in Duck's regard. "Are you familiar with them?"

Duck shook his head and said, "No."

"Well, I assume you've read them. So what do you think?"

Duck thought hard but not long before answering. "They address character."

Gordon Ryan nodded. "Go on."

"And not making excuses, or whining as you endure things along the way. . . . And being responsible for your outcome in life." Gordon Ryan didn't reply so Duck thought to continue. "And not giving up. Being decent. And learning from defeat."

Gordon Ryan nodded approvingly. "Defeat is only possible when you quit. You're the first felon in three years to ask me about those poems. And yes, if I weren't a community placement officer they would still be in my office." Gordon Ryan paused a second. "There's a book you should read called *Man's Search for Meaning* if you're truly interested in motivational literature."

"Man's Search for Meaning?" Duck repeated, searching himself for a pen he knew he didn't have.

"Here." Gordon Ryan reached over his desk, jotted the title down on a yellow piece of paper, and then passed it to Duck.

Duck thanked him, believing he'd changed the man's attitude toward him, then left the building realizing he forgot to ask about the clothing voucher and bus card his cellmate had told him about. Oh well.

He trotted along and caught the bus, leaving Renton for downtown Seattle, where the Sheriff's office was. The eighteen-mile bus ride would be an hour. It was ten o'clock, and the day was beginning to get warmer.

"King County Courthouse," the friendly bus driver announced, pulling to a stop. The parking brake hissed. The double doors butterflied open. Duck had been standing by the driver, holding onto the floor-to-ceiling pole. Duck nodded, thanking the man, who'd been telling jokes through the PA system the entire ride.

Ducked stepped off onto Third Avenue between James Street and Yesler Way where the archaic, concrete building was. The twelve-story structure made him think of a mental ward. He shifted his attention to the people in front of him —four transients loitering at the bus stop, sharing a sleeved bottle of what he assumed was alcohol.

He passed them unnoticed, but a man with blood-clotted eyes and dry lips stepped up from the sidewalk and asked if he had any spare change. Duck ignored him, walking cautiously around him and the group of juveniles smoking a blunt.

A flock of pigeons feeding on breadcrumbs flew out of Duck's way. They were being fed by an obese bag lady, who probably lived in the homeless encampment of ragged tents set up on the south side of the property.

Duck kept his head down and continued walking toward the building.

Inside he emptied his pockets, dumping his belongings into a gray tray before two armed security guards who were also King County deputies. Duck passed through the metal detector and recovered his property, then discreetly asked where the sheriff's office was located.

He walked straight ahead and then made a left as directed. The cathedral-like building was buzzing with lawyers and criminals and law enforcement officers, moving in all directions on the shiny brown and beige kaleidoscopic marble floor.

He came to a door that said: SHERIFF'S OFFICE and turned the knob. His heart racing. A dry lump in his throat. Three men were seated to his right with their heads lowered. One of them was filling out papers. The other two looked shamefaced. Behind the counter was a short old woman in a tan uniform. There was a loud fan oscillating and blowing wildly on the counter. She shut it off with one push of a button. The action of the fan tapered off into silence.

"What can I do for you?" she asked.

"I'm here to register," he mumbled.

"Do you have your prison ID?"

He nodded, then handed her the green and white Department of Corrections inmate card.

The woman took it, then pushed over a clipboard with a sign-in sheet. "Sign in here."

Duck printed his name and signed, writing out the date and time, while she quickly made a copy of his prison identification.

She returned, then reached under her desk and pulled out a clipboard attached with forms. She clamped the ID in between the papers. "Fill this out and let me know when you're done."

He sat down and recorded his full name and alias, "Duck," his current address, his date of birth, and the date and place of the supposed crime. After the other men were processed, Duck was fingerprinted, photographed, and sampled for blood by a woman who was referred to as the registration specialist. The blood would go into their database to help catch him for any future crimes.

Future crimes. He scoffed at the idea of him being guilty.

Still, he'd been officially marked for life.

He arrived back in Renton at one-fifteen. Hungry and exhausted, he stopped by the McDonald's on South Grady Way and ordered a meal with the money Grandmother had given him. He sat down to eat, wondering what to do about work when he needed to take classes. He decided to work part-time on the weekends, thinking he couldn't get in trouble for that. He got up and asked the clerk for a job application, filled it out while eating, and then got to the question: *Have you ever been convicted of a crime? If yes, please explain.*

He wrote yes, and started to explain. Scribbled it out, and tried to explain again. Scribbled it out, scrawled *child molestation in the first degree*, looked at it, and decided that he wouldn't even hire himself. He tore up the application and asked for another. Again he circled yes, but instead of explaining he wrote, *Class A felony. Will explain upon interview.* Hopefully, that'll work.

He left and walked under the warm blue cloudless sky, listening to the birds chirp songs of jubilee. The sound was like childish, playful laughter. A celebration of living. He slowed to observe the creatures. They leapt from branch to branch in a tree blooming purple flowers on every upturned limb.

Life was beautiful. He was home and free in spirit. There were no boundaries to lessen him. The birds then took off together—flapping and flittering. Dipping and rising and turning playfully close to each other like jets at an air show.

He spent the next few hours filling out job applications at every neighboring fast food restaurant on Rainier Avenue and Grady Way, answering each felony question the same way as before; vague with invitation. He went to the library afterward. Tried to log on to Facebook using the password he and Alexa once shared, only to discover it didn't work, as if their profile had been deleted.

He created an account of his own and searched for her. When he couldn't find her he thought about stopping by her old job, then dismissed the idea quickly, recalling the consequences of being on the grounds of a daycare. Plus he would hate to see Amy.

He logged on to Indeed and searched for more jobs, then considered the time and left wondering if he should stop by Ms. Davis's again.

He did. The first time he'd stopped by was on his first day home, late in the evening. The house was dark and no one had answered. This time the blinds were open and the curtains were parted. Lamps were on in the living room. A red car he didn't recognize was parked in the front. The sight of it scared him into thinking they might have moved. But then he reminded himself that Ms. Davis owned the house, and she wasn't the type to suddenly sell.

He stepped up to the porch, tingling. He rapped on the door softly, anticipating the answer, and seeing Alexa's face. Would she be happy to see him, or still be questioning his innocence? What did she look like now? Did she have more surgery? Was she still taking medication for pain? Did she go back to school or start a business like she wanted? Or did she return to the daycare to work with the children? Was she happy?

There was a sound. Footsteps! And then movement— muffled, as if someone were pressing against the door, carefully watching him through the peephole. A torturous pause followed. Now the door was being unlocked. What would he say to her?

"Yes, Carlos," a voice said coldly.

It was Alexa's mother, staring with contempt behind the thin crack of the doorway. He looked past her into the house. She stepped into his line of sight, pushing the door so that he was now struggling to see beyond a narrower opening.

He focused on her instead. She looked as though she had aged a decade, and the left side of her face seemed to droop. Had she had a stroke? "How you been doing Ms. Davis?"

She cocked her head and said, "Fine. Now what do you want?"

Okay. She hadn't changed a bit. "Is Alexa here?"

"No, she isn't."

He tried looking behind her again. She shifted her body, annoyingly obstructing his vision. He focused back on her tired face. "Do you know how I can get in touch with her? Her number's changed, and I just wanna know if she's okay. I left a note—"

"I got the note, Carlos, and she's fine. She's moved on with her life and so should you."

Moved on?

"Now, if you'll excuse me. I have company." She shut the door abruptly.

He stared at it, frozen.

Moved on? What did she mean by that? Had Alexa gotten married? Did she have children?

In his heart, he felt Ms. Davis was lying, or maybe he misunderstood her. Maybe she meant Alexa had moved on past the attack. Maybe Alexa had left the incident behind her. But no, it was the way Ms. Davis had said it as if Alexa *had* found someone better, better than him.

He staggered off the porch and caught the bus home to his grandparents' house in a consuming daze, suddenly noticing every couple and family the bus passed by. He saw a man with a baby strapped to his chest walking with a woman Duck imagined to be Alexa. That's what her new life was like now. She had a family with a husband who cared for her. Should Duck be happy for her?

He made it home and fell into bed in a slump.

The next day he couldn't shake it out of his mind. If Alexa had moved on, he had to know for sure.

He renewed his driver's license, receiving a temporary paper one until the real license came in the mail, went to the bank, and discovered the five thousand dollars he had saved was still there, but had accumulated little interest. He withdrew a few hundred dollars, requested a new debit card, and returned home with a cell phone, and a battery for his car.

The motor started as loud as a diesel-fueled tractor engine. Dark clouds of smoke spewed out of the exhaust pipe, filling the garage with blackness. He stood outside the car, watching carbon monoxide roll out into the street, polluting the neighborhood.

Finally, the racket began to settle down into a vibrant purr. He climbed in, put the gear in reverse, and stepped on the gas, but the car remained in neutral. He again tried to back out, flooring the pedal. The engine whined and then died. He restarted it and went through the same motions to no avail, got out, and slammed the door shut.

He knew the transmission was busted. He had wasted two-thirds of the day worrying about his car, and still needed to see a doctor to receive his medication. He caught the bus to the first mental health clinic circled on the list, checked in, filled out paperwork, and waited to be scheduled to come in the next day for an assessment.

Seventeen

The next morning he met his psychiatrist, Dr. Austin.

He sat across from her inside her office.

"So what brings you in?" she asked.

He looked at her. Hadn't she read his chart?

He sighed and tried to relax. "I was just released from prison. The doctor there told me y'all could help me. I was prescribed Seroquel, but I'm out of medication."

"Seroquel?"

"Yes, ma'am."

She referred to the paperwork he filled out the day before. "So you were diagnosed as schizophrenic?"

"Bipolar, but my mom is schizophrenic. I told my p-doc that when I was locked up."

"Interesting," she said, jotting a note. "Well, Seroquel can be used to treat both illnesses. When did you last take the medication?"

All right, straight down to business. "A day before my release, on Friday."

"So four days without it. How are you feeling?"

He remembered vomiting on and off on Saturday, not being able to sleep, and being extremely agitated when he got into the fight on Sunday. He remembered cursing when he spilled chicken broth on the stovetop while stirring a pot of soup, and Grandmother telling him there was no need for him to get upset. He was just trying to help and it was the first time in years he'd used a stove. He remembered how yesterday morning he felt dizzy. Today it came in waves, but was he getting better? "Nauseated," he said. "Irritated."

She nodded. "That's very common for withdrawal." She clacked on her keyboard. "How did you feel about the medication?"

"It was okay, I guess. I didn't like that it made me tired." He rubbed his hands and inched forward, perceiving that she may be helpful. "I still want to be able to work, you know."

She nodded, documenting another note on her computer. With curious eyes, she looked at him again. "How exactly, were you diagnosed in prison?"

He repeated the story he told Gordon Ryan.

"I see." She typed rapidly, then flicked her gaze back to him. "Outside of depression, do you ever have any thoughts or ideas that conflict with your normal pattern of thinking?"

Conflicting thoughts? "Yes."

"Can you give me an example?"

"Uh . . . it was a long time ago, but I saw a license plate once . . . that told me people were trying to kill me."

She typed more notes, then looked up, concerned. She cleared her throat. Folded her hands. Leaned closer. "Do you ever hear voices or sounds that no one else around you are hearing?"

"Yes."

She eased back in her seat and prepared to type. "Can you describe them?"

He never really had anyone to talk to but Alexa about his hallucinations. Not even the prison doctors. All this was new to him. "I don't know. Maybe."

She peered at him. He blinked and gulped.

"Sometimes I hear animal noises," he said. "Sometimes I hear children screaming. Sometimes I hear my name being called. Sometimes I hear a man. A child-like man. And it kind of feels like I know him. Sometimes he says things to make me believe that I'm worthless. Sometimes he tells me to hurt people."

She typed furiously. "And does he have a name?"

He thought for a moment, then wondered why the voice, who called him Lucky Ducky, never told him his name. He frowned, then answered, "I don't think so."

She nodded again and typed.

"Do you know where you are right now?"

He smirked. The question seemed silly but he knew that she was serious. They never asked him these types of questions in prison or the county jail. "I'm in a mental health clinic."

"Good." She folded her hands again, then took a deep breath. "To be diagnosed for any mental illness, two or more symptoms have to be present for thirty days or more. Now I know you came here for help, and we are going to help you. At this point, however, I think we should monitor you weekly, for thirty days at least, before prescribing you any medication."

He dropped his head, then looked at her for mercy. "If I don't get any meds, they're going send me back to prison!"

"I understand that you're worried. I'm just a bit concerned about how you were diagnosed. Now these are the necessary steps. I'm going to send you down to the lab so we can do some blood work. Now is there anyone I can speak to who may have witnessed any dramatic changes in your behavior?"

"My grandparents," he said. "And my girlfriend at the time . . . and her mom."

"Okay," she said. "I'm going to need their contact information. And I'm going to have to contact the prison to get a copy of your mental health record. I just need the name of the institution, and the name of the doctor who treated you."

He provided what information he had. Later he was assigned a caseworker, who came to visit every Saturday, documenting his behavior. For four weeks Duck complained about not finding a job. He had been including Grandmother as a reference and decided it was because of her. She was telling the employers bad things about him, he told the caseworker. Duck recently had luck getting one interview, but when asked about his felony, he stammered, saying it was something he'd been accused of and would like to put it behind him. The interviewer then asked him for details. Duck started to explain, then stopped in mid-sentence, losing confidence in himself. The interview ended with the man standing and extending his hand, saying: "Thank you for coming. We'll give you a call." Duck had walked out feeling assaulted.

In the meantime, he searched for Alexa. He had called the daycare asking for her, disguising his voice, but some new girl there told him there was no one by the name of Alexa who worked there. Risking violation, he stood across the street from the daycare the next day after 5 p.m. to see if the receptionist was lying. If Alexa had gone back to work there, she no longer had the same shift, at least not on that particular day.

That following Sunday, he stopped by Ms. Davis's neighbor's house. An old widow he remembered who had been nice to him. He had cut her lawn once after the landscapers she hired to cut her grass weekly hadn't shown up for a month. Afterward, she insisted on paying Duck, forcing a fifty-dollar bill into his hand, even though he said she didn't have to. Her only companion was her dog, and from what Duck gathered she never received much company.

He pressed the doorbell twice.

She answered, "May I help you?" holding the small white, fluffy dog.

Duck fixed his voice to sound polite and his demeanor to be as non-threatening as the Bichon Frise she was holding. He stood back from the door, in a relaxed posture, smiling, so as not to alarm her. "Hello, ma'am," he said. "I'm sorry to bother you, but do you remember me?"

"No," she said.

"I'm Alexa's old boyfriend, Duck."

She squinted at him, scratching the fidgeting dog's head.

"You know your neighbor, Ms. Davis?" He pointed at the house. "I was dating her daughter. Alexa. Remember, I cut your grass?"

Her face brightened. "Oh, yes. Come on in." She pushed the screen door open for him.

He entered behind her as she turned with her dog. She shuffled forward very slowly and gingerly toward the living room. "Have a seat. How's Alexa been? I haven't seen her in years." The old widow sat down with her pet, facing Duck. "Would you like some tea? You'd have to get it yourself. There's honey in the cabinet."

"No, thank you." He sat down in an antique armchair. She had inadvertently answered one of his questions. He and the old lady had a long conversation, but ultimately she knew nothing.

He then used his phone to go on Facebook and messaged four of Alexa's friends from high school to see if they had heard from her. Only one of them responded, saying Alexa had gotten married and moved to Atlanta, where her husband was from. The person who said this was a male friend of Alexa's, so Duck wondered if his word was true. Duck looked into the information anyway, going online, searching the White Pages for an Alexa Davis in Atlanta. There were five Alexa Davis's listed. He called every one of them but none of them were her. If she was married, he needed her spousal name. He messaged her male friend to see if he knew but the guy wouldn't respond.

Duck created an account with every social media site he could think of and continued to search for her, but he still couldn't find her.

At the end of week four he asked about his medication. The caseworker said she would consult with Dr. Austin, who would probably extend the observation period by another sixty days since he was doing so well.

This news disappointed him.

Five minutes after the caseworker left the house, there was a knock on the door. Duck and his grandparents were sitting at the dining room table talking when it happened.

Grandpa answered and returned. "It's for you."

"For me?" Duck asked.

B came in, wearing a blue and gold fringed uniform. A thin beard was on his face, and he looked clean like he was free from marijuana.

"Shalom, Grandmother," B said, smiling. He came over to her. She stood slowly. He hugged her and then kissed her on the cheek.

She tugged on his uniform. "What do you have on?"

"They're fringes, part of God's dress code, to remind us of the commandments," he said. "Duck, can I holler at you?"

Duck rose, wondering what B wanted, hoping he wasn't there to talk about Fats. He didn't need that right now. They went outside. Duck closed the door behind them.

They stood on the front porch, looking around at everything but each other.

"So what's up?" Duck asked.

"My brother Noah has a moving company and he's hiring right now. I know you need a job with that felony."

Duck frowned and shook his head.

"No?"

"I'm too busy with classes."

"So what, you takin' classes all day?"

"Yeah, something like that." Duck shoved his hands into his pockets and looked away at the clouds, turning so that his back faced his cousin. Duck was glad B was making positive changes in his life, but how could he associate with Fats?

"Look, brother, forget all that stuff that happened with Fats," B said as if reading Duck's mind.

Duck faced him. "Is that what you came here for?"

"No, I came here to tell you about this job."

Duck shook his head again. "I'm good."

"You're only saying that 'cause you're still beefin' with the brother. I think if you work with him, you'll learn to forgive him."

"Forgive him?" How could he ever forgive Fats? He peered at B. "Man, I'm done with this." He turned and went inside, retiring to his room.

An hour later, the squeak of door hinges woke him from his nap.

"I'm going to pick up this pizza," Grandpa said. "You wanna ride?"

"Yeah," Duck said rising lazily. "Sure."

They drove to Corina's, a local pizzeria he remembered Grandpa liking.

They walked in.

"Welcome to Corina's!" everyone chimed.

"I'm here to pick up an order for Carl," Grandpa said.

"Carl!" the clerk repeated with great enthusiasm. She hurried back to the heat rack for his order just as a small Asian lady came darting to the front.

"Hey!" she said excitedly. "How have you been?"

"I've been blessed," Grandpa said humbly as the pizza was handed to him by the clerk. Grandpa and the lady, who Duck assumed to be the manager, talked for half a minute before the small woman turned her attention to Duck.

"Who is this?" she asked Grandpa. "Is this your son?"

Grandpa laughed. "My grandson," he said, correcting her, looking modestly down.

"Ohhh! Your grandson!" She returned her attention to Duck. "I remember you now. I haven't seen you for a long time. Where have you been?"

"On vacation."

"Vacation? Very big vacation!"

"Yeah, you can say that."

Grandpa cleared his throat. "He's looking for a job right now. Do you have anything for the weekends? Something part-time?"

"Oh, yes! We need drivers."

A girl skipped forward and handed Duck an application before the small lady had a chance to turn around. He thanked the girl as she stared, twirling her curly hair, grinning with wide sparkling eyes.

"Thank you, Nia," said the manager. The girl then returned to her place behind the counter.

"Are there any other positions available?" Duck asked. "I'm asking because I may not be able to drive right away."

"No, we just need drivers right now. Can you not drive?"

"No, I can drive. I just have some issues with my car." Which was true. The estimated price for the transmission was $2,600. Plus he'd have to get tabs. He decided weeks ago that he'd junk the vehicle and buy another, as soon as he was able to use his license.

"Well, we always need drivers. Weekends are very busy."

"All right, I'll fill this out as soon as possible, but it may take me a while to get my car fixed. And oh! What was your name?"

"Liem."

"Lee-Anne?"

"Lim-Lim," she said, smiling. "Everyone calls me Lim-Lim."

"Lim-Lim. Okay, Lim-Lim. Thank you. I appreciate this very much."

He grinned and thanked Grandpa repeatedly as they exited the store.

The following Monday, Duck visited Gordon Ryan and told him about the opportunity. The CPO responded by reminding him he needed to focus on STOP and SAA for another two months, before working. Then added that he still needed a signature from a doctor permitting him to drive.

Duck left angry. He wasn't free at all. He hoofed along to the bus stop and out of nowhere rain started to fall. This upset him more because earlier it was sunny. And because it was sunny, he'd left the house without a coat.

He hurried in his V-neck T-shirt but soon he was soaked. He muttered, looked back and saw the bus, raced ahead toward the stop, and raised his hand yelling as it shot by. He cursed the driver and continued to walk, thinking he had plenty of time to make it to STOP. He marched along through puddles, rain pelting his face, falling sideways, showering his arms. The wet T-shirt now stuck to his chest and the wind was blowing mercilessly hard.

He wiped his face. Nothing was working out right. Every corner he turned, there was a wall. Ms. Davis wouldn't let him find Alexa. Gordon Ryan wouldn't let him get a job. Dr. Austin wouldn't give him medication. And now he had to attend group therapy with a circle of sex offenders just to move on.

This was about Alexa. No one wanted him to be with her. They all wanted him to fail and be unhappy, especially Grandmother. That's why she treated him like a child. She thought he was dumb and incapable of living on his own. He grabbed his head, ran a few feet, and stopped.

She is the fallen angel, the one they call Lucifer . . . And you are a god.

He boomeranged back in the opposite direction, clenching his hair and shrieking under the rain.

Show them you are a god.

He looked at the cars flying by. A tractor-trailer sped up to make it through the yellow light. Forty, fifty, sixty miles an hour.

Jump in front of the semi and show everyone you're a god.

He squeezed his eyes shut as the rig stormed by.

He wandered for hours, roaming the streets. Soon he found himself at the USA Gas Station by Walmart. He'd applied to work there and failed the interview. He loitered around the pumps until nightfall when the third shift clerk finally came out and told him to leave. Duck relocated to the parking lot, where he roamed and lingered absently until the next morning.

He came home later that afternoon, soaked and hungry, passing his grandparents, who greeted him with questions. He went straight to his room. Immediately, there was a knock.

He sat down at his desk.

The urgent knocking continued.

Grandmother let herself in. "Where have you been?"

He ignored her, squaring a notepad, holding a Bic.

"Is everything okay? You've been gone since yesterday. And you're all wet!"

Water dripped from his hair onto the desk, spattering the notepad cover. The downpour from yesterday had never stopped. He smoothed his hair back into a ponytail and squeezed a pool of water onto the floor. He cleared his face with the crook of his arm and wiped his hands on his wet lap. He turned to a blank page and started with the word, *I*, then scrawled the word *am*.

"Carlos, where have you been?" Grandmother repeated softly.

He stopped, slammed the pen down, and rose. "You are not my grandmother! I am a god!"

He strode over, shooing her out of the room, shutting the door behind her. He returned to his desk and wrote *a god* on the notepad.

"What is going on?" Duck heard Grandpa ask Grandmother.

"He's acting all strange and rude again."

They continued, taking the discussion somewhere deep into the living room. Duck hurried through the letter, then searched for his gym bag. He found it in the closet, then went around the house filling it with tennis shoes.

He returned to his room to change into dry clothing. Soon after he did so, someone tapped on the door. Duck was sitting on the edge of the bed, examining the pair of sneakers Grandpa used to mow the lawn. The door opened. Duck put the pair in the duffle bag next to him and rose to sit at his desk.

Gordon Ryan entered with two police officers. Grandmother and Grandpa squeezed in behind them.

Duck moved from his desk back to the bed, sitting Indian style, saying nothing. He noticed the black gothic device his community placement officer was holding. It looked like a garage remote with durable plastic straps.

Gordon Ryan stepped forward with it. "What's going on here, Duckworth? I get a call here saying you didn't come home last night . . . and you're skipping therapy?"

Duck didn't answer.

Gordon Ryan studied the room, then approached the bed. He snatched the duffle bag at the foot of it and set the ankle monitor down in its place. He unzipped the bag, curiously pulling out several pairs of tennis shoes.

"You going somewhere?" he asked.

"I'm tired of being treated like an animal," Duck said. "I'm a god!"

Gordon Ryan picked up the anklet and set down the bag. "You know your conditions and what can happen if you violate." He switched the hideous device to his other hand. "Now . . . I'm not going to send you back, but I have to monitor you more closely."

"This man is very nice, Carlos, and he's being very fair," Grandmother added nervously.

"I'm going to confine you to a GPS monitor for thirty days," Gordon Ryan said. "Now give me your leg." He reached for Duck's leg, holding the anklet.

Duck slapped it away and turned his back.

"All right," Gordon Ryan said. "Cuff him!"

The two officers seized Duck's arms. He pulled away.

"You are not my grandmother!" Duck cried. "I am a god!"

He struggled to stand and to keep his hands in front of him as the cops fought to wrestle him down. The three of them tussled from the bed to the dresser, thudding against walls and furniture, grunting, panting. Finally, Duck was facedown, sore, and out of breath with a knee in his back. They cuffed him promptly. When they lifted him his grandparents were gone. The police and Gordon Ryan led Duck out into the hallway, gripping hard on his upper arms.

Grandmother was standing there speaking into the cordless phone. "Wait a minute," she cried at the officers, signaling for them to stop with her hand. "I'm on the phone with his psychiatrist, right now. She should be here any second. I spoke to her earlier, before I called you, Mr. Ryan. Please don't take my grandson to jail."

Just then the doorbell sounded followed by an urgent knock.

"You're here?" Grandmother said into the phone. "She's here. Carl, get the door!"

Gordon Ryan nodded to the officers, agreeing to wait.

Grandpa opened the door for Dr. Austin. She stepped inside immediately, holding a leather briefcase, heading straight toward Duck and the officers. She offered her hand to Gordon Ryan. "Hello, I'm Dr. Austin and this is my client. Sorry, I couldn't get here sooner." She passed her badge to an officer, who glanced at it before handing it to

Gordon Ryan. He examined it carefully, then returned it to her, introducing himself.

She explained why Duck was not taking any medication and how he could be having a psychotic break. "I understand he is under your supervision," she said. "But I need to know that he is okay. If I can just have a moment with him, please?"

Gordon Ryan agreed. Duck, still hand-cuffed, sat down on the couch.

"Carlos, are you willing to talk?" asked Dr. Austin.

Duck nodded slowly.

"Can you tell me about what happened?"

He nodded again.

Break the cuffs, turn invisible, and escape.

"That's impossible," he said.

She stared with grave curiosity. "What's impossible? Carlos, you can tell us. What's impossible?"

"Turning invisible," he mumbled with his head lowered. He then grunted, trying to break the cuffs. A heavy hand landed on his right shoulder and squeezed. Another clapped onto his left. The two officers eased him back onto the couch.

"Try to calm down, okay, Carlos," said Dr. Austin. "We're here to help."

Her voice was soothing.

The awkward seating seemed to tighten the manacles. He doubled over to relieve the biting pressure as she went through her briefcase, revealing a yellow steno pad and a push pen. "And you're right, turning invisible is impossible. Did someone tell you could do that, Carlos?"

He mumbled, "No" but nodded yes.

She jotted something down on paper. "Can you tell us where you were yesterday? We were all worried about you."

He kept his head down, glancing at the floor, wanting everyone to go away. "I took a walk."

She waited a moment. When he didn't add anything, she said, "I understand. You just needed some space. We all need that from time to time. It's just that . . . you're under strict conditions . . . and people were concerned about you."

There was a long wait. He felt the party eyeing him in the stillness, fidgeting, waiting for his reply. Weighted down in turmoil, he imagined his escape. He shimmied his shoulders like a bound magician submerged in ice water, now understanding why she had sampled his blood. He was invincible and had superhuman strength. He twisted his wrists, trying to snap the metal restraints again, ignoring the viselike pain. He let out a groan, and then a grunt.

One of the officers reached over and palmed Duck's arm. "Sir, you need to calm down."

His partner turned down his shoulder radio and then touched his gun. Duck looked at Grandmother and Dr. Austin, who blinked at him. He felt vexed. Judged. Deflated, he sighed. The officer let go of him.

Dr. Austin continued with more questions, wanting to know every bit of detail about Duck's thoughts and mood.

He answered wearily, and reluctantly. But he complied. Several minutes passed. His hands felt numb. "These cuffs are tight," he said.

The psychiatrist turned to Gordon Ryan, who had the cuffs removed.

After Duck confessed his idea for departure, Doctor Austin searched his room. She returned asking about the shoes and the letter explaining to his grandparents that he was a god. Duck said no one respected him, and that he was going to run away to Atlanta to find Alexa. She was his girlfriend and would help him. When asked about how he was going to get there, he said that he was going to catch a Greyhound and walk, which is why he had filled the bag with sneakers.

"So," Dr. Austin said, "I believe the correct diagnosis for your condition is schizoaffective disorder. You have had two or more symptoms occurring for a period of thirty or more days. There have been some changes in your behavior during the time we have been monitoring you. Today especially, because the stress you're under has set you off —which is unfortunate, but at least now we have a diagnosis. I'm going to prescribe you Haldol. It's going to be a little different from the Seroquel, but we'll give it an eight-week trial run to see how it works for you. We're going to start you off with five milligrams, which you will take daily." She paused, looking at Gordon Ryan. "And you also have to wear the ankle monitor that Mr. Ryan has brought for you. Are we okay with that?"

Duck nodded.

"Good."

She inserted a tablet into his mouth. It was dry without any flavor. A second later Gordon Ryan knelt to strap the ankle monitor to Duck's leg.

Eighteen

Duck stepped off the bus, then crossed the street, and entered the mental health clinic. The two young women behind the counter smiled as they greeted him. He smiled and greeted them back, then signed himself in. The receptionist on his right made a quick call, then hung up. "She's ready for you." He thanked her, then went around the corner and stopped short of the doorway, listening to the Classical music coming out of the office.

He crossed his arms and listened closely. Slow-fast the melody. High-low the tone. A cry of music that said to him the pianist had lost someone he loved and was trying to communicate to the world that he missed her. Maybe he'd lost his wife or failed in his marriage. Maybe this song was an effort to express both love and pain.

Duck thought about Alexa. How she once was a pillar in his life; accommodating him, nursing him, encouraging him to be more than what he felt he was. He prayed for her and that he'd find a companion, then tapped on the open door.

Dr. Austin turned the music off and waved him in. She wiped her mouth with a napkin and closed the Styrofoam container she'd been eating from, then pushed it aside.

Duck had been scheduled to see her every Friday, from 2:00 p.m. to 3:00 p.m., for more than two months. Last week he'd missed her because of the Fourth of July weekend. Her office had been closed.

He took his seat. Often he came ten minutes early, catching her relaxing to music he frequently inquired about.

Today she was listening to a favorite he'd asked about before—Enrique Granados's "Spanish Dance No. 2."

She folded her hands. "How was your Fourth?"

He sighed and said it was all right. In truth, it was lonely and miserable. He had stopped by Ms. Davis's house to see if she would give Alexa a letter he'd written her. But as he stood at the door, speaking, Ms. Davis had interrupted him, saying she was not sending her daughter anything. She then threatened to call the police if he ever showed up at her house again. If Alexa was married he wished the best for her.

He massaged the back of his neck. Over the weeks it had grown stiff and tight. Heavy spasms had started over his forearm, and his mouth would get so dry that he could spit nothing but white froth. Last night he couldn't sleep because of the medication, plus he was thinking of all his responsibilities: SAA meetings, weekly reports to his CPO, seeing his psychiatrist, and group therapy. If Alexa was there, she would have told him not to worry, then stroked his back until he fell asleep.

"You seem to have a lot on your mind today. Is everything all right?"

"I'm fine." He stopped rubbing his neck and sat still. Dr. Austin was always studying him.

"Is there anything in particular you want to talk about?"

"No. Not really." He sighed and tried to relax. "But can I have a cup of water, please? The medication makes me thirsty."

"Sure." She rose and got him a cup of water from the water dispenser she kept inside her office, handed the cup to him, and then returned to her seat.

He thanked her and downed the cold water greedily. He exhaled and crushed the paper cup, then tossed it into the waste bin across from him on the side of her desk.

He felt more at ease.

"How's your arm?" she asked. "Are you still having spasms?"

"Yes." He extended his arm to show her. "It's the medication."

"We know it's the medication, Carlos." She made a note. "It has been helping with your hallucinations, correct?"

"Yes."

"And sleep?"

He shook his head.

"Would you like to go back to Seroquel then?"

"No, because I want to be able to work, and all Seroquel does is make me sleepy."

"Well, we're doing our best, Carlos. Just give it a bit more time. Sometimes it takes a while for your body to adjust to the medication."

"But it's been two months already!"

She stared at him, then blinked.

"I'm sorry. I'm just . . . frustrated."

"I understand, but everybody responds differently, Carlos. The bottom line is that the Haldol is working. What I could do is prescribe you Amitriptyline if you're having trouble sleeping. It'll help with your anxiety as well."

He recalled what Eddie Blodgett said at the group meeting. He was right. She was already trying to add another prescription on top of the medicine he was currently taking. Duck remembered the anti-depressant drug from prison and how, like Seroquel, it made inmates sleep all day. This is what it meant to be a pill junkie. At first, he was a person. Now he was just a patient.

"I want a job," he said. "My ninety-day thing is up, and my CPO is letting me work. I have a driving job waiting for me, but I can't drive until you okay it with a signature."

She looked surprised for a minute, then touched her desk, picked up a pen, and twirled it in between her pale fingers. She set it back down carefully. "You're talking about driving, Carlos . . . That's a whole different matter."

"I know, but I need this job. I'm going to get an apartment and start my own business, but I can't function right if I'm on this medication, or if I'm on Seroquel." He stretched the truth a little but felt he had to.

She sat back, examining him, then leaned forward, folding her hands. "I admire your drive for independence, Carlos, but I don't know if you're ready to be behind the wheel. There are a lot of risks. For example, how would you respond if a voice told you to do something dangerous as you're driving?"

"I would pull over and call you or my grandmother or my CPO. I know when something is wrong now. I just need a different medication. Something that won't cause spasms, dry my mouth, or put me to sleep. I already have my license. I just need your written consent." He stopped. "I've never missed a session with you. Never. And I'm always on time or early."

"If you want to drive I think you should pass a written road test first."

He opened his mouth to protest.

She raised her hand to finish.

"You will also need to complete driver's ed to show that you can be a safe and responsible driver."

"But—"

She raised her hand again. "I understand you want to drive, and I'm glad you're showing initiative. But it's my responsibility to protect you, as well as the public. We will try a different medication, and if this works there will be no more changes until *I* say so. And if you're going to be behind the wheel, I expect you to have insurance. And I expect you to stay med-compliant. No exceptions."

He nodded.

She examined him more carefully, folding her hands over the desk. Squinting. "There is a new drug called Rexulti that's been on the market for about a year. I think it might work well for you. It has fewer known side effects and you can take it in smaller doses. We'll start you off with one milligram, then move you up to two."

He nodded, feeling happy and hopeful.

"It is a bit more expensive. But if need be, you can get insurance through Blue Cross Blue Shield. They will help you."

He smiled. Fist pumped. "Thank you."

He weaned off of Haldol, then started the new medication, passed the written road test, and completed driver's school within a month, then returned to Corina's, the pizzeria, to see if they were still hiring. Two driving positions were still available. He applied in the store. The manager hired him on the spot and asked if he could start that Saturday. This was on a Thursday. He said yes and left, immediately using his phone to search online for a car. (He had scrapped his old one for a hundred dollars.) He checked locally and found a Jeep Grand Cherokee that he liked. It was in his price range and not too far from his grandparents' house. Just two and a half miles away, on Sunset Boulevard, next to a neighboring used car dealer with poorer reviews.

He hurried in that Friday morning.

The salesman stood up. "Hey, buddy. How can we help you?"

"I'm here to buy the Jeep," Duck said. "The online special, for thirty-five hundred. You still have it?"

"I'm sorry. We just sold it yesterday. But we do have a beautiful MDX. Low miles, one owner."

Duck looked away, flustered.

The salesman got up and grabbed a pair of keys. "Let's go take a look at it."

He stepped out. Duck followed. The salesman opened the door, popped the hood, and started the motor. He stood outside it and let it purr.

It was black, shiny, and sleek. An expensive SUV. "I don't want this car."

"You haven't even driven it yet."

"It's triple the price of the Jeep."

"Sure, but it has fewer miles and it's a newer model." He reached into it, stroking the upholstery, looking back at Duck. "You have heated leather seats. And a moon roof." The salesman climbed in and pressed a button to show off the moon roof.

"I don't have that much money," Duck said. "I came here thinking that I was going to buy the Cherokee."

The salesman killed the motor and stepped out with the keys. "I'm sorry, but our cars go fast." He looked sympathetic and shrugged. "I wish we had something for that price, but we don't. We rarely do." He turned slightly and then faced Duck again. "I tell you what, why don't you look around. Tell me what you like and we'll work something out."

Duck went around uninterested, kicking tires, and sitting inside some of the vehicles. There was a BMW Seven series with a wood grain interior that he felt big and important in, but again the price was steep. There was a tan Honda CR-V that was unpriced and locked, which made him more interested. He peeped inside. It was dirty. Maybe it was a personal vehicle. But why was it on the lot with the rest of the inventory? There was a 2002 Chevy Cavalier for $5,500. He went back into the office disappointed.

"So, what do you like?"

"I don't like any of these cars," Duck said. "But I need one for this job."

"I see. You had your mind set on the Jeep and I apologize for that, but that's business. You said you need a work vehicle. What type of work will you be doing?"

"Delivering pizzas."

"I see. So you want something good on gas mileage. Something economical. What did you think about the Cavalier?" The salesman reached for the set of keys on the plywood board to his left.

"It's okay." He thought the car was too small for his body.

"Let's go take it for a ride."

Duck got in with the salesman, checking the AC and the radio, nearly feeling the roof of the car touch the top of his head. The Cavalier drove smoothly without any noticeable issues. He parked after the drive, got out, looked under the hood at the engine, and then slid underneath the car to check for damage and leaks. Nothing obvious.

"So?" asked the salesman.

"I mean, it's all right but it's still more than I want to pay."

"How soon do you need a car?"

"Now."

"Okay. Say you wait for a car to sell at the price you want, do you think they'll hold that job for you until then?

Chances are they won't. They'll fill that position as soon as they can, just like we sell cars as soon as we can. That's life. You have to seize the opportunity, buddy. And right now you have the opportunity to put down what you have. I'll hold the vehicle for you until you get the rest. Then you can tell your employer you have a car so you can go to work and make money."

Duck looked at the man, short in stature, but big in confidence. It was hard to argue with him.

"You'll hold it for me?" Duck asked. "I can't just give you this money and drive it off the lot?"

"Not without financing."

Duck turned to the side, like he was consulting with someone, and thought. A few potential buyers nosed around, looking inside the vehicles. One of them stopped and peeked into the Cavalier.

"All right, but I'm going to need a receipt or something on paper."

"Of course." The salesman smiled.

Duck followed him to the office and fished in his back pocket for the thick envelope of cash he had withdrawn earlier from the bank. He sat down, rethinking his decision as the salesman stood whistling behind the desk, pulling out various sorts of papers from a file cabinet. The salesman sat down with the paperwork and turned one set around, pushing it toward Duck, pointing with a pen, summarizing what he'd be signing.

Duck wondered how he'd get the rest of the money and how soon, then thought Grandmother might help him. But that was selfish—she had helped him enough. He didn't need to be a burden. And there was no guarantee that she'd have the money anyway. And if Grandpa found out, he'd make a fuss about it. With that Duck changed his mind about the Chevy.

"What about that Honda out there? There's no price on it."

The salesman looked at him and grimaced. "The CR-V? That's a trade-in we got in late yesterday. It still needs to be cleaned and inspected."

"Well, I'm looking for something more like that."

The salesman disregarded the papers and pondered, rubbing his chin. "Okay, I tell you what. I'll sell you the CR-V for the same price as the Jeep, as is, since you came all this way. Is that a deal?"

"Well, I have to drive it first to see if I like it."

The salesman leaned back and let out a hearty chuckle, then smoothed his shirt, regaining his business composure. "All right, buddy. Let's go drive that CR-V." He rose and fetched the keys.

Duck drove the CR-V to work that Saturday, feeling good. He had a car again. It was dirty, but it didn't leak, ran and stopped smoothly enough, and had enough headroom that he didn't feel hemmed in. He was starting a job and was doing well on the medication. He followed Lim-Lim to the back where she handed him a bright red polo shirt with *Corina's* stitched in white cursive on the left breast. He went to the bathroom to try it on and stepped out feeling official in the snug polyester.

He was proud. He was working.

Lim-Lim looked down at his jeans. "So you're supposed to have on khakis, but you're okay for now. This is my husband, Caesar."

"Oh my goodness, you're our new driver?" Caesar said.

Duck shook his hand, looking down at the middle-aged Latino. He had a glowing face and seemed to be genuinely kind and friendly. Caesar gripped him on the shoulder and commented on his strength, laughed, and then politely excused himself.

Duck then followed Lim-Lim around the store. She introduced him to several drivers and clerks, and the four-person crew working the make line. They were from all over the world— India, Turkey, Mexico, Bulgaria, Brazil— and felt like a large extended family. Everyone was cordial but short with their words, as they were too busy to chat. Drivers sprinted out with their deliveries, as others rushed back in for their next. There was panic on the make line as a large order came in. The pizza cutter yelled at his teammates for making a mistake. The phones rang constantly as one of the service counter girls ran up to Lim-Lim to inform her of a customer's complaint.

A driver sped past Duck. "You came right on time."

Lim-Lim handed Duck twenty dollars in ones. "This is your bank. Hosea will be training you."

"Hosea?" Duck asked.

"Welcome to hell," a voice said beside him. "I'm Hosea." Hosea knifed his hand out for a shake. "You come right in time for the dinner rush. Are you ready?"

Duck nodded.

Hosea led him to the heat rack, where many pizzas were boxed and ready. "Always double-check your order." Hosea double-checked the order he was taking and then stuffed it into a heat bag. He marched out of the store. Duck hurried behind him.

Hosea put the order inside the back of his car. He was a solid man but oddly shaped. Five feet four inches tall with a compact upper body and little legs. When he walked, he moved like a penguin.

"Get in," Hosea said.

Duck climbed into the white Accord and buckled his seatbelt.

"Do you have a cell phone?" Hosea asked, starting the car.

"Yeah."

"Good. Three things you need: a cell phone, flashlight, and Pepper Gel."

"Pepper Gel?"

"Yes. Sometimes you get robbed or bit by dogs." Hosea lifted his pants leg to show him a vicious bite wound. "And you need a phone for Google Maps and to call the store because sometimes you get lost. And you need a flashlight because at night it's hard to see the addresses. People don't leave the light on for you. Stupid people." He shook his head, released the e-brake, and reversed out.

They arrived at the house. "Right here." Hosea parked, yanking his e-brake. He jumped out of the car and reached in the back for the pizzas. Duck followed him to the door. Hosea knocked. A man half-dressed in his A-shirt and boxers answered, blowing marijuana smoke into their faces.

"Hello, sir," Hosea said with scripted joviality. He turned the heat bag around, ripped the Velcro part open, and pulled out the man's order. The man paid in cash and then shut the door promptly.

They hustled back to the car. Hosea mumbled under his breath, cursing about not receiving a tip. He then turned to Duck. "You got it? Easy. Now you do the next one."

Within hours, Duck had the hang of it. The next day, he bought work pants and a high-powered flashlight. The weekend after that, he bought Pepper Gel. He worked the weekends and saved whatever money he could as he continued seeing both his community placement officer and psychiatrist, while still participating in group therapy and SAA meetings. As the months passed, he became a store favorite.

By January, he was counting down the days to when he finished the obligatory treatment program. In three months, he'd receive his certificate. Then, he'd no longer have to attend group therapy for sex offenders or participate in twelve-step meetings for sex addicts. He'd finally be free to work full-time, he hoped.

Corina's was buzzing with chaos. It was Saturday, snowing, and the Seattle Seahawks were preparing to play the Green Bay Packers in the first playoff game of the new year. The game would start within an hour. It was twelve-fifteen, and the lobby was crowded with customers asking about their orders. Duck helped them and answered calls on hold until the rush calmed. And because he stayed and helped, Lim-Lim sent him out with the next big order—ten large pizzas going out to the Renton Senior Activity Center. She helped carry the load to his vehicle, wishing him luck and telling him to drive safely. Two drivers had called out, saying they couldn't drive in the snow. Luckily, Duck had a CR-V with four-wheel drive and new winter tires.

He drove carefully, staring into the hypnotic snowstorm, mesmerized by the oncoming flakes. The snowy roads were tracked, but a wind had started. He navigated through a psychedelic tunnel, seeing images. A Butterfly. An Angel. A snake.

He skidded, rounded a corner, regained control of the car, and drove slower. Large flakes continued to fly at the windshield. He pulled over, remembering the last time he drove in the snow was when he had the incident with Amy.

He searched the glove compartment for the pill box of Rexulti he kept in the vehicle and took an extra two milligrams, then waited, trying to decide whether or not he should return to the store and call Dr. Austin. The customer was waiting. A minute later, he re-entered the traffic.

Finally, he turned into the parking lot, tires crunching on compacted snow. Every car parked was blanketed by six inches of the white stuff.

He got out and carried the first load of five pizzas to the half-glassed double doors, which were locked. He kicked the bottom of the door twice, hoping the hard thuds didn't sound rude or give them the impression that he was being impatient. He wasn't, but the pizzas were getting heavy. And it was cold. And he was blinded by the blizzard. He kicked the door again, spacing out the thuds, attempting to communicate his patience.

Finally, a young woman appeared. The two froze and locked eyes. She pushed the door open to let him in, never breaking her gaze. Her soul was without any blemish. She stared, smiling. Everything about her spirit was innocent.

He blinked himself out of paralysis, remembering that he was working. Remembering he was cold. Remembering the order was heavy. He stepped inside, stomping snow off his black work boots.

"Sorry. Hope you weren't waiting too long." Her voice was soft and graceful. Her skin caramel. She was five feet two. Slim-bodied but curvy.

"No worries," he said, eager to engage with her. "It's all good."

She smiled a subtle smile that made her brown eyes brighten.

"This way." She turned, maneuvering around the receptionist's desk to their left, her long black ponytail swaying. She walked, appearing to have a defect. He hadn't noticed it at first. But she hunched forward slightly as if she couldn't keep her back straight.

He followed her to a dining area, and when she faced him again, he saw in her a certain kind of humility that could only come from endured pain. Yet she seemed happy. She was a woman without vanity. Everything about her was natural. She wore no make-up or extended eyelashes. She had no tattoos, at least none that were visible.

He saw in her compassion. She was working, or volunteering at a senior center. And she was wearing a small gold oval pendant around her neck, of what he believed to be the Virgin Mary. Was she Catholic? If so she believed in God and must have some set of moral standards, like Grandmother. Like Alexa. He looked away from the necklace into her eyes. He realized she might think he was he was being inappropriate. He panicked, hoping she didn't get the wrong impression.

"I'm sorry, I wasn't . . . I was looking at your necklace," he said. "Are you Catholic?"

She smiled and touched one of the tables. "You can set them right here." He set what he had down, removing the warm boxes, feeling hotly embarrassed. He looked around as he went out for the rest of the order. The game had just started, and some seniors were watching it. Others were dispersed, playing cards and board games. Two very old men were engaged in a game of pool. Old women sat in rocking chairs, crocheting. He smiled, thinking of his grandparents.

He went to his CR-V and returned with the rest of the order. As she signed the credit card receipt he watched her, making note of her lax posture and how she held the pen like it was a paintbrush. She handed him the receipt, touching his fingers. Again they shared a glance.

"Did you guys need any napkins or paper plates?" he asked, hoping she said yes so he could run out and come back and spend more time with her.

"No, we're fine," she said. "We have plenty in the kitchen."

Just then an elderly woman appeared and asked for her help with something. The girl thanked Duck smiling, then went with the old lady—and just like that the opportunity was gone.

He went out into the snow, hoping he'd see her again soon. Odds were he wouldn't.

Nineteen

"Congratulations, Carlos!" The instructor pumped Duck's hand.

Duck glanced at the certificate that was handed to him, then returned to his seat, joining the circle of others. Another name was called and the routine was repeated until the last sex offender got his award. Afterwards they walked single file alongside a table—talking—loading their paper plates with food.

Duck joined them and tonged a fried chicken wing onto his plate.

"Carlos," a soft voice called beside him. It was Jeff, the bespectacled white man who was always trying to converse with him. "So what's the plan, seeing that we're all done with this?"

Duck sidestepped down the line, taking a drumstick. The plan was to work full time and start saving for his apartment, now that he was done with *school*, as he would tell Lim-Lim.

Jeff huffed at the silence.

Duck continued to ignore him, adding mac and cheese, a sweet roll, and coleslaw onto his plate.

"How did you even get your certificate?" Jeff shook his head, then turned with his plate to join the group of mousy men eating with each other.

Duck sat alone and ate, glad he no longer had to be around them. They were sick, and their sins would forever burn in his mind. Still he was grateful. The experience had given him perspective, and an understanding to darkness. A darkness much like his own. For they too were driven by compulsion, alone in a universe of conflicts, with unwanted thoughts they couldn't control.

The next day he presented the certificate to Gordon Ryan, who in turn reduced Duck's visits to once a month and confirmed that he was no longer required to attend SAA meetings. He found he would actually miss them, because the stories they shared had humbled him, and often made him think, in terms of addiction and sickness, that he really didn't have any problems at all. That weekend he started his full time work schedule.

"Delivery up!"

"Carlos, your delivery's ready," Lim-Lim echoed.

Duck finished washing a deep dish pizza pan at the three-compartment sink, dried his hands, double-checked the order, then slid it into a heat bag and went out the door. It was May and raining in sheets. Sunday, an hour before closing. The roads were clear and the day had been slow.

He got in his car, looking at the name on the order. *Gabby Reyes, new customer*. He thumbed the address into his phone, then stuck the delivery tag on a sheet of cardboard beside him on the passenger seat and drove.

He made it to the house, hiked the stairs, and rang the doorbell, thinking about dieting and getting back into weight lifting as he wheezed. He had seen Dr. Austin two days ago. She had checked his blood sugar level, weighed him, and suggested he watch his food intake or see a dietician, which he could not afford. The sound of footsteps progressed to the door.

Someone struggled with the lock and then opened the door.

The two stared at each other like before.

"Gabby Reyes?"

She smiled. "Yes." She was wearing the gold pendant of the Virgin Mary and touched it. Her short fingernails were plum colored, and her long hair was wrapped in a bun.

"How's your night going?"

"Good," she said, smiling. "I'm just hungry."

He grinned and said, "Right. . . . Well, luckily there's Corina's."

She nodded, then raised herself on her tippy toes. He closed his mouth, then handed her the receipt and a pen for her to sign. She signed and wrote in a tip, then handed the pen and receipt back. He opened the heat bag and gave her the order. "Here you go."

She took it, then looked at him, smiling.

"Do you remember me," he said, "from the senior center?"

She blinked. "I do."

"That was a while ago, so I wasn't sure. My name is Carlos, by the way." He offered his hand, then instantly thought it was bad luck to shake if you were interested in the woman. Her fingers were soft and smooth though. And her curved grip was loose and dainty. Truth was he just wanted to touch her.

"Nice to meet you, Carlos." She held the pizza under her arm in a careless way that concerned him.

"You don't wanna hold it like that." He pointed at the box. "You'll mess your pizza up."

She adjusted the way she held it, then looked over her shoulder as if she heard something inside the back of the house.

Maybe she had children, or a boyfriend she was listening for, or parents they had awakened. Duck wanted to talk longer but took her distraction as a cue for him to leave. She probably had to get back to whatever she was doing anyway. "Well, I don't want to hold you up." He slowly stepped back a pace, and then added, "It was nice to meet you."

"Sorry," she whispered, returning her gaze. "I was just listening for my client."

Client? "Are you a caregiver?"

She nodded, touching her pendant again.

He then wondered if she had two jobs or was volunteering at the senior center. Either way he felt more respect for her. And more admiration. "That must be hard."

She sighed. "I have my tough days, but I don't mind."

"You like helping people."

"I do."

"Yeah?"

"Mmhm."

They stared at each other. He side stepped, shifting the heat bag to his other hand. "Well, I really don't wanna hold you up. . . . It's late and I know you're hungry."

"I am." She tilted the pizza again.

He looked over his own shoulder, and then down at the door mat, thinking it was inappropriate to flirt with a customer. But he wasn't flirting. He was genuinely interested in her. And she must be interested in him, too. Why else would she still be standing there with the door open? When else would he get another opportunity to exchange numbers with her? And what were the odds that he would ever see her outside of work?

Maybe this was fate.

He cleared his throat, then looked her in the eye. "I don't mean to be inappropriate, but . . . I was wondering if you'd like to exchange numbers?"

She smiled, touching her neck charm. "Sure, we can do that." She turned gracefully, and disappeared into the house, then returned with her cell phone in hand.

He waited a few days before calling.

Nervous, he cleared his throat as the line rang.

She answered softly. She had just gotten home from work. He asked about her day and she said it was good, then began talking about her client, who was a twenty-five-year-old lady with multiple sclerosis. She was confined to a wheelchair and lived alone with a small dog. Gabby said she had to bathe and dress the woman, take her dog out for a walk, and return to make her lunch, and sometimes dinner.

She said the day they exchanged numbers she had to pull a double because one of her co-workers had called in sick. He let Gabby talk, discovering they had a lot in common. Like him, she had no siblings. She loved to eat and cook, enjoyed reading, watched PBS, and liked foreign movies. Following Latin tradition, she held two surnames, the first from her father, the second from her mother. So she was named Gabby Lee-Reyes. Her father was black, and her mother was Guatemalan; both raised in Renton, Washington. Duck always assumed he too was biracial, even though he never knew anything about his dad.

Gabby's parents had decided to wait until their forties to have her. Their older age and health issues had a lot to do with her career choice and volunteering at the senior center. Her mother had given her the pendant before she died of breast cancer, which happened when Gabby was twelve years old. After that, she began nursing her father, who was diabetic and had both his arms and legs amputated by the time she was eighteen. He died a year ago from complications.

She was now twenty-three, the same age as Duck, and was passionate about her job as a state certified nursing assistant for the elderly, sick, and disabled. She wanted at least two children and was working on changing her diet as she was afraid of winding up like her parents.

They spoke for hours, laughing at one another and at the embarrassing childhood stories they shared.

"So . . . why are you single?" she asked.

He wasn't expecting a question like that. "It's a long story. Basically we had a misunderstanding. Something I never got to clear up. So . . ." He shrugged and shook his head, as if Gabby could see him. "She's moved on, I guess."

"Oh." Gabby paused for a long second. "Sounds like you still love her."

"No. I mean . . . hey, that's the past. Let's talk about something else. Like me and you."

Suddenly he felt deceitful and disloyal all at once. What if he ran into Alexa? What would he say to her, after now taking interest in Gabby? Did he still love her? He thought back on how hard he'd he tried to find her. He'd done everything he could think of. He even went to Greater Glory, the church Ms. Davis attended, and sat in for Sunday service, hoping he'd see Alexa there. No dice.

Gabby then asked about his parents. He told her that his mom was disabled and that he was raised by his grandparents, who he still lived with for the moment. He decided to wait to tell her about his illness. He just met her and didn't want to scare her. Plus he wanted to get to know her better.

They FaceTimed every day that week, then got together on his next day off. He took her to Coal Creek Natural Area, a park he knew she would like. They walked a trail between tall trees snowing down yellow pulp. They talked. Mossed branches stretched high above, protecting them from the white sun. The air smelled of fresh dirt and along the narrow trail were tiny chips of coal. He stopped to pick one up. It was remarkably light and brittle to the touch.

"Look." He handed the piece to her. She giggled as it crumbled between her fingers. They continued along. Strange bushes boarded the walk. Thickets of centipede leaves stretched out to the ground, reminding him of a jungle. He then thought of snakes and spiders. Tarantulas and brown recluses. King cobras and pythons.

"Shit, I hope there aren't any snakes out here," he said.

She snatched his arm and looked about. "Why would you say that?"

"I'm sorry."

She clung closer. He felt the warmth of her soft body and liked that she was pressed up against him. Her arm was linked around his bicep, with her hand squeezing gently. He felt strong and trusted. He smiled. It's been years since he's been touched by a woman.

"If we see a snake, you're going to protect me, right?"

"If I see a snake, I'm going to run."

She gasped and tagged him playfully, still holding onto his arm as they walked.

They stopped to observe a monument on their left. "This place used to be a coal mine," he said, reading the historic information that was framed and mounted between two pillars of wood. "This is where they'd turn the locomotive around . . . with men!" There was a sepia picture of a locomotive on a turntable, with a man on either end, pushing against a long bar. Behind the monument was a slab of concrete matted with dead leaves and rusted rebar worming out of its sides.

She said something in her sweet voice but her reply was lost. A calliope whistled nearby, or perhaps it was a screeching hawk soaring high in the sky. He closed his eyes, then looked up at the height of the trees.

"Did you know Renton used to be a forest?" he asked.

"Yeah, my dad said there was an Army base out where he grew up. They would sneak through a fence and play in this restricted area where the tanks were."

Duck imagined himself as a child, playing break-in, running between tanks, and climbing them. Standing on top, shooting energetically with a big air gun. He inadvertently made sound effects with his mouth.

She shook her head, smiling, then surprised him by taking his hand. They continued walking, passing hikers and joggers and other couples and families with small children in strollers.

The two said nothing for a while. They just held hands and walked, looking around at trees and foliage and listening to the sounds of nature. Creatures moved in the woods. Birds sang and chirped and cawed. A waterfall plunged in the distance.

He glanced at her, observing her sloping posture, wanting to ask about her back, but decided against it, thinking it would be rude. Besides, the moment was too good and he felt that it would badly alter the mood.

Next week, they went to dinner, deciding on a Punjabi restaurant they both wanted to try. He ordered chicken curry with basmati rice. She picked the lamb chop with the same side dish and was eating while talking about the cost of medication, saying it was sad and unfair for people who paid thousands of dollars to die.

Duck wanted to listen, but the voices in his head were louder than usual. More active. Foreign music played in the background of the restaurant—sitar pinging, cymbals clanging and crashing and gonging. He ate slowly, wincing. The drums sounded like stampeding elephants. Silverware clinked loudly against plates. Chatter stormed around in echoes. And somewhere in the restaurant, an infant cried over and over and over.

Gabby scraped her dish with her fork. He looked up, wanting to snatch it from her. She was eating rice, chewing greedily. Humming. She scraped her plate again. He rubbed his throbbing temple, then scratched his drumming chest. He saw himself thrash the table and storm out in a roar.

Breathe. Focus.

He breathed in . . . and out. Like Dr. Austin had taught him. It was just the noise he was sensitive to.

Take a deep breath, and breathe slowly. Focus on calming your heart.

He inhaled and exhaled accordingly, feeling the rhythm in his chest mellow down. Finally, he was able to listen to Gabby, though traces of cacophony remained.

"You know doctors get incentives for prescribing certain medications?"

Just then the waitress refilled their glasses with water, routinely asking if they were satisfied with their food.

Duck turned away, shielding his face from the waitress. Her black eyes were bleeding pitch. Her smiling lips were painted in blood. Her yellow teeth were kernels of corn. He stammered, shaken by the sight. "C-c-could you guys turn the music down, please?"

The waitress conceded kindly, then dispersed.

"Are you okay?" Gabby asked.

"Yes, I'm fine." He sipped his water, then finished his coffee, then sipped his water again. His hand trembling like an alcoholic's. He thought of running to his car to take another pill, but didn't want to make a scene or cause any concern. The date was going fine. He just had to keep her talking and stay calm. He thought about what she had said about doctors getting incentives to prescribe certain drugs. He chanced a look at her and saw that her face was unaltered.

"What did you mean about doctors getting incentives?" he asked.

"Well," she said, "sometimes pharmaceutical companies pay doctors to prescribe a new drug, to help get it out on the market."

He looked down and poked around at the remains of his food. "How do you know all this?"

"Uh, Google. Plus I learn a lot from my clients. Are you sure you're okay?"

He squared his plate. "Yeah, I'm good. Do you know anything about antipsychotics?"

"Not really."

He thought about it, then decided it was best to tell her now. "I'm taking this new drug called Rexulti."

"Rexulti?"

"It helps me manage my illness."

"Your illness?"

"I'm um . . . I'm schizoaffective." He paused to swallow. "I need to run to my car." He hurried out of the restaurant and returned hoping she would still be there.

She was.

He sat down at the table. "I'm sorry. It's just . . ."

"It's fine," she said. "I just hope you're okay."

"I just needed to take another pill. Sorry." He looked away out the window, thinking he'd scared her off. He expected her to gather her things and leave with an excuse.

She folded her hands over the table, then hunched forward. "What is . . . schizoaffective, exactly? Is it like schizophrenia?"

He looked down at the sweaty glass of water and then gazed up at her. She was genuinely interested. But where should he start? He answered, giving her the definition according to the DSM-5. Then told her about his symptoms, and then opened up about his mom. He talked about his first episode and told her it had only been a year since he'd been properly diagnosed. He mentioned the different medications, but left out the part about prison. While talking, he wondered how he would ever tell her about that. He knew he was required by state law to inform anyone he was intimately involved with of his offense. She was nice, but couldn't possibly understand *that*.

He reasoned that he was not obligated to tell her anything yet. They were still only dating. Not even making out. He would go into his conviction some other day. He didn't want to overwhelm her.

He went on about the illness, explaining how it caused depression. "Sometimes it messes with my mood. I get depressed, but my psychiatrist says I'm lucky. Because I can work. Some people with my condition can't work at all." He watched condensation roll down his glass, then sipped his water. "You're not mad?"

"Why would I be mad?" She touched her necklace. "I can see that you're different."

Different?

"What do you mean by that?"

She laughed. "It's not bad. You just . . . you blink a lot, for example."

"I do?"

"Yes!" She laughed again. "But I'm not perfect either." She shrugged. "Mother Teresa said that, 'if you're too busy judging people, you'll never have time to love them.'"

Love? Woah.

She couldn't possibly love him already. She had to be speaking in a general sense.

She then got up and sat down beside him, taking his hand. "I'm just saying that nobody is perfect, and we have to accept others for who they are. So I'm not judging you."

He thought he understood her better and nodded, then cleared his throat. "I wanted to ask you about something."

"Okay. So ask."

"But I don't want to offend you."

She cocked her head and gave him a look. "Ask."

"All right. I was wondering what happened . . . with your back?"

She laughed. "Why, do I walk like an old lady?"

"No, not like that."

"No? It's not that bad?" She giggled, and then her face smoothed into a look of seriousness. "It's my breasts."

He glanced at them. "Really?"

She smirked. "No. It's just the way I walk. Why, does it bother you?"

"No. I was just wondering. Sorry, I shouldn't've asked."

"No, you're fine. It's something people want to know about. I understand."

"No, I shouldn't've asked. That was . . . that was wrong of me and insensitive."

"Oh my god. Do you want dessert? What do they have for dessert?" She reached across him for the small menu at the end of the table, then waved the waitress over and ordered dessert.

Twenty

Fireworks exploded in the night, booming one after another; flickering, popping, crackling. Great dandelions of the Nation's colors fizzed away into ribbons of smoke. Three more cannons sounded, and the night lit up with another balloon of sparks, and another, and another. Delighted onlookers cheered, clapping at the sight. It was the Fourth of July again.

Duck and Gabby sat on a blanket in the grass at Seward Park, watching the fireworks burst over Lake Washington. It was a warm night. Peaceful. People stood laughing, socializing in clusters. Small, excited children mounted the shoulders of proud fathers, pointing at the display. Folk sat in lawn chairs, drinking. Couples lay sprinkled across the park grass, making out.

Gabby cuddled against Duck beneath an elm tree, holding his hand. "It's so pretty."

Under the glitter of mushrooms, feeling warm and complete beside her, he looked into her eyes and saw the child-like expression of joy in them. Within the past three months, he felt freer than he had his entire life. He looked away at the sky again, trying to remember if he'd ever felt this way, or this strongly about Alexa. Then he felt guilty for having forgotten her, and even guiltier for thinking about her while he was with Gabby. He met her beautiful eyes again, then kissed her.

She smiled, squeezing him tighter.

He took her home afterwards, to a two bedroom apartment she shared with a nice girl who waitressed at

Shari's. Duck met the girl two months prior. Kelsey. Kelsey was gangly and bubbly and wore lots of make-up, and now had a pot smoking, Rock loving boyfriend, who'd promoted himself to practically living at the apartment. The two met a few weeks ago on a dating site called Plenty of Fish.

The boyfriend had three feet of silken hair that shielded both sides of his face. He wore a pea green jacket and always carried an acoustic guitar. After the couple got high in Kel's room, he would begin to practice. When he was done strumming, he'd play thunderous Rock music until Kel would remind him that she *did* have a roommate and neighbors that lived across from them and below them as well. Gabby said the pot didn't bother her but sometimes the music did.

She unlocked the door and switched on the lights. To their surprise nobody was home.

Duck followed her to her bedroom. They took off their shoes, lay on the bed, and talked quietly while listening to 80's music play lightly from her TV. Michael Jackson's "Thriller" came on. They cuddled, Duck with his arm around Gabby.

"Have you ever seen a ghost?" she asked suddenly.

"What? No. And I don't want to either."

"My mom used to see ghosts all the time. She called them apparitions."

He tapped her so he could move. She rose. He lifted himself up, removing two of the pillows from the pile on her bed. He tossed them onto the floor, then repositioned himself, getting more comfortable. She rested on his chest again. He relaxed with his hands behind his head. She continued talking about her mother and apparitions.

He remembered he needed to email Dr. Austin. He was now seeing her once a month, and corresponding with her weekly about how he was doing. She had increased his daily dose by a milligram, and he'd been feeling much better ever since.

Gabby sat up and nudged him. "Are you even listening?" She searched him with pouty irritation, which was a sign he'd been asked a question.

"I'm sorry. What was the question?"

She muted the television. "*I said*, what if your illness is not an illness at all?"

What? He stared at her. Sometimes she said things that were compelling and sensible. Other times she said things that went over his head. This time she just didn't make sense. He remembered how she'd researched the side effects of antipsychotics and agreed with his doctor that Rexulti was probably best for him.

He propped himself on his elbows then, attuned. "How can it not be an illness, Gabby?"

"Okay." She crossed her legs Indian style. "So you know I've been researching. Whatever you see and hear is real to you, right? And they've done scans that show that when hallucinations do occur, those parts of the brain are actually active. Like the feeling part, the hearing part, etcetera. So whatever a schizophrenic sees or feels or hears *is*, in fact, real. So where does it come from, right? What-if . . . what if what you're seeing and hearing are spirits. Or voices from beings in another dimension? What if your brain is evolving? What if you're hearing from the dead?"

The idea scared him. Then mildly intrigued him. He thought about the baby he heard crying at the apartment when he was with Alexa, then remembered the dog he heard barking in prison. Were they real sounds from other dimensions communicated to him especially?

But still . . . "I don't . . . I don't know about that, Gabby."

She took a deep breath. "You know in the fifteenth century, Guadalupe appeared to Juan Diego and told him to build her a shrine, and when he went to the bishop with the news the bishop didn't believe him. The bishop wanted proof, so she visited Juan a second time and told him to gather some roses, which were growing out of season. He did and returned to the bishop with them. When Juan Diego released them from his cloak, an image of Guadalupe appeared on the front of his tilma."

He stared at her and blinked. "Who is Guadalupe?"

"Oh, my God." She pinched her gold pendant and held it out for him. "Our Lady of Guadalupe! The Virgin Mary! The people could have said he was crazy, but he wasn't. And dozens were there to witness the miracle."

"So you're saying I'm a prophet?"

"You could be." She shrugged, unmuting the television.

"Have you been smoking with your roommate? I haven't seen anything like the Virgin Mary, and if I did I wouldn't feel like a prophet."

She lay on his chest, then kissed him. "You're so funny, sometimes." She slipped her hand under his shirt, rubbing his stomach. The sensation of her touch helped him relax. He then wondered if she ever felt his scars. It sometimes seemed like her tender fingers were searching for them. Some nights, when he was alone, he rubbed his own stomach, seeing if he could detect them. But they were imperceptible. Smooth, like the rest of him.

He moved, spooning her closer. "You shouldn't say things like that."

"I know but there are a lot of people who believe that. And I'm not just talking about schizophrenics."

He sat up. "Yeah, but . . . you don't know what that's like . . . to hear something that scares you. Then to believe that it comes from *God?* Or another *dimension?* That *sounds* crazy."

"Okay, I get it. I'm sorry." She shrank into silence.

He lay back down, thinking about the mystery of God, then remembered the prayer he sent forth asking for a companion. Was it a coincidence? Or had God answered? Duck chose to believe the latter. Maybe he and Gabby met on a spiritual plane, in pre-existence somewhere. Predestined.

She lay, resting on his chest again. Her hand back under his T-shirt, soft on his sternum. He turned to observe her. Her eyes were closed and her face was peaceful. She smelled of summer blackberries, but always swore she wore nothing but her natural scent. He turned on his side, scooting down to her eye level, thinking it was time to commit. He kissed her, then sniffed in between her collarbone and chin.

She giggled and squirmed sleepily.

In the next moment, he was cupping her breasts, sucking her long, protruding nipples, and tasting her exotic skin.

He leaned back to look at her. Her areolas were large. He licked around them gratefully, pacing himself, thinking it'd been so long since he'd been with a woman. He gazed into her lustful eyes and slipped inside of her slowly. She was like a wet, rubber ring around him. Pulling and gripping him tightly.

Shit.

He worked his hips, trying not to come too soon. He moaned softly, then leaned forward to kiss her.

She whispered, "Harder."

He grabbed her hair and pulled and drove into her hard. She cried yes, slapped his butt repeatedly, and wrapped her legs around him. He felt the tingly sensation of orgasm building up in him. He tried to think of something distracting, something unrelated, like cartoons.

Why do some adults love anime? And what the hell is Teletubby?

That worked.

"Put your arms around me," he said, panting.

She looked confused but held on to the back of his neck.

With a surge of energy he picked her up. He stood strong and steady, gripping her butt, spreading her cheeks apart. He lifted her slightly, then pulled her down onto his thick member rapidly, over and over, until she cried out for God.

They fell onto the bed where he pressed her legs back. Her knees met her shoulders and he fell into her deep. She let out a loud scream, cursed, then grabbed his face with both hands and kissed him. She bit his bottom lip and he felt it. She choked him until he saw stars.

He moved her hands and held them down at her sides, rocking his hips faster, grunting. She tilted her head back, clenched her teeth, and squeezed her eyes shut. Tears fell from them. She said something quickly in Spanish.

"Gabby, I'm coming!"

She jumped up from underneath him. Suddenly he felt the inside of her warm mouth.

He convulsed uncontrollably hard. He heard himself shout, "Gabby!"

She moaned and kept doing what she was doing to him, gulping loudly three or four times. Squeezing his sack with one hand, and palming his cheek with the other. He cried out involuntarily with every short and powerful burst. She caught the corner of her mouth, and then continued. Weak and light headed he collapsed.

They rested for a long time after, kissing; laughing at what they'd just done, and how they had done it. He couldn't think of a time he had sex like that. And he thought Gabby was Catholic.

He stroked her long, thick hair as they cuddled in the nude. She was so warm and soft and fleshy. And loving, lying on his chest, listening to his heart, tracing one of his scars.

"I'm losing weight," he said, feeling her forefinger graze over his belly.

They'd been going to the gym together, three days a week, for the past month. But it wasn't fitness he was thinking about. He was thinking about how he got the scars that she was touching, how stabbing went down. He'd made the comment to divert her attention away from the marks. She was now drawing a heart on his chest.

"Someone keeps calling you," she said.

He turned over and listened, then heard the soft tone and vibration coming from the pocket of his jeans. He reached down to the floor for his phone.

It was eleven o'clock. Four missed calls from Grandmother. He moaned, remembering his curfew. He called her back and told her he was at Gabby's and would be home soon. He set the phone down beside him and lay back down, pondering before getting dressed. Sooner or later he'd have to tell Gabby the truth.

"You have to go?" she asked.

"Yeah. I'm sorry." He told her a while back that his grandparents' early retirement to bed was the reason for his curfew.

She sighed. Pouted. "Why don't you just stay the night?"

"I can't. They would worry."

"I don't understand why you don't just get your own apartment."

"I told you I'm saving up for it." He lied. He had spoken to Gordon Ryan a month ago about getting an apartment, but Gordon rejected the idea, saying it would be best for Duck to continue living with his grandparents, as they had been helpful with assisting Gordon in his supervision of Duck. It would be another nine months before Duck would be able to move and even then he expected to have a hard time getting a rental application approved.

He recently thought of buying a house with the money he was saving. No one could deny him that, as long as his credit was good. And if Gabby ever decided to start her own home care business, he would have a house for her to do it in. But then he remembered his criminal charge again. If the house was in his name, would she be able to operate there? And what if they married and owned property together? How would that work?

He sat up and reached for his drawers, hating that he couldn't be honest with her. He had already lost Alexa, and they had known each other since high school.

"We're not moving too fast, are we?" Gabby asked.

He looked at her. "Oh, no." Then he felt ashamed. It was the first time they had sex, and he was leaving. He hoped that she didn't feel used. He tossed his drawers back and climbed into the bed, facing her. "We care about each other, right? I mean . . . I know I care about you." She was looking down, fondling her necklace. "I wouldn't've had sex with you if I wasn't serious, Gabby. I want us to be together."

Her face lifted to his. Her brown eyes sparkling with immediate approval. She kissed him. He kissed her back and held her warm body close.

They snuggled quietly for a minute.

Duck thought about the house again. If he paid cash he wouldn't have to worry about debt. But the average home price in Washington State was $400,000. Maybe he'd invest in rental property instead. That would generate income and still give him the option to sell. Duplexes in Texas sold for $150,000, he saw on Zillow, and he'd already saved fourteen grand, ten of which he had invested in an index fund, as Warren Buffet had suggested. If Duck and Gabby both got higher paying jobs and worked together, they could buy a house in Washington, own rental property in Texas, and ultimately run a home care business.

"What do you think about becoming a registered nurse?" he asked.

She sighed. "I've thought about it."

"You should do it. I've been thinking about getting my CDL."

"Your CDL?"

"Commercial driver's license. For truck driving. I'd make a lot more money, plus I could help you pay for your schooling. The CDL class is only, like, five thousand dollars."

She propped herself up on her elbow, lying on her side, resting her head in her hand. "That sounds like a good idea, but what about your condition?"

"What about it?"

"I mean . . . would you be okay driving those big trucks?"

"I'm okay now, delivering pizzas, right?"

"Yeah."

"Then I should be fine driving semis. I'm still driving either way."

"I don't know." She wriggled her mouth as she often did in quick thought, then sat up and grabbed her phone from the nightstand. She reclined, and began doing some research, he supposed.

After a minute she said, "If I go to school it'd have to be in the spring quarter of next year. It's too late to register for the fall. And tuition is really cheap. Only fifteen thousand dollars . . . or twenty-five hundred per quarter. And you might not have to pay that if I get financial aid."

He nodded. "All right. Let's make that our goal then. I get my CDL this year, and you get your RNA license next year."

She set her phone back down on the nightstand and faced him. "Don't truck drivers spend a lot of time away from home?"

"I'd be driving local, not out of state."

"I don't know. It just seems dangerous."

"I thought you said it was a good idea."

"It is, but . . . maybe you could drive for UPS. That'd be safer, right? I heard they have good benefits, and they pay well."

"Yeah, but if I get my CDL, I'll have credentials. I'd be making myself more marketable."

She nodded, then cuddled closer, tracing over his scars. He could feel her wondering about them. She was going to ask about them soon. He saw himself explaining them, and the lie that put him in prison, and her not believing him, and leaving him to be lonely again.

She quieted, then sat up to study the marks. "What happened right here?" She looked at him.

He swallowed, sat upright against the pillows and headboard, thinking of where to start. How to start.

I was stabbed in prison.

She would then ask why he went to jail.

I was arrested for a crime I didn't commit.

What crime?

Child molestation.

He opened his mouth and said, "I . . ."

Just tell her you were stabbed, and don't mention prison. No, start with Amy. No, start with Alexa.

He opened his mouth again. "I—"

A woman's voice called out in the apartment. "Hel-lo?" It was her roommate. Drunk.

Duck and Gabby covered themselves with the bedclothes.

"Is anybody . . . Oh, God." The roommate cursed as she knocked things over in the living room. Duck wondered if she had turned on the lights. She thudded around the apartment, staggering closer to the room.

Suddenly she pushed the door open.

Gabby spun around with the sheet held close to her naked breasts. "Kel, what the fuck!"

"Ohmygod, I'm so sorry." Kel stood in the doorway, swaying. "Ineedsomehelp. Garrett is passed out in the car."

"Okay, but you need to get out!"

Kel staggered away without shutting the door. Gabby got up and closed it. Duck and Gabby got dressed and helped Garrett inside.

The rain took a day off. The sirens didn't. It was fall now. October. Duck was driving to Gabby's after she called him over to talk about something important she didn't want to discuss over the phone. He thought maybe it was about him not getting his CDL. He had enrolled in the course and had been going to school part time on the weekends for the last two months. In the beginning he failed the permit test, having to retake the air brake section twice, then he had a difficult time driving the semi. He had issues with double clutching and backing, and when tested by his instructor, Duck failed simple directions and went over a curb once. He'd failed the road test three times. Any time you took the test after that there was an additional charge.

Gabby kept saying God was telling him something. And maybe she was right. Maybe truck driving wasn't for him.

He did like working at Corina's. The money he made was decent, and the staff loved him. His only issues were car maintenance expenses. Still he didn't want to be complacent. And this is what he suspected Gabby wanted to talk about, him moving forward with finding a career, or a higher paying job.

She let him in, then headed toward the dining room without saying a word. He shut the door behind him, slowly followed her to the dining table, sat down across from her, staring at her, wondering what was up. She rubbed her palms together nervously. He then surmised the meeting was not about truck driving school. Afraid, he wished that it was.

"Hey," he said. She must have found out about his conviction, probably by doing her online research. Or maybe she had seen his picture on one of those sex offender notification fliers you sometimes see stapled to power poles or taped to corner store windows. Duck's heart was thumping in his throat.

He thought he'd start off by telling her why he decided to give up on getting his CDL, which would gradually lead to the subject of his conviction. Then he would explain the story behind his arrest, and why he kept the criminal charge a secret. Then it would all feel like a confession, and not like something he'd been hiding from her. Then she would forgive him. He hoped.

"I'm sorry," he said. "I know I said I'd get my CDL but I changed my mind about it."

"What? Why?"

"You were right. It's not for me. Plus I was thinking about the long hours on the road. If I had an episode driving one of those things . . . I could . . . I could kill somebody, you know."

She looked as though she understood, then dug inside her purse and handed him a folded sheet of paper. The notification flier.

"What's this?" he asked.

"Open it."

He unfolded the paper and was surprised to see no mugshot of himself. He read: *Valley Medical Center. Pregnancy confirmation letter. Patient: Gabby Lee-Reyes. Positive pregnancy test confirmed.*

He looked at her. "You're pregnant?"

She smiled. "Yes! You're going to be a dad!"

He dropped his shoulders and sighed. He was . . .

He was going to be a father! He was going to have a family! "Wait a minute. How long? Since when?"

"And I'm going to keep it, Carlos. I don't believe in abortions."

He stood. Raked his hair back and ruffled it. Looked at her. Reread the letter. Set it down and paced. He'd never been a father before. He would need to marry her. And buy them a house. And work longer hours. And hope his child didn't grow up to be schizophrenic.

She stopped him from pacing, grabbed his face, and kissed him. "Calm down. Everything's going to work out. We're going to be fine."

"Okay. I have to move out of my grandparents'—so we can get us a place together."

"Wow!" She grinned. "Gold star for *you*."

He ignored her, wondering how he could move out without his CPO knowing about it. Duck hadn't even told him about the relationship. Would Gordon send him back to prison for not disclosing his conviction to someone he was intimate with? What would Gordon say about Duck having a baby? Would Gordon alert Gabby of Duck's charge and spoil their relationship, thus taking Duck's family away from him?

January fifth. Thursday. No flakes this winter but still cold. Duck had been promising Gabby that they'd get a place together soon. In November, he learned the apartment manager was a Sounders fan, bought four tickets to the MLS Cup, and invited the man and his wife to come with him and Gabby. That night the Sounders won the championship for the third time. Now every time Duck and the apartment manager saw each other, they would shout, "Go Sounders!" When it came time, he'd pay the man three months of rent in advance, plus first, last, and the deposit, and $40 for the application fee. Then, the apartment manager would move him in without question. In the meantime, Duck was still trying to figure out what to do about Gordon Ryan.

Gabby was now in her second trimester, with a pronounced baby bump. She and Duck had just come from her monthly prenatal visit. Both took the day off from work. They left the doctor's office happy to know they were having a boy, who, so far was healthy. They celebrated by shopping for baby clothes, then stopped by the public library to see what used books they could buy for their son.

Gabby went to the restroom. Duck stood at the bookshelf. Finding what he was looking for, he began picking through a row of children's books.

He couldn't wait for her to come out. He had accumulated quite a collection: *Where's My Teddy*, *The Snowy Day*, and *The Old Man and the Sea*. *A Christmas Carol* and a book by Dr. Seuss called *My Book About Me*.

He happily dropped five dollars in the coin box for what he'd selected.

Finally she came out of the restroom.

He faced her, handing her the books.

She smiled as she went through them. "Oh, he'll love this one," she said of *Where's My Teddy?*

Duck agreed and put his arm around her, then kissed her on the cheek as they turned to go out. This is what it felt like to be a family. Smiling, Duck stopped to push the handicap button on the door for an old woman who passed them.

Gabby then took his hand. They went through the corridor to exit.

"We need to stop by Safeway," she said. "I want to make that chicken breast with asparagus you like. And get some pickles and orange juice."

One of her stranger cravings. But that meal sounded good. Maybe he'll make lettuce wraps for her lunch tomorrow. He mentally added avocados and ranch sauce and cherry tomatoes and romaine lettuce to the grocery list.

It was four in the afternoon when they arrived. Duck parked, noticing the crowd of bearded black men in fringed uniforms handing out leaflets in front of the west entrance of the store.

"Shit."

"What?"

"Nothing."

Duck and Gabby climbed out of the car.

He took her hand and headed toward the east entrance. "Let's just get this stuff and go. I don't want to be in here all day."

"O-kay. What's gotten into *you*?"

"Nothing. I'm just hungry."

They went in and took a handbasket and filled it with organic food: pickles, boneless-skinless chicken breasts, asparagus, and orange juice. Cherry tomatoes, avocados, romaine lettuce, and ranch sauce. They waited ten minutes in the only available line. He paid, then took the bag of groceries as she walked ahead of him, starting west toward the sliding doors.

"Let's go this way," he said.

"Why would we go that way when there's an exit right here?"

"Because we're parked over here."

She shook her head, turned, and walked out before he could stop her.

He hurried out behind her, flustered.

"Shalom, sister," Fats bellowed, handing her a handbill.

Duck snatched it from her and crumpled it. She spun around and faced him.

Fats was unfazed by the action.

The men with him stepped up as if to protect him. All eight of them. Bearded and adorned in blue and gold. All hardened ex-convicts, ex-drug addicts, and former gang members. Now religious and militant.

B clapped Fats on the shoulder, then greeted Duck. "Shalom, brother. How you been?"

"Good," Duck spat. "Always good." He then leaned into Gabby's ear and whispered, "This is why I wanted to go the other way."

"Shalom, sis," Fats said. "I see you wearing a pendant of Our Lady of Guadalupe around your neck. You Hispanic?"

She looked down at her religious medal. Duck tugged on her arm.

She pulled away. "Yes. Well, I'm biracial."

"And what are you mixed with, sis?"

Duck snarled into her ear, "Let's go."

She faced him. "No. Hold on. Geez." She quickly returned her attention to Fats and the congregation. "Black and Hispanic. Well, my father was black and my mother was Guatemalan."

"All praises," Fats said. "So that means you're an Israelite from the tribe of Judah."

"Thaaat's riiight!" the congregation chorused.

Fats glanced down at her pendant again. "I'm guessing you were raised to be Catholic. Do you know about Juan Diego?"

She smiled. "Yes."

Duck tapped her on the elbow. She shrugged away from him.

"Calm down, brother," Fats said. "Can't you see the sister and I are talking?"

Gabby turned to Duck. "Yeah, just give us a second, please."

Duck sighed, clenching his teeth.

"Do you remember how Juan Diego described the Virgin Mary?" Fats asked.

"I do! He said she had dark skin."

"That's right. So if the Virgin Mary was black, then the Messiah must've been black, too, correct?"

Duck then seized her by the hand and hauled her like she was a fourteen-year-old child hanging out with cigarette-smoking misfits.

Back in the car, he asked, "Why aren't you listening to me? I said, 'Let's go,' and you wanna stand there talking to them. I don't want you talking to them."

"Why not?"

"I just don't want you talking to them."

"Well, I don't understand what the problem is. They're just talking about religion, and they acted like they knew you."

"Why do I always have to explain things to you?"

"Excuse me?" She reached back as if to slap him and he flinched. "You don't have to explain anything. As a matter of fact—you have a hard time answering my questions. You think I don't notice, but I do. Because you just run around them, and you never make any sense."

"Gabby—"

"No. You never want to talk about anything interesting, and whenever *I do*, you act like it's boring to you. Like I'm boring to you. I can't even have a five-minute conversation with other people without you interrupting. That was so rude."

"I'm sorry."

She put her hand up, blocking his face.

He stopped talking and started the motor.

She looked out the window, crossed her arms, and mumbled to herself in Spanish.

He then drove to her apartment, playing three of her favorite songs. He sang terribly but comically along with them. So by the time they arrived, she was in a better mood.

He held the bag of groceries, waiting for her to unlock the door. She switched on the lights as they entered.

"What the fudge?" she said, staring into the living room.

The sofa, television, coffee table, and end tables were gone, as well as the small dining room set, which all had belonged to Kelsey.

Duck came in behind Gabby and set the groceries down on the kitchen counter. He then followed her to Kel's room. "What happened?"

Gabby pushed the door open. He looked in over her. The room was empty but littered with a few articles of clothing and a bag of garbage.

"That *bitch*." Gabby turned to Duck. "She moved out without telling me."

"Why would she do that?"

"She probably went to move in with her boyfriend. What the hell?"

Duck followed Gabby into the bare living room. "Why would she do that without telling you?"

"She knows I can't afford this on my own."

"Well, when is your lease up?"

"In a couple of months, ugh."

"Just post an ad on Craigslist. You can always find another roommate."

She spun around and punched him on the arm. He grabbed where it hurt and rubbed.

"Why would I look for another roommate, *Carlos*, when you can just move in? I'm fourteen weeks pregnant with *your* baby. God."

"Right. I wasn't thinking." But he was. He was thinking about how he could move without Gordon Ryan finding out. And was Duck ready to try his luck with the apartment manager? Would Duck be able to sign a lease without exposing his supposed crime?

And if he had to tell her, how could he? After hiding it this long?

Monday morning, before work, he reported to Gordon Ryan with those very issues on his mind.

Duck appeared at the doorway to see him clacking away at his keyboard. Duck tapped on the door.

Gordon looked up. "Mr. Duckworth! Come on in."

Gordon Ryan, cheery? A good mood?

Duck sat down across from him.

"How have you been?" the man asked.

"I've been good," Duck said. "I've just been busy with work." And having a girlfriend. And starting a family.

Gordon Ryan cleared his throat and studied him. Duck stared back. He then mentally prepared himself to ask about moving again.

"So how's home life?" Gordon Ryan asked.

Duck sat up, then leaned back in his seat. "Home life is good. . . . You know my grandparents." He crossed his legs, then uncrossed them. "I uh, I wanted to ask you something."

"Yeah, well, that can wait. You do have a good family. And a good doctor, who you do know I keep in contact with."

Duck rubbed his mouth. Grandmother must've told Dr. Austin about Gabby, and Dr. Austin must've told Gordon, who was now going to send Duck back to prison. Duck remembered signing a waiver for his CPO to communicate with his doctor back when Duck first met her. Therefore, Gordon knew all about the pregnancy.

"I've got some good news and some bad news, Carlos."

His heart was pumping hard.

"The bad news—" Gordon Ryan reached into a drawer beneath him and placed a clear plastic cup on the desk. The cup had a green lid and white tape alongside it. "—is that I'm leaving. I'm sorry, but I'm joining the police academy. The good news, depending on who you are, is that I have a caseload of forty or so parolees who cannot all be transferred. So that means I have to release some people. And since you've been doing so well, and because I trust your psychiatrist, I have considered releasing you three months early."

Duck felt a smile crawling up his face.

"Yeah, well, don't get too excited yet," the man said. "There's a condition. If you can pass a urine test today, then you're off of paper. Do you think you can do that?"

"Yes, sir."

"All righty then." The man stood up and handed Duck the cup.

Duck followed him to the restroom and submitted a urine sample for the last time.

Twenty-One

The congregation had expanded by five since B had become a member. Two middle-aged men from Seattle and three young men from Tacoma had joined and stayed within the past few years. (There were some others—including women—who came and went.) Twelve Hebrew Israelites now filled Noah's living room every Sabbath to attend class and congregate. And each Sabbath they confabulated deep into the night, drinking wine as permitted while poring over scriptures.

Fats was second in command now and acted as secretary, proudly assisting Noah in all of his affairs in order to keep the group organized and well structured, while also helping the family business, Noah and Sons, grow by overseeing all accounts north of Tacoma. He and B, now Brother Benjamin, and the two brothers from Seattle had their own twenty-four foot box truck that Noah had invested in.

Occasionally, after work, they would find locations to hand out leaflets. As Fats learned from Noah, the best places were inner city grocery stores and churches. Fats embellished these notions by adding to his grounds DSHS offices, liquor stores, cannabis shops, Work Source, and even McDonald's. His people needed to be saved, and by all means, he would help them.

Valentine's Day. Noah's house. Noah and Fats were webcasting a class on the subject of paganism and lust. (Both men had been given the honorable duty of teaching an online class every Wednesday and had been doing so now for the past six months with the blessings of the elders in New York, who sometimes picked the topic, or approved of the one that Noah chose.)

Noah was at the computer. Fats was sitting beside him, reading from the Bible whenever commanded, as Noah routinely stopped him to demystify the scriptures. Hundreds of people were logged in for the lesson.

Two hours later Noah ended the lecture and asked if there were any questions. Dozens came in at once. He and Fats took turns answering for the next sixty minutes.

"All right, we got a question from a sister—Gabby." Noah looked into the monitor. "She's new and local. Out there in Renton. All praises. No picture. Okay, if you're new we encourage you to add a picture so we all know what you look like. She says this is her first time attending class. Well, welcome, sis." He read, "'In your sermon, you used the word betrothed. What does betrothed mean?' All right, sis. Betrothed means to marry or a promise to marry. Today in this Western world we say engagement. If a man was interested in a maid, or young woman, he would betroth her. But before he betrothed her he made sure he had property and other means to take care of his wife and family. There's not supposed to be all this baby daddy, baby mama stuff you see today."

He paused. "Okay, she's typing again. All right. She says . . . 'Okay because I'm pregnant right now, but we are not married. Does that mean we are sinning?' Well, sis, first of all, you two are supposed to be equally yoked, meaning you're both supposed to be Israelites, walking in the truth. And, like we discussed in class, if he was righteous, he would have already married you, *before* you got pregnant. But that's okay. He can still repent and do the right thing. And I know you just coming to the Truth, but does *he* know who *he* is? Does *he* know that he's an Israelite? Hell, is he even black, Native, or Hispanic?"

Noah waited for her to answer. Took a sip of his bottled water and read, "'No, he does not know. And he is black, or mixed. Does not know who his father is.'"

Fats said, "Sis, if you attending class, he needs to be there with you, so you *both* can be learning the truth. And let me add, that if you two are *not* married and having sex then you are fornicating and prostituting yourselves, according to scripture. All this broken home stuff needs to stop. He needs to marry you and come to the Truth. That's it." He clapped Noah's shoulder, excusing himself. With that Noah ended the session.

It was 9:01 PM.

Duck clocked out from work at the pizza shop at 9:20 p.m. He was exhausted from eleven hours of labor and had been working overtime six days a week, ten to twelve hours a day, for the past month.

He texted Gabby saying he was off, then stopped by Target to buy her a gift and a crib that he would later assemble. He then drove home to her apartment where he had successfully moved in and converted Kel's old room into a child's. He and Gabby had painted it baby blue and set up a colorful car mobile. He himself had cleaned the carpet, which was now cluttered with four bags of baby clothes, two boxes of baby wipes, and three boxes of size N diapers.

He came in with a bouquet of roses and a heart-shaped box, trying to contain his excitement. Gabby was on the couch, facing her laptop, quickly muting whatever it was she was watching. It was a routine he'd gotten used to, coming home late in the evening from work. She then rose to greet him at the door.

"Hey." She kissed him, rubbing his arms. But she cocked a critical scowl at the flowers, as if they were blackened by death and rank with rot.

"Sorry I had to work today, but—" he handed her the heart-shaped box and the dozen roses, excited by the prospect of her reaction once she opened the box. "Happy Valentine's Day."

She took them, half-smiling, into the kitchen and set them down on the counter. He scurried out, remembering he'd left the baby crib in the Honda. He returned and set the box down, removed his work coat and shoes at the front door, carried the box into their son's bedroom, and sat down on the couch.

She sat down next to him. "How was your day?"

"It was fine. Busy. Where's your gift?"

"It's in the kitchen."

"Well, bring it here. Open it."

"Why?"

"Because."

"It's just chocolate, Carlos."

"Well, bring it here."

"For what?"

"What do you mean for what? It's Valentine's Day."

"Yeah—well, we shouldn't be celebrating it anyway."

"Why not?"

"Because it's a pagan holiday. It's not of God."

He scowled and huffed, then went into the kitchen and came back with the box.

"Here, open it. I love chocolate."

She tossed it on the coffee table. "It looks like it's already been opened. But I'm serious about that, Carlos."

"About what?"

"Celebrating holidays. The only holidays we should be celebrating are the High Holy Days mentioned in the Bible."

"Gabby, what in the hell are you talking about? Open the box." He retrieved the heart and placed it on her lap.

"I'm not eating any of this." She set the box back on the table. "If I do that means I'm celebrating. And I can't accept the flowers either, Carlos."

He shook his head. "Okay. Whatever. Just open it to see what kinds of chocolates are inside."

She looked at him, then brightened as if she were catching on. "Fine. Why's it such a big deal?"

He watched her face intently as she pried open the red cardboard top.

In the center was a small black box, about the size of one of the chocolates.

She flashed a look at him, then picked it up. Her hands shaky as she opened the small box. She gasped at the tiny cluster of sparks, then gazed at him, happy-eyed, covering her mouth. It was just like he pictured. Like a scene from a romantic movie.

He took the box with the engagement ring, stood her up, moved over to where there was more space, and said, "Ever since I've met you, my life has changed for the better. You've taught me compassion and given me strength. You're smart, eccentric, and caring. Every moment with you is special, and I want those moments to last forever." He knelt and took her hand, slipped the ring onto her finger. Looked up at her. "Gabby Lee-Reyes, will you marry me?"

She nodded frantically and said, "Yes!"

Yes!

The next Wednesday, after class, came the questions. Noah left to shower, leaving Fats alone to answer the students. A query came in from Gabby Lee-Reyes, the sister from Renton, Washington, Fats remembered. He answered her question, but she typed in another. He answered that one as well. She typed in a third, and then a fourth. She was inquisitive, like he was when he first joined. He then looked at her profile and immediately recognized her as the woman he'd seen with Duck.

"How long have you been in the Truth?" Fats asked after answering her last question.

She replied that she had been studying for a little more than a month, off and on, watching YouTube videos of them on the streets preaching to people.

"All right, because I see you have a lot of questions. And that's good. But let's do this. Let's exchange information. Send me your email address and cell number so we can do a one-on-one. Some of you brothers and sisters online can exchange information with this sister as well. She's new and needs all the help that she can get to understand the scriptures." He paused to type in his own email address and phone number. "All right, sis. Now you have my information. Do you know about the dietary laws and the dress code?"

I'm familiar with them, she typed.

"Okay, good. So hopefully you still not wearing pants, or eating pork or shellfish. Or catfish. Or any of that stuff. You sisters and that shellfish, I tell you. Y'all hate to give up that crab. And that shrimp. Especially that *scrimp*." He chuckled to himself. Peers online shared his humor, responding with a scroll of LOLs.

"Now . . . I remember last week you were asking some questions about marriage. Whatever happened with that?" He sat back, sipping Dasani, waiting for her response.

She typed, **He proposed to me on Valentine's Day.**

Fats sat up. "Now that's an abomination, sister. Did he offer you a ring?"

Yes.

"Wedding bands are not permitted in Israel. That is a custom of ancient Egypt, later adopted by the Romans. Savages. Heathens. Pagans. So you give that ring back to him. Or toss it or pawn it. Whatever you do, don't accept it, because that is a sin, according to scripture. 'Be not conformed, and learn *not* the way of the heathen . . . for the customs of the people are vain. Keep your own tradition.' Now, did you invite him to class and tell him that you need to be equally yoked?"

No.

"Sister, when you come into this truth, you have to surround yourself with others who believe. Otherwise, you will succumb to the lust of non-believers. You have to be strong. Now ask yourself, what is his interest? Because if his interest is of the world, and yours is not, then he is costing you your inheritance, which is eternal life in the Kingdom of God."

He lectured for half an hour more before she suddenly logged off. It was fifteen minutes after nine.

On Sunday, Duck and Gabby went to visit his mother. Initially, Duck planned to tell his mom that he and Gabby were going to get married, but Gabby had asked him to wait. She wanted to have a baby shower and make the announcement then, she had told him.

She was looking very beautiful that Sunday, wearing a black and teal handkerchief dress, showing a prominent baby bump.

Mom let them in.

"Look at you!" she said to Gabby, who smiled shyly in return.

The two women embraced one another. They hadn't seen each other in months.

Mom stepped back a foot and re-examined Gabby, then touched the skirt of Gabby's dress, rubbing the colorful fabric between her fingers. "It's so pretty." She looked at Gabby curiously. "Did you make it?"

"Lord, no." Gabby smiled. "I wish. But you know, I have been thinking about sewing."

"Sewing?" Duck shut and locked the door behind him then turned to face the women.

"Yes," Gabby said. "I would like to sew if that's okay with you?"

Duck ignored her sarcasm.

"Did Carlos tell you I used to make his clothes when he was a toddler?" Mom asked.

Duck side-glanced Gabby and whispered, "She did not make my clothes when I was a toddler."

"I did too," Mom said. "You don't have to be embarrassed. I still have my sewing machine somewhere. Where is it?" She drifted away to search for it. "If I find it, you can have it. Then you can make clothes for my grandson!"

Mom spent less than five minutes digging through a closet. "Here it is! "Ducky!"

Duck rose from the couch he and Gabby had settled into while Mom had gone off to find the Singer. He came around the corner to the hallway and knelt to help her pick up the heavy machine. He then carried it into the living room and set it down on the coffee table until he and Gabby got ready to leave.

Mom made fish tacos for dinner. *Friday* flickered quietly on the TV, while R. Kelly jammed on in the background. Mom smiled, reminiscing about Duck's childhood at the dinner table. She kept them laughing.

Duck and Gabby returned home hours later, exhausted. Mom had talked their heads off, but Duck was glad they'd seen her. She was doing well, and he could tell that she was happy and excited to be a grandma.

He set the Singer down on the coffee table, wondering if Gabby would ever use it, or if it would just take up space in *their* closet and collect dust.

They settled in and then sat down on the couch. He picked up the remote and turned on the television.

She grabbed the remote from him and turned it off.

"What are you doing?"

She turned to him. "We need to talk."

"Okay. About what?"

They both grew quiet. He waited on the words. She hesitated, twisting her lips. She rubbed her palms together nervously. "Don't be mad, but—I have to give you the ring back. I can't accept it."

"What are you talking about?"

"I just—I just don't know about us getting married right now."

"You don't know? What do you mean you don't know?"

She sighed. "We're supposed to be equally yoked, Carlos."

"What?"

"I think you should start attending class with me."

"Class? What class?"

"The Hebrew Israelite class."

"What?"

"They're pretty interesting. I've been watching them on YouTube."

He sighed. "Why are you even watching them, when I specifically told you to stay away from them?"

"I can make up my own mind, Carlos. I'm not a child."

He shook his head. "Have you been talking to them?"

"Yes, I've been talking to them."

"Okay, Gabby, just stop."

"You have to repent and accept Israel as your nationality. And follow the laws, statutes, and commandments."

"They're a cult, Gabby!"

"No, they're not."

He scratched his head. "Okay, then tell me why you're so interested in them. Please."

"It's the way they teach the Bible. I was raised Catholic, and the church never taught me that I'm an Israelite, that Jesus is black, or that the Gentiles are the lost tribes of Israel. Those lost tribes are our brothers and sisters, Carlos! Native Americans, Mexicans, and Haitians. Puerto Ricans and Guatemalans!"

He stood, drew in a deep breath, and paced. "This is crazy." He stopped and faced her. "Look, my focus is on the baby and yours should be, too. Think about what's important to *us*. Think about what's important to our family."

"I am thinking about what's important, and what's important is that we inherit the Kingdom."

He sighed. "Do you even hear yourself right now? Those dudes are a bunch of clowns. Drug addicts. Failures. That's why they're saying that stuff. You believe them the next thing you know you'll be drinking a cup of Kool-Aid laced with cyanide. Most of them dudes are criminals, Gabby. Just look at them." He pictured Fats, remembering what he did to Alexa. Duck pursed his lips, making a fist. "That stuff is dangerous. Shit, they're already brainwashing you."

"How can it be brainwashing when the Bible says that we're chosen? What's dangerous is believing that we're not."

"I can't have my son around this." He sighed. If this was a phase how long would it last? A few months? A year? He shut his eyes and slid his hand down his face. "Look. I love you, but this is interfering with our relationship. If you need something to believe in, believe in yourself. Isn't that enough?"

"Believing in yourself won't get you the Kingdom."

He stared at her and blinked, not knowing what else to say to her. He shook his head, then shuffled off to their bedroom.

The rest of the week was calm.

Wednesday, after the webcast, Fats got a text message from Gabby saying her boyfriend wouldn't be able to attend class because of his work schedule. Fats quickly reminded her that there are no boyfriend and girlfriend relationships in Israel and that if her child's dad was too busy during the week, then he could always attend class on the Sabbath, a day no Israelite should be working. That day was designated for the Lord, Brother Yehuda told her.

She repeated this all to Duck, who ignored her. Growing cold, the two began focusing on their selves.

March.

April.

May.

Duck continued working six days a week, getting overtime, saving money, and refurnishing the apartment. Gabby was still nursing clients, attending Israelite classes, and seeing her doctor every month. One rainy day, Brother Yehuda had called asking when she was going to congregate with them. She had been corresponding with him and others within the online community for three months, but no one in the church had met her in person yet, and they had been persistent, though respectful, in asking when she was going to become an official member. Three brothers had strayed from Noah's camp, and one was suspended for misconduct. So Fats and Noah were fishing for potential members again. Gabby promised to soon join them.

Wednesday, May 12th.

Duck came home from work tired. Gabby sat, very pregnant on the sofa. Earbuds in her ears. Laptop on the coffee table. Her face a span away from the monitor.

He smacked involuntarily, opening his mouth and closing it, like a fish. Most times he did it unaware. Probably a side effect of his medication.

He stared at Gabby. She reminded him of a child sitting too close to a television, watching cartoons. He saw that one of his T-shirts was hanging over the arm of the couch, on top of a dress of hers. Both garments had blue fringes sewn into them with a border of blue. Next to her on the seat cushion was a red baby polo, also stitched with blue fringes.

He shut the door. "Hey."

She didn't respond.

He removed his shoes and coat and walked over to her. "I said hi." He waved his hand between her face and the monitor.

She jerked back, looking up at him, unplugging her ears. "Oh, hi. You scared me!"

"What are you watching?" He peered at the screen.

"Class." She turned the laptop toward him. "It's almost over." She pressed a button on the Mac Book Pro. A voice came blaring through the Bluetooth speaker.

Duck looked away and took his shirt from the couch. "Turn that off, please. It's annoying." He examined the thick ropy strands on the clothes, recognizing them as what Fats and the others wore on their clothing. "What did you do to these shirts?"

"I made them godly, to remind us of the Law."

The voice was blaring still. He leaned across and pushed the laptop shut.

She looked up shocked.

"That's annoying, I said."

"You're being rude." She reopened the laptop.

The loud voice was back on. She tapped a button twice to turn it up.

Duck grabbed the laptop and slung it across the living room. "I said, shut it off!" It crashed into a wall and landed on the floor, the screen shattered.

She sat still with her mouth open.

He clapped his head, realizing what he'd done. "I'm sorry. I just wanted you to turn it off."

Without looking at him, she said, "You need to go."

"I said, I'm sorry."

She threw a look at him. "If you don't leave, I'm calling the cops."

"I just lost control for a second, Gabby. I'm good."

"No. You need to leave." She got up and shoved him lightly. "Get out!"

He backed away, apologizing repeatedly.

"I don't care, Carlos. Get out!"

He asked to get some of his things. She said no. A second later he reluctantly left.

Fats had just wrapped up class when he got a call from Gabby. He listened as she told him everything in one breath. Afterward, he offered to come over to talk.

He made it there in thirty minutes, and saluted her at the door, saying, "Shalom." He entered with Bible in hand, observing her somewhat old folks posture as she turned to escort him into the warm living room. He sat down on the couch with her and opened the Bible to go over scriptures about men of violence. Men given to anger. Hot-tempered men. Men with loose tongues controlled by strife.

After forty minutes he stopped. He was too distracted by the irony. He looked at her lustfully. "I'm sorry, sis, but have we met before?"

"Yes. In front of Safeway—in Renton. We were talking about Juan Diego and the Virgin Mary. Remember?"

"Oh yeah, he said, feigning recollection. "That's right!"

He made a few comments about that day, then stood and walked around, surveying the apartment with her shadowing and narrating a brief history of anything he took interest in. The mint green, electric typewriter Duck bought from Goodwill (for home decor purposes only). The life-size cardboard standout of Kobe Bryant. The canvas print of an Air Force-One sneaker on the wall, six feet across from a poem called "If." The framed poster of Scarface shooting a machine gun. All in the living room as if it were a bedroom belonging to a teenage boy. There were some female touches, too, such as the black and gold Chinese vases with dragons on them and the fabulous wall art.

Fats walked over and gazed at the bookshelf. It was full of children's books, cooking magazines, and Jack Reacher novels.

Fats was surprised Duck read anything at all. There was one book that stood out from the others. *Man's Search for Meaning* by Viktor Frankl. Fats picked it up and skimmed through the pages, seeing a few highlighted sections. The book must belong to Gabby. He put it back and turned around.

And there it was. The gilded Madonna and Child statue: A white Mother Mary, standing, holding a white baby Jesus, on the end table next to the couch.

Abominations!

Fats would discuss it later. He came around to the mantelpiece. There he picked up a framed picture of Gabby and Duck. Fats stared at it. It looked like a booth photo taken inside a mall. Their heads joined together, close to the camera. Duck was tight-lipped with a distant look in his eyes, but Gabby was smiling, appearing bright and alive, and enjoying the moment.

How could she like someone like Duck?

"How long have you known this brother?" Fats asked regarding her.

"About a year."

He grunted, then put the picture back, wondering if Duck had ever mentioned him. Obviously, not.

Fats returned to his seat on the couch while she sat down at the opposite end.

"You know," Fats said. "I know that brother. Carlos Duckworth. Did he tell you we used to work together, at my dad's shop, doing oil changes?"

"No," she said. "He didn't tell me that."

"Yeah, we sure did." Fats sat up and cleared his throat, then licked his lips.

"I'm sorry," she said standing. "Can I get you something to drink?"

"Sure, sis. Ice water is fine."

She went to get the ice water.

She must not know about the acid attack or anything else regarding his and Duck's history.

"I see he still has his demons," Fats shouted toward the kitchen, where she was pouring his beverage. "Did he tell you that he was incarcerated?"

"Incarcerated? No." She returned, handing him his drink.

He thanked her, took a sip, and then set it down on the coffee table. "Is that his seed you carrying?"

She looked down at her stomach and said, "Yes . . . "

"And he never told you he was in prison?"

"No," she said looking worried. "Not at all."

"I see you don't know much about this brother, do you?"

"Well . . . what did he go to jail for? Was it bad?"

"I'll let you be the judge, sis. All you have to do is google his name. There are websites you can go to, to see if someone has a criminal record. I'm sure you know that." He paused a second to let her think. To let her be curious, so she would later discover Duck was someone she couldn't trust. Then she would join the congregation when she had nowhere else to go. "He tell you about his ex-girlfriend, Alexa?"

"No. I mean . . . a little. What about her?"

He shook his head and said. "Someone threw acid all over her face. But no one was arrested for it. I'm thinking it was him. I think the brother did it because she wanted to leave him."

Gabby pinched her medal, looking worried, afraid and appalled.

He noted the gesture and said. "That thing is a form of idol worshipping, you know. You might be attached to it, but you need to get rid of it, along with that statue over there. You know what the scripture says about graven images, right?"

She nodded.

"But you need to do a check on that brother. He's already shown you he can be violent. Ask him about his ex. But don't be surprised if he denies it or blames someone else for it. You know what the devil does. He lies and deceives. If this boy's spirit was right he'd be in the Truth. But do a background check on him and see what he did time for. He shouldn't be living with you anyway. Remember you have to be married for that, and equally yoked."

She looked at him as he rose. "Well, sis. I'm tired and gotta work in the morning. If you need anything remember you have a family right here with us. But you need to come congregate. Meet the rest of the camp. Every Sabbath we get together. And Sister Sarah could use some help in that kitchen." He chuckled.

She walked him to the door. He turned around saying, "Shalom," and then stepped out.

It was raining.

Twenty-Two

Duck returned home Friday, hoping Gabby had forgiven him. He had bought her a new laptop and had mailed her a four-page letter, apologizing, saying what she and the baby meant to him. During the past few days he tried calling, but she ignored him, only responding with vague text messages.

When he got there, the lights were off as if no one was home. He set down the laptop, which was still in its box, and then switched on the lights. Surprised, he saw that Gabby was sitting on the couch, hunched forward with her hands folded. Big. Pregnant. There was a sheet of paper before her on the coffee table. He could see that it had a picture of him.

A mugshot. His criminal offense.

He didn't bother to remove his coat. He swallowed hard and muttered, "Hey."

She calmly picked up the notification and stared at it. A single tear ran down her cheek. "My son's father is a child molester?"

He stepped forward cautiously. "C'mon, Gabby. You know I wouldn't do something like that." He stuck his tongue out without trying to.

She shook her head. "No. No, I don't."

He took another step.

"Don't." She rose with the paper and looked at him with wet eyes, warily scanning his face.

"Gabby, you have to believe me."

"You. Are. A registered sex offender!" she yelled shaking the notice at him. She then slung it, turned her back, and wobbled away.

"Gabby, stop it."

She was sobbing in anger. "I'm so stupid. How could I fall in love with a monster?"

"Gabby, listen to me."

"No!"

"I'm telling you I didn't do that."

She turned to him. "Get out of my life! I don't want you here."

"Just listen to me for a second."

"No!" She sobbed, then doubled back to the couch for her purse and got her phone.

"Who are you calling?"

"Give me your key." She sniffed and held out her hand and made a call with the other.

"Gabby. Who are you calling?"

"Yes, brother," she said into the phone. "You said to call if he doesn't leave."

"Gab, I'm sorry I didn't tell you about it, but—"

She held the phone to her chest and said, "You need to leave."

"Just listen to me!"

"No! You're a liar. I can't believe I ever trusted you."

He stepped toward her. "I never lied, I just—"

She evaded him. "Don't touch me."

"Who do you have on the phone?"

She spoke into it. "He's not leaving, Yehuda. He's in the living room harassing me."

"Give me the phone," Duck demanded extending his hand.

"Why? Are you going to throw acid on me, too?"

"What? What the hell are you talking about? Are you talking to Fats? He's the one who threw acid at Alexa, not me! Give me the fuckin' phone, Gabby." He took hold of her arm and pried the phone out of her hand as she shrieked.

A booming fist then hammered at the door. A male neighbor yelled, "Gabby, is everything okay?"

"We're fine!" Duck shouted.

The voice behind the door said, "I'm calling the police." Footsteps clomped away.

Duck looked at the phone, ended the call, and tossed the phone onto the sofa. "I'm not a child molester. I never touched that girl. Okay. Alexa was working at a daycare and had this boss there who liked me."

"I can't," Gabby said. "I just can't." She walked away.

He wanted to finish explaining it to her but sensed the police were on their way.

He fled out the door.

Sirens wailed in the distance.

Fats peered over his shoulder at the backseat where Gabby sat. Pregnant, returning a gaze, crossing her legs, and placing her hands upon her lap. Shaken. Noah, driving, shot a glance at Fats. Fats felt it, then focused on the drive again. He stared out his window at the shiny asphalt that was slick with rain and covered by darkness, then at the railing as they turned onto the freeway ramp going south toward Tacoma.

He was thinking about her call again; the panic in her voice and how she confided in him, abiding by *his* advice, and relying on *his* assistance. Then he remembered Duck apologizing fruitlessly, and her disregarding him. Fats felt a sense of power then. The fact that she ignored Duck and depended on him made him feel godly. He turned to peek at his prize again.

"Lower your gaze," Noah said.

Fats returned his attention to the traffic. "How many months are you?"

"Seven," Gabby answered. "Seven months."

"That baby is an abomination," Fats snapped. He looked back at her.

She put her head down shamefully.

"The sister wants help," Noah said. "So we're here to help. Not to condemn."

"Well, she needs to know that she was dealing with the devil and that that baby was created out of wickedness. That boy may not even be an Israelite. Didn't you say he doesn't know who his father is? His father could be an Edomite. Or a Hittite. Or a Canaanite."

Noah turned up the volume on the stereo. Israelite music played two decibels louder.

Fats stared out at the traffic again.

Noah looked up at the rearview mirror. "So, you don't drive, sis?"

"No, I don't."

"Why not, if you don't mind me asking?"

She was silent a moment. Long enough for him to decide to switch lanes.

"I just never got my license. When I was in high school, I got into a really bad car accident."

Noah nodded. "I understand."

Half an hour later they arrived at his house. Fats hoisted her luggage out of the trunk, hauled it up the stairs, and went inside with her trailing behind him. Noah brought in her backpack and called the boys down to help with the boxes of baby wipes and Pampers. His sons, now tall young men, tumbled down the stairs, blazing by their mother, who had come out into the living room to greet Gabby.

Sarah was wearing a white and gold shawl over her head and her chocolate, round face was grinning. The white dress she had on had gilded embroidery around the neckline. Swirly, intricate gold designs ran down the sleeves, and frilly, gold fringes circled the hem. She hugged Gabby to her right, and then hugged her to her left, saying, "Shalom. I am Sarah."

"Gabby."

The boys returned with the boxes of baby paraphernalia and set them down on the sofa.

"All right, I'll see you brothers tomorrow," Fats said, grasping Noah's hand and embracing him in one sweep. Fats took one last look at Gabby, then headed out to his car, feeling supreme.

After he left, Duck drove to McDonald's and ordered a number three. While he was eating, flashing prowlers sped down the street, hunting for him, he assumed. He watched with dread and excitement, feeling both lucky and clever yet offended that they thought he could be such a menace. He would never hurt Gabby or any woman, for that matter. Well, he had pushed Amy, but that was different.

He ate and waited an hour, then went back to his CR-V, trying Gabby on the phone over and over; trying to see if he could come home, trying to see if he could explain things without arguing.

No answer. Straight to voice mail.

He ended each call, leaving no message, then drove back to his grandparents', deciding to stay over the weekend. Maybe that was best.

Three days later, he still hadn't heard from Gabby. He came home Monday, thinking he'd waited long enough. He was impatient and restless but also sorrowful and repentant. He had 72 hours to reflect and understood that he had every opportunity to be honest with her but had decidedly kept things from her instead. He had shown cowardice and, in a sense, lied to her, betraying her trust by never giving her the chance or choice to believe him. He understood she needed the time to think.

But three days? Three days had to be long enough.

He switched on the lights. "Gabby? Gabby, are you home?" No answer. It was just him in the silence. Cold. He went to their bedroom and saw the middle drawer sticking out of the dresser. Empty, when it once had been filled with her underclothes. On top of the dresser was the black velvet ring box. He picked it up and opened it. The once sparkling ring now seemed evil and dull. He set the box down, hyperventilating, his throat clogging. A fist closed around his heart. He turned to their closet and found that all of her outfits were gone; strode to the bathroom to discover all of her hygiene products were missing; stormed to their son's room and found that she had even taken the baby clothes, boxes of wet wipes, and diapers.

How could she believe him over me?

He banged the heel of his hand against his forehead repeatedly, yelling at himself. Cursing.

Why couldn't you just be honest?

He tried calling her again, leaving a voice message, apologizing, and asking her to come home. He ended the call thinking maybe she was at work. Maybe she had a new shift and was working swing or graveyard. Maybe she'd taken on a new client.

He called her employer. The automated answering service came on. He would try again tomorrow. But then, he found himself in his SUV, stopping by the house of her last client. Duck knocked and rang the doorbell. An African Muslima came to the curtained window, looking confused. Duck asked if she knew where Gabby was. The Muslima shook her head as if she didn't understand him, then closed the curtain abruptly.

He tried calling B. Maybe he had heard from Gabby. Where else would she go but to the congregation? B had to know something. But he wouldn't answer either.

Friday morning, Duck went to visit Dr. Austin. He sat across from her at her desk, looking away at a wall, smacking, mulling over why he couldn't find Gabby. Earlier that week, her employer had told him they couldn't provide any personal information about any employee. No matter who the inquirer was. Duck didn't curse but ended the call angry.

"Carlos? Are you okay?"

He blinked and looked at Dr. Austin. "Yeah."

"I asked you a question," she said. "But I'll ask again. How long have you been displaying these symptoms of TD?" Tardive dyskinesia is a neurological disorder caused by the use of certain antipsychotics. A side effect characterized by involuntary movements, such as arm flapping, lip smacking, sticking the tongue out of the mouth, rapid blinking, puffing the cheeks, frowning, grunting, and lip puckering.

He looked away. "I don't know. Months, maybe."

She sighed, then quickly referred to his file. "Let's see, where do we have you? You're currently at three milligrams. So, let's take you back down to two. See if we can stop this. This side effect can be permanent, and we don't want that. I'm sorry, but I didn't anticipate this. God, I hope we don't have to switch medications again. And the Rexulti was working so well for you." She rubbed her temples, then leaned forward, folding her hands over the desk. "You're going to have to come in for weekly visits again until we get this thing under control. I'm sorry, but we need to monitor this."

He nodded. "Whatever."

Duck went to work afterward and tried B, using the pizzeria phone in the back.

B answered, "Shalom. Who is this?"

Duck sat down at the table. "You're ignoring my calls now?"

B's voice turned cold and flat. "What's up, cousin?"

Duck tongued his bottom lip and smacked twice before saying, "I need to know where Gabby is."

"I'm sorry, but I can't tell you that, brother."

"So you know where she is then?"

B sighed. "I think you should be more concerned about pleasing God. You need to congregate with us."

"All right. Where do you guys congregate?"

"Tacoma."

"Where at in Tacoma?" Duck picked up a pen.

B chuckled. "Nice try. You can start by attending classes first."

Duck slammed the pen down. "You're a piece of shit, bro. The least you can do is tell Gabby the truth. You're supposed to be my cousin, and you're over there kicking it with Fats, praising Yah-yah or whatever it is you do. You *know* where Gabby is. And I know it was you that told Fats about my conviction—like I did that shit. Gabby needs to know I didn't touch that girl. This is not a game, man. This is serious. This is my family!"

Just then Lim-Lim appeared. She stood with her arms akimbo, frowning at the sight of him sitting down, chatting on the work phone.

He covered the mouthpiece. "Sorry. It's a family emergency. It won't take long."

"You have a delivery waiting." Then she stood there staring until her name was yelled. She left back up to the front.

B's words became a blur. He said he wasn't at the daycare that day to know what happened and had believed Duck because they were cousins, but felt that these trials were a part of a curse, according to scripture, and a sign for Duck to repent.

Duck hung up, got his order, delivered it, and returned to deliver more.

Within two weeks, Fats and the congregation had convinced Gabby to transfer job locations, had persuaded her to change her number, instructed her to wear a headscarf, and advised her to save money to move into Fats's apartment complex in Lakewood, where he said the rent was cheaper than anywhere else in Tacoma. She agreed, calling the home care agency, requesting to be transferred, and asking that they not disclose any information to Duck, who might call asking about her. They understood and transferred her to their Tacoma office, where she was given two clients. One in Sumner, the other in Lakewood.

Fats promised her transportation so she wouldn't rely on the bus. But Noah insisted on taking her, as it would have been difficult for Fats with his moving schedule. Noah and his family agreed to let her stay in the bedroom upstairs with their now five-year-old daughter until Gabby had enough money saved to get her apartment. Noah calculated that it should take her no more than a few months. Fats said that he would help her if it took longer.

Duck was washing dishes at the three-compartment sink, smacking but trying hard not to. He thought he should've asked Dr. Austin how long it would be before the TD would stop once he reduced his dosage. He guessed a month. Then he remembered her saying the side effect could be permanent.

He considered not taking the pills altogether. Look at what they were doing to him. In just a few short years, he'd lost his muscles, gained weight, and now had an involuntary tic. He felt defeated but then was happy to be at work where he could escape self-pity by keeping himself busy with things like dishes. A duty most drivers hated was a task he was most grateful for, as it allowed him to work in peace and solitude while he attempted to hide himself from his coworkers until he was physically normal again.

The dinner rush was over and had been for more than an hour. Laughter erupted by the make-line and cut table. Someone had told a joke. Most likely Caesar. The owner was always telling funny stories. Sometimes, they were about customers, former employees, or old Caesar himself. But now—Caesar was probably making fun of Duck.

Yeah. That's why they were laughing.

He washed, rinsed, and sanitized another deep-dish pizza pan, grateful to be working alone.

But in came Nia, the service counter clerk who was so eager and happy to hand him a job application that day he came in with Grandpa. She eased her way into the dishwashing area where Duck was, wearing lots of make-up, fake nails, long lashes, and loud perfume. Talking rapidly about a customer. Once a high school cheerleader, then an assistant cheer coach for her alma mater, Liberty High School. She was outgoing and bubbly. Duck thought he remembered her saying she was once on a debate team. He could imagine her winning her arguments, not by being articulate, but by verbally exhausting her opponents.

She stood next to him, chewing gum, breaking policy. "What are you eating?" She blew a bubble. It popped and stuck to her upper lip. She licked it off and kept chewing.

He focused on scrubbing a pizza screen. "Nothing." He started smacking again. He concentrated hard on controlling his jaw.

She stared, squinting at him. "Looks like you're eating something." She placed her hand on her hip. "Are you high?"

"No, I'm not high. Don't you have something to do?"

"Um, excuse me? Don't be rude."

The boss appeared. "Carlos, are you ready to clock out?"

He turned and looked at the wall clock. It was early, not even eight o'clock.

"Meth kills," Nia mumbled, striding to the front where she worked as a customer service representative.

Duck dried his hands on the black apron he was wearing. "It's still early," he replied to Lim-Lim.

"Yeah, but it's slow. And we have too many drivers already."

He thought maybe she was upset about the phone call he made earlier. He went to his small locker anyway, got the money he'd collected from cash orders and the receipts from those that were prepaid, and sat down with her in the back to cash out.

"Sorry about the phone call," he said, handing over the signed credit card receipts he'd collected.

"No worries." She logged on to the computer to tally up the tips he made. "Is everything okay with you?"

He wondered why everyone kept asking him that, then realized he was involuntarily opening and shutting his mouth again. How long had he been doing that in front of her? He jerked his head away sharply, trying to stop. "Sorry, I'm fine."

She was staring at him. She scooted closer, folding her hands over the table of clutter. "We all like you here, Carlos. Caesar likes you. I like you. The crew likes you. But you've been acting very strange lately. . . . And . . . as you know, we have a no drug policy here."

"I'm not on drugs!" he said through clenched teeth.

Her brow lifted, eyes bright with alarm and shock.

He sighed, then sat back, recomposing himself. "I'm sorry, but I'm not on drugs." He then reached into his pocket for the pills and set the bottle down on the table, turning it so that she could read the label. "I'm schizoaffective and on meds. Mouth clapping is a side effect. Half the time, I don't even know I'm doing it. If you'd like, you can call my psychiatrist. She can tell you all about it."

"No, that's okay. I'm sorry for assuming. Do you need a few days off?"

He relaxed and thought it over. "Actually . . . yes. I can go for that. Thank you." He could use the time to search for Gabby.

After work, he drove by the Safeway on North East Fourth Street in Renton to see if the Israelites were there. He didn't know what he'd do or say if he saw them. But as he expected, not a single one of them was present.

In the morning, he drove to Seattle, by the church on Twenty-Fifth and Jackson, where he first saw Fats and the congregation street preaching to people. Duck hardly recognized the city. The streets had been narrowed and cluttered into one-lane sections for the construction. The strip mall between Twenty-Third and Twenty-Fifth and Jackson had been demolished. The Red Apple grocery store that was once a staple in the community was being replaced by a high-rise apartment complex. Traffic was more congested, and judging by the amount of civilians he saw in the neighborhood, the population seemed to have doubled.

He stopped by the Safeway in Renton again, then headed to Tacoma, taking the Fife exit. He drove through the city aimlessly, refueling once, stopping occasionally to ask strangers if they had seen or knew who the Israelite brothers were. To his surprise, they were well known. He then stopped by every location he was told he could find them street preaching, from the strip mall off of Eighty-Fourth and Hosmer to the Safeway on South M Street.

Unsuccessful, he went home and logged on using the laptop he bought Gabby, registering with the Israelites' website to attend their daily classes. He would continue the search routine for weeks thereafter, sporadically on weekdays after work and all day on Sundays.

No luck.

Three weeks later. Fats and the congregation stood in front of the Safeway on South M Street in Tacoma. Nine of the men stood aligned and upright. Listening to Noah speak, they kept an eye on the growing crowd. Fats stood beside Noah, holding his Bible, ready to read the next line of precepts. Noah spoke vehemently, drawing people's attention with charismatic ease. Fats listened to his mentor carefully.

Swift was the monologue, hot were the scriptures. "Give me Proverbs twenty-four, verse ten."

Fats flipped to the scripture. "If thou faint in the day of adversity, thy strength is small."

"Again."

"If thou faint in the day of adversity, thy strength is small!"

Noah pointed to a black woman. "Now, what is King Solomon saying right here?"

"Uh, he's saying not to give up."

"That's right. King Solomon is saying, like gold, we will be tried through the fire, and if you faint in the day of adversity, you are a *weak* man—or a *weak* woman. And how do we know we are giving up? We know because we get drunk. We know when we smoke crack or meth or marijuana, or when we prostitute ourselves, gangbang, or hustle."

The crowd nodded.

"For what does the scripture say? 'He that is cruel troubles his own flesh.'"

The crowd nodded again.

"Give me second Timothy, chapter two. Start at verse three."

Fats read accordingly, then tapped Benjamin on the shoulder when he was done. "I gotta piss and take this insulin." Benjamin nodded and stepped into Fats's place. Fats grabbed his backpack, stuffed his Bible into it, and then headed inside the grocery store.

He walked by the registers, noticing the red-faced store manager working check stand six. The manager swiped an item, looking dead at Fats. Fats kept walking. The manager reached for the store phone.

Fats strutted down an aisle and pushed through the black double doors where he knew there was a bathroom. He locked himself in it and quickly relieved himself, then opened his backpack, pulling out his kit of diabetic supplies. He filled a syringe with 80 units of insulin just as he heard an urgent knock at the door.

"Yeah, I'll be out in a second!" Fats lifted his shirt and stuck himself below the navel, injecting the insulin into his body, tossed the syringe and needle into a small trash can set in the corner, strapped on his backpack, and then opened the door.

"What are you doing back here?" the manager asked.

Fats walked past him, saying nothing.

"This area's for employees only."

Fats kept walking.

The manager followed. "What do you have in your backpack?"

Fats turned around. "Nothing, you racist faggot!"

The manager shrank back appalled. "What did you call me?"

Fats grinned. "You heard me. I didn't stutter."

"You . . ."

Fats stepped towards him. "Say it."

The manager turned quickly, stalking off into the restroom.

Fats shook his head and turned to leave.

The manager shouted after him. "Hey! Are you doing drugs in my bathroom?"

Fats faced the man again, trying his best to hold his tongue. Trying not to give in to anger, but instead of providing *a soft answer* which *turns away wrath,* he said,

"I'm diabetic, dumbass. Haven't you ever seen an insulin syringe?"

The man darted by Fats. "I'm calling the cops."

Whatever. Fats walked out and rejoined the congregation. He put his backpack down and pulled out his Bible.

The manager came out five minutes later. "You guys are loitering and I want you to leave!"

"We'll leave when we're done educating our people," Noah said.

The manager cocked his head, then walked across the parking lot and stood, watching them with his arms crossed.

Noah turned to Fats. "What's wrong with him?"

"You know what's wrong with Esau. He's wicked. First, he accused me of stealing, then said I was doing drugs in his bathroom."

Noah sighed, shaking his head.

Three minutes later the police arrived. One cruiser at first, then two others. And two more after them.

The manager pointed out Fats. Five officers approached him.

"Sir, we need you to step aside," one of them said.

He stepped aside. "What's this about? I haven't done anything."

"We just need to check your belongings."

"Check my belongings for what?"

"Did you come into the store?" a female officer asked.

"Yeah, I came into the store. I came in there to piss and to take my insulin. Not to steal from this devil."

"If you haven't stolen anything, you have nothing to worry about."

"We're just doing our jobs here," another cop added.

By then, brothers from the congregation were shouting questions at the police in the background, wanting to know what the issue was.

Fats started to walk away back toward them.

"Sir."

"You ain't searching shit," Fats said over his shoulder. "I know my rights."

An officer then grabbed him by the arm and seized his backpack. Fats spun from the grip and snatched it back. There was a scuffle. The officers quickly brought him down and handcuffed him.

"What exactly is going on?" Noah was asking. The rest of the camp had gotten behind him, repeating the question, adding that the officers were harassing Fats and had no probable cause to search him or his belongings.

The police, out of breath and irritated, told them to leave for they were trespassing.

Noah said, "For us to be trespassing, we would have to be ignoring some sort of signage posted by the legal owner of this property. And there is no such signage on this building. We know the law. This devil—" He pointed at the store manager. "—says we're loitering, but none of us are lingering or hanging out without a purpose. We have a purpose here."

"Thaaat's riiight!" the congregation chorused.

"He also accuses our brother of stealing," Noah said, "and then calls you guys, the police. No, what we need to do is stand here and make sure our brother is safe."

A crowd of spectators thickened. Shoppers coming out of their cars to enter the grocery store or just leaving had stopped to witness the exchange. Other onlookers were from the audience Noah had earlier or civilians passing by.

They all amassed quickly, drawing closer to law enforcement. Forming a mob.

"Stay back!" An officer reached for her gun.

Fats lay on his stomach with his face to the pavement, watching. Two officers were on top of him, resting their knees on his back. He grunted and struggled for comfort.

Another prowler pulled up, parking on the corner. The two officers lifted him and threw him into the squad car.

"Why y'all arresting him?" a man in the crowd asked.

There was a stir. Several people wanted an answer, charging the officers with racism and false arrest.

"Stay back," an officer yelled.

Fats watched from the window of the squad car. One of the officers searched his backpack, finding nothing, of course.

"Y'all need to let him go," Benjamin protested. "We ain't committin' crimes. We out here working for the Lord."

"Everybody needs to remain calm," an officer said.

"Fuck you!" someone shouted.

Something was thrown at the cops, hitting one of them square in the face. From what Fats saw it looked like a banana. The officers scrambled angrily, confused at who was throwing what. A cop's voice then blurted through an intercom, "Everyone needs to disperse. Anyone who doesn't leave will be arrested."

The crowd advanced instead.

Noah was in the front, shouting and pointing with the others. The police rushed him, took him by the arm, and ordered him to turn around to be arrested. The crowd yelled for them to leave him alone. Noah broke away from the hold and faced the cops.

They whipped out extendable batons and surrounded him. One of the officers swatted him on the elbow. He winced and nursed it. Another officer went to tackle Noah, but Noah stuffed the move, and the two began to wrestle.

Fats scooted closer to the window.

Several officers swarmed in on the fight, a mass of uniformed bodies clubbing at one. Pandemonium spread through the crowd. People were shoving and pushing each other out of the way. Members of the congregation were shouting at the officers. Benjamin was closest to the scuffle, looking as though he might jump in.

An officer raised his gun. "Back up!"

Benjamin receded with the rest of the crowd.

More squad cars had come and the officers were gaining control, pushing people back into smaller groups and clusters.

Noah was now visibly squirming on the pavement.

His sons were yelling for the officers to get off of their dad.

"Stop resisting!" the police shouted at Noah.

Small groups of the crowd advanced.

"Step back!" a cop ordered.

People held out their cell phones, recording the arrest.

"Stop resisting!"

Fats was struggling to see, then heard a *pop*.

Pop.

Pop.

The crowd drew back screaming. Noah's sons yelled for their father.

"Back-up!" the officers shouted, pointing their weapons.

Fats shrieked and banged his head against the window.

"Everyone calm down!" the police demanded.

Officers radioed in. Fats could see two of them kneeling now, putting pressure on the bullet wounds from which

Noah bled on his upper and lower back. Noah was taking short breaths and his sons were crying.

Shit! God help him, please!

Fats lowered his head then lifted it, hoping he'd see something different. But he did not.

The crowd had swelled, and more cops had arrived.

Noah was taking quick breaths, and then suddenly, he stopped.

"He's dead!" someone shouted.

Noah's youngest son ran at the officers, yelling, his brother joining him. They were swinging and connecting, punching two individual officers in their faces. The officers fought back with expandable batons, their colleagues helping, beating the two boys and others who rushed to attack the police. Benjamin backed away peacefully.

People in the crowd picked up rocks and bottles, shouting as they threw them at the officers. Fats watched, crying in anger.

"Please, please, please!" Benjamin and small groups of others begged.

To no avail.

Twenty-Three

After a day of burning and looting and a week of protests, the city had calmed down. A little. Brothers from New York came down to show support. Led a few rallies and stayed for Noah's funeral, then flew back to the Big City.

Fats sat down at the computer station in Noah's living room, scrolling through the many comments responding to the article he just read about Noah's murder. One comment said that Noah shouldn't have been resisting. Another suggested he had a gun. Others supported the cops for doing their job and accused the Israelites of being a hate group. He scrolled down further.

Stop committing crimes and you won't get shot.

Looking at the video, I think it's safe to say that this guy was no future laureate.

What do you expect when you don't respect authority? POC need to take responsibility for their actions. They rally against the police, but not against the gangs killing each other. Funny how that works.

Stop blaming the cops. They're the ones being targeted. Violent crimes are disproportionately committed by black men. Think about that next time you call for help because you've been robbed, raped, or shot—by your own "brother."

Benjamin appeared at the side of Fats, leaned forward, read a few lines, and said, "You gonna drive yourself crazy reading that crap."

Fats scrolled down further still. "Surely oppression makes a wise man mad." He turned and looked up at

Benjamin. Benjamin frowned nodding, as if he understood the reference, then quietly shuffled off.

Fats swiveled around to see what the others were doing. Two brothers were on the couch reading scripture. Gabby was consoling Sarah in the kitchen. And Noah's daughter, Abigail, was on the tiled floor, halfway playing with a black doll. She sat with her legs crossed and stooped with her head lowered. Fats remembered when the girl was an infant. Now she was five years old and already fatherless. The thought of that made his eyes burn.

Noah was a great father and leader. Noah had saved his life. Noah never judged him or mistreated him. He loved Noah more than he loved Dad. Fats rubbed at his eye and turned away. The boys were upstairs he assumed. He checked the time on the computer and then rose.

"Shalom everyone, it's time for class."

He logged on, then grabbed the snake-like horn that Noah used to blow into and faced east, blowing into the trumpet. The congregation gathered, prayed standing with their hands raised, then sat down facing the monitor.

There was a panel of five men on the screen. Elders. The bearded bishop in the center spoke first.

"Today's topic is patience," he said. "We're going to open with second Timothy, chapter three. Start from the top."

The elder sitting left of the bishop spoke. "'This know also, that *in the last days,* perilous times will come.'"

"Stop. Now give me the book of James, chapter five, verse seven."

"The book of James, chapter five, verse seven. 'Be patient . . . unto the coming of the Lord . . . for the coming of the Lord draws nigh.'"

"Stop. Now Jeremiah chapter fifteen, verse twenty-one."

"The book of Jeremiah, chapter fifteen, verse twenty-one. 'And I will deliver thee *out* of the hand of the wicked, and I will redeem thee *out* of the hand of the terrible.'"

The bishop raised his hand for the reader to stop. "There's been a lot of noise this week. A lot of grumbles. A lot of talk. A lot of questions about what's happened to our brother in Tacoma. But as we just read here in this Bible, the scripture clearly states for us to remain patient. The Most High is our redeemer. *He* will deliver us from the hand of the wicked. *He* will deliver us from the hand of the terrible. But we have to continue to endure in righteousness and wait for the coming of our Lord. There is no need to call for violence or to take matters into our own hands. That would be foolish, people. For vengeance is mine, says the Lord."

Class ended three hours later. The congregation had vacated, leaving Fats alone with Gabby and the family. He straightened the living room and vacuumed, mulling over the sermon.

Vengeance is mine, saith the Lord?

Their day of calamity *is* at hand.

He finished vacuuming and then searched the kitchen cabinets and refrigerator. Seeing little food in either, he walked out to the master bedroom, addressing the women.

"Sarah. Gabby."

They stood. "Yes, sir."

"I need you sisters to get groceries." He handed Sarah five twenty-dollar bills from his wallet. "Sun's down. Sabbath is over."

"Yes, sir." They got their coats, covered their heads with blue shawls, and headed out the door. He watched them leave, then hurried back to the master bedroom once they were gone.

He searched the closet pulling down boxes, sifting through each one, and putting them back quickly. He checked under the bed and pillows, searched between the box spring and mattress, then rose from his knees and sighed with his hands on his hips.

Where would he put it?

He listened for the boys upstairs. He was not worried about the daughter. The boys were quiet. He scanned the room and then noticed the set of keys in the cup on top of the dresser. He grabbed them thinking he'd solved one-half of his problem, then searched the drawers, going through the layers of clothing. He got to the last drawer and yanked it out, then reached into the opening, snatching the black case on the floor. He put the drawer back. Went through the set of keys and stuck the smallest one into the keyhole.

He unlocked the case.

He grabbed the Sig Sauer and held it, then put it back. He removed the tiny key and pocketed it, then raced out to his car, and tossed the case inside the trunk. He ran back inside and headed downstairs to the basement.

The door was secured with a padlock. He sorted through the keys, trying out different ones. Heard creaking above and stopped. Tried another key and twisted it. The lock popped open. He locked it back and removed the key, then stuffed it inside his pocket.

He crept up the stairs and peeked around the corner, then stepped foot into the kitchen. Noah's oldest son, Josiah, was looking in the refrigerator.

"Your mom is getting some food right now," Fats said.

The young man turned, startled.

"She should be back soon. I'll let you know when she gets here."

Noah's daughter, Abigail, then came down the stairs saying, "I want my Dad-dy." She hurried over to Fats carrying a child's book, then hugged his middle.

He stiffened and looked at Josiah.

Josiah lowered his head.

Fats looked down at the child. Not knowing what to do, he patted her on the crown.

She broke away, then ran into the living room and sat down on the couch.

Noah's youngest son, Malachi, then came down looking for her. He saw her in the living room and went in to join her. Fats and Josiah followed from the kitchen. Malachi sat down on the sofa, next to his sister, who opened the wide book. Fats stood watching. Josiah plopped down on the other end of the couch, also sitting close to his sister. Abigail stretched her neck to see Fats, flipping pages, rubbing them with her tiny hand.

Malachi reached for the book.

"Nooo!" she cried, pulling it away.

"I was going to read it to you," Malachi said.

Fats strode over to the office chair and sat down scooting close to them.

Maybe this was his purpose. To be a father to the fatherless. To lead like his mentor did. But then, his real purpose had already been chosen. His whole life led up to this.

"You want me to read?" he asked, taking the book.

The little girl nodded, then pushed her brother Malachi aside. "Moooove."

They all laughed, Fats chuckling the hardest.

Fats and Malachi switched seats. Fats read the story twice and two others before the women returned. He heard the car pulling up and rushed the boys out to help with the groceries. Abigail followed after them.

Fats then scurried to the master bedroom, putting back the set of keys.

On Monday it was announced the cops involved in the shooting would not be charged. An internal investigation determined they had followed procedure. Body cam footage would now be released to the public, and the cops would return to work as if nothing had happened.

Fats called Benjamin after the news.

"Shalom," Benjamin answered.

"I need you to meet me at Noah's tomorrow. At one."

"One?"

"That's what I said."

Benjamin grunted. "For what?"

"What're you questioning me for? I'm your elder. You just be there at one."

Benjamin sighed and said, "All right. But what's going on with work?"

Fats looked at his phone. Brothers from all over kept texting about the news. "We'll discuss that tomorrow."

"I'm saying though, what are we gonna do about the business?"

"We'll discuss it tomorrow," Fats said. Then he recalled that tomorrow was New Moon.

They met accordingly. Fats sat with Benjamin on the sofa, watching Gabby and Sarah check on lunch, which they'd started making three hours ago. Matzah ball soup served with mashed potatoes and steamed broccoli.

Fats thought about his plan as Benjamin went on about the business, saying they should continue running it but would have to talk to Sarah, as he was unsure of what to do about taxes. They'd also have to figure out ownership. Not once did Benjamin bring up the news.

Fats cut him off. "I think the boys should be here for this." Even though he'd just sent them to take their sister to a park. The day had been sunny, and they hadn't been out since the funeral.

"Right," Benjamin said. "I guess the business is technically theirs."

"They're smart, like their father. They'll figure it out."

Benjamin nodded. "Right."

"You hear the news?"

Benjamin sighed. "Yeah. Shit's fucked up. But what can you do?"

"I spoke to Sister Sarah about it yesterday. She wants to move on, but—"

Just then, the women appeared, bringing each a plate of unleavened bread and a glass of red wine. Fats smiled and thanked them.

Benjamin stuffed his mouth quickly and sipped.

They finished the appetizer and Fats rose. "Let's take this somewhere else. I got something I wanna show you."

Benjamin stood reluctantly.

Fats narrowed his eyes at him, then signaled with his head for him to follow, led him down to the basement, went through his keys, and slid the one he was looking for into the padlock.

"What you wanna show me that's down here?" Benjamin asked.

Fats removed the lock and pushed open the door.

"What's down here, ach? Damn, you can't even see in there."

Fats stepped in. "I swear you worry me sometimes."

It was dark and cold and musty. Fats searched blindly for the string to the light switch and pulled.

Click.

A bulb buzzed illuminating the dungeon. Fats clasped his hands, then strode over to the long table in the center of the basement, reached under the table, and pulled out a keyboard-sized black case from the lower shelf. He set the case atop the table, along with a cardboard box. "Push that door closed."

Benjamin shut the door, but it fell open an inch.

Fats dug into the box and held up a heavy tactical vest, then laid it down on the table. He unlatched the case and took out an AR-15. Raised it to his shoulder and pointed it. One eye on the sight. Focused. He set it down and started filling a magazine with cartridges.

"Brother, what's going on?" Benjamin asked.

"What's going on? Come. Come closer." This was Noah's stash of weapons that only Fats and Noah knew about. A MAC-11 was mounted on the wall before them with a pegged Draco facing it. The mini AK-47 was Noah's favorite. He and Fats sometimes went to an outdoor shooting range, where they practiced on tin plates instead of paper targets.

Fats pulled out a map and unfolded it, smoothed it over the table, and then held it down by placing a magazine on each corner. "I have a plan."

Benjamin was staring at all the artillery.

"Are you paying attention?" Fats snapped.

Benjamin nodded and looked at the map.

"The store manager gets off at five." Fats checked his phone. "That's two and a half hours from now. Safeway is here. The precinct is here. The freeway is here. We're off of Cushman. Now—"

"This is wrong."

"What the fuck you mean, *this is wrong*? These mothafuckas are responsible for Noah's murder!"

"This is not the way to handle things, brother. You heard the Elders."

"Man, fuck the Elders!"

"Yehuda, this is crazy! We were just talking about the business. What about that, huh? And—and think about what this will do to Israel. This will give us a bad name. This will bring heat on us."

"After this, they'll know not to fuck with us."

"After this, they'll be calling you a coward. No one will respect this, Yehuda. *No one.* Not even Israel. Look, I know you're pissed. I'm pissed. We're all pissed. But this is not the way to handle things. They'll hunt you down."

"I don't give a fuck about that."

"We should forgive our enemies, Yehuda."

Fats laughed. "You sound like a Christian."

"You sound like a Muslim!"

They stared at each other.

Gabby knocked and entered.

"What the fuck do you want?" Fats yelled.

"I . . . I'm sorry." She turned to leave.

"Stop," Fats said. "Close the door."

She closed the door and faced him. Again the door fell open an inch.

"What the hell did you come down here for?" Fats asked.

"Um, lunch is ready . . . and the brothers in New York are trying to get ahold of you. People are protesting all over the Country."

Fats frowned but nodded, finished loading the magazine, then snapped it into the rifle.

"Brother, this is not the way to handle this," Benjamin said.

"Then how do we handle it?" Fats pulled the T-charging handle back. "All we do is talk. No action."

Benjamin snatched the map. "I'm reporting this to the Elders in New York." He headed for the door.

Fats raised the rifle and pulled the trigger.

A deafening *bang!* filled the basement.

The back of Benjamin's head exploded. His body jerked forward and collapsed. Chunks of gray matter and blood splattered all over the wall.

Gabby screamed, wide-eyed, trembling, clutching her stomach. Her stunned face was spotted with red mist.

Fats set down the rifle and put on the bulletproof vest, then loaded himself up with extra magazines. He strapped a holster onto his right thigh, loaded the case with the AR-15, grabbed it by the handle, and headed toward the door. He stopped short of Benjamin's body and recovered the map, where a rose-colored pool of blood had formed. He folded the map and stuffed it inside his pocket, then looked down at the head, marveling at the size of the crater.

He stepped over the corpse. "Come on." He snatched Gabby's hand. "Let's go."

They went upstairs.

Sarah sat stiffly on the couch, eyes big as two planets. "W-w-where's Brother Benjamin?"

"He's downstairs," Fats said. "Now get up."

"Please!" She clasped her hands.

"What the fuck are you begging for?" He set the case down and marched toward her, reached under her arm to stand her up, and then heard a splashing sound followed by a deep groan. He turned around and looked at Gabby. She held her medicine ball-sized belly, quivering, eyeing the puddle growing beneath her blood-speckled dress.

"Jesus fucking Christ!" Fats cried. "Come on you guys."

He dragged them outside, holding both of them by the arm. Gabby moaning. Sarah crying. He ordered them into the car and ran back in to grab the rifle, then hurried back and popped the trunk, threw the long case into it, and reached inside for the .40 Caliber Sig Sauer.

Gabby sat in the front passenger seat, taking short quick breaths. Sarah sat behind Fats, mumbling prayers. He started the motor and reversed into the street. Drove fast, then stopped at a red light.

"Brother, please." Gabby groaned. "Please take me to a hospital."

Fats gazed at her, noticing the stains of blood on her face and dress. At the hospital, they would ask questions. The light turned green. He sped along, weaving through the traffic.

"Yehuda, please slow down," Sarah cried. "No one knows but us."

He thought about what she said. Speeding would bring attention and cause an unnecessary traffic stop that might end up in a shootout before he could accomplish anything. He eased off the pedal, and adjusted the rearview mirror, seeing his own eyes peering back at him. Dark. Evil. He adjusted the mirror better, checking the tailing traffic.

"We won't say anything," Sarah said. "We swear. She just needs to get to a hospital."

He looked at Gabby.

She groaned, rolling her head toward him, looking pained and desperate. She was sweating profusely now.

"Brother, please," Gabby said.

He looked away. The baby would be born on New Moon.

He opened the glovebox and gave Gabby a fistful of napkins and the bottled water that was between them in the center console cup holder. "Wipe your face." She did, trembling, but got the blood off.

He drove to Tacoma General Hospital, which was not far from Safeway or Noah's house. He pulled over by the Emergency entrance and shouted, "Get out! Both of you. Get out!"

Sarah pushed the door open in a hurry and ran around to the passenger side to help Gabby. Fats reached for the passenger door and closed it, checked the rearview mirror again, then sped off.

Renton, Washington.

An hour later.

Duck worked cutting pizzas. Dropping the dosage of his medication had made the TD go away, so Lim-Lim trusted him up front now. Nia stood at the heat rack, to his left, raking her long fake nails across the aluminum rungs.

"So you still haven't heard from her?" Nia asked.

"No, Nia."

"That's crazy. You think she would've called you by now. And you said you knew him?"

"I said I saw the dude before. I didn't know him. We weren't friends."

"Wow. That's crazy. Do you think the police should've shot him?"

"I don't know, Nia."

"When do you think she'll call you? Probably after she has the baby. Do you think the baby is yours?"

He side-eyed her, saying nothing.

"I'm just saying. If that was me I would've called you by now. I wouldn't've even left you. I'm just saying. Have you tried going to a protest? They're, like, protesting all the time now. You might see her at one of those rallies."

"She's pregnant. She's not going to be in a protest."

"Well, you never know. She did join a cult. And you might even see your cousin, or that other guy you were talking about. What's his name again? Fats?"

"Nia, please," he said firmly through clenched teeth.

"Pizza!" she shouted.

He turned around with the pizza shovel and saved the pizza from falling out of the oven just in time. He laid the pie down on the cut table just as his phone began ringing. He set the pizza peel aside, reached into his pocket, and saw that the call was from an unknown number.

He answered quickly saying, "Hello?" Then stepped out of the workstation, signaling for somebody to cover him. He hurried outside with the call.

"Shalom, is this Carlos?" a woman's voice asked.

"This is Carlos. Who is this?" He heard muffling on the other end and then a familiar voice.

"Hello?"

"Gabby?"

"I had the baby." She sounded tired. And her voice was hoarse.

Tears surfaced to the rim of his eyelids. He wiped his face. They were quiet for a moment. He felt jittery and exhilarated and relieved all at once. He thought about how much he missed her, then realized why she might be calling.

"Is he . . . is he all right?"

"He's healthy."

Duck then heard his son in the background, making newborn baby noises as if the infant were trying to say hello to him. Duck listened smiling, right as she began to sob.

"What's wrong?" he asked.

She sniffed, saying nothing. The muffling in the phone returned. There was a long wait. A long drawn-out pause.

"He killed him," she said finally.

"Who? The cop? I know. I saw the—"

"No." He could hear her sniffling and swallowing. "Yehuda." She seemed to get some control of herself. "He killed Brother Benjamin."

A swelling seized his throat. He scratched his chest, paced, and then stopped himself from crying, believing he misunderstood her. He took a deep breath.

"Who? What are you talking about, Gabby?"

"Fasir." She sniffed. "He shot your cousin." She started crying again.

"Where are you at?" he croaked.

The phone was then transferred to someone else. "We've already called the police," the strange woman's voice said.

"Where are you guys at?"

"Tacoma General, room two-seventeen."

He ended the call and turned to see Nia and Lim-Lim plastered to the window.

He went inside with his throat feeling clogged. His head stretched and heavy. His eyes wet, brimming with tears.

"Everything okay?" asked Lim-Lim.

Duck shook his head. "I have to go. She's had the baby. And she needs me."

"Yes," Lim-Lim said. "Go. We'll clock you out."

He hurried out before he started crying in front of Nia and Lim-Lim, wept in his car for several minutes, then left, driving as if fleeing a monster, on the freeway, in and out of lanes, eighty miles per hour. He replayed the call in his mind, wondering if Gabby was there, an actual witness to the murder.

Why?

He whipped around a Geo with a bike rack. Switched lanes to go around a semi.

Honked at a slow pickup hauling a horse trailer.

He made it in thirty minutes, hurried inside and squeezed into a closing elevator, got off on floor two, and searched for two-seventeen. Found it and rushed in to see two police officers along the bedside of Gabby, to the left, taking notes as she lay with the baby.

The officers turned and glanced at Duck.

"He's the father," Gabby said to them in a low voice.

Duck greeted them and took a seat next to a woman in a fringed dress, who quietly introduced herself as Sarah. He clasped the ends of her fingers and shook, staring over at his son. His skin was the color of tree sap. His puffy eyes were shaped like almonds. He looked no bigger than a football and wore a sky-blue beanie on his head. His cheeks were chubby, and his whole body was wrapped tight, like a mummy's.

He was entirely perfect.

"He didn't deserve that," Gabby said to the officers.

"Well, we've got officers looking for the shooter, ma'am."

"I think he's going after that store manager at Safeway," Gabby said. "And the police."

"The police?"

"Yes. I heard him say something about the precinct. He had a map."

One of the officers radioed in a coded message.

His partner said, "And what kind of car is he driving?"

"Chevy Impala. Black. Five or six years old."

The other officer turned to Sarah. "You've contacted your children, is that correct?"

"Yes, I told them to go to their aunt's."

"Okay. Thank you ladies." They shoved their pens and pads into their breast pockets and started to leave. One of the officers stopped and turned, addressing Sarah. "I'm very sorry about your husband, miss. I understand he was a good man. That should have never happened."

She pursed her lips and nodded meekly, forgivingly.

The officers left.

Duck went to Gabby and carefully took his son from her arms. The child was warm. Cute. Weightless. And had that newborn baby smell. Duck cradled him close, holding him tight but gently. He didn't want to hurt him by squeezing him, but he also didn't want to drop him. He looked at the newborn's features and giggled.

"He's got my lips," Duck said.

"Yes, he does," said Gabby.

Duck kissed his son on the cheek for the first time. The child smiled. His dark marble eyes adjusting, then half-closing to puffy eyelids. "He's tired, I guess." Duck lay down with Gabby in the small hospital bed. "What did you name him?"

"I named him after his father."

He looked at her. "So you named him after me?"

"Yes, I named him after you, silly."

"Carlos?" He stared down at his son. "Little Carlos."

She stared at him, smiling. Eyes glistening.

He made himself more comfortable, cuddling with his family.

Fats headed to Safeway. The busy traffic ahead of him slowed and then stopped. After a minute it slowly moved again. He inched on impatiently, cursing, thinking there must've been an accident. He was three blocks away from the grocery store but could already see himself there. Parked, waiting for the manager. He inched closer, seeing cars being detoured by a traffic cop. Right, left, turning away. Protestors had blocked the streets ahead of them. He took the alternative route, nodding and smiling at the traffic cop directing him.

He drove in the crowded parking lot, proud of the activity he saw.

A black man shouted through a bullhorn. "Hands up!"

Black people raised their hands. "Don't shoot!"

The police stood by, watching.

He waited ninety minutes, watching protesters in front of the store and the policemen patrolling them. He imagined going in shooting the manager. Fats would walk in, brandishing his pistol, seeing wide-eyed terror in the man, who'd start screaming, begging for his life. Apologizing for calling 911. Apologizing for falsely accusing Fats of a crime. Apologizing for getting his friend killed. Then Fats would say he forgave him, then smile, and shoot him. Several times in his body. Then in his throat. Or in his face. Maybe put the gun in his mouth. Fats couldn't decide.

But then he'd be without his rifle, and quickly outnumbered and outgunned, as he would have left it in the trunk so that he wouldn't be seen carrying it inside the store.

So he'd follow the manager home instead. Fats imagined catching him at a red light, pulling up alongside his car, and letting him have it. There would be traffic cameras, but by the end of the day, that footage would be irrelevant.

Officers cocked their heads to their radios, then turned alert, as if warned of a bomb threat. One of them grasping his receiver, responded to dispatch. They glanced over the protesters and the parking lot, then gathered in a circle, arm's length apart.

Fats sat up. Something had shifted.

One of the officers pointed at the vehicles, then pointed toward the detour, where more cars were parked. Two prowlers eased in.

Fats leaned forward and started his motor. Something was wrong. It was time to leave, time to regroup. He was at the far end of the parking lot, where the crowd was thick at the exit. It would be hard getting out. The cruisers crept by each car, hunting closer and closer to his.

Fats eased out of the parking lot, watching the cruisers in his rearview mirror. The people shouted, pounding his hood, and smacking his windows. He bucked, making a left. They parted like ants around an obstacle, filling the parking lot, and yelling at him. He accelerated as the crowd walled themselves, creating a pathway. He checked the rearview mirror again. Red and blue lights whirled with the *whoop* of sirens.

He mashed his foot down on the accelerator and clutched the handgun. The crowd screamed as two or three pedestrians bounced off the hood of his car. Prowlers wailed behind him, advancing fast.

He dodged into the main street, swinging into the wrong lane to get around a long bus. An oncoming car honked at him. Fats swerved out of the way, cutting in front of the bus just in time. He sped up. The police, slowed by the obstruction, were just a string of lights in his rearview now.

He squeezed the wheel. Gabby. It was *she* who came downstairs to the basement being nosy. It was *she* who saw the map and guns. It was *she* who witnessed the shooting. He did wonder how long she stood behind the door eavesdropping. Because of her, his enemies would get away with murder.

He turned onto Martin Luther King Jr. Way. The car fishtailing with cruisers behind. He made another turn, nearly hitting the pedestrians in the hospital lot. He slammed on his brakes and skidded, crashing sideways into an Ambulance Entrance sign.

He popped the trunk and got out. Police swarmed. He snatched the long case and fired randomly with the handgun. People ran and screamed and covered themselves. Officers scrambled, shooting back. He hid behind a pillar. Bullets hit the cement protecting him, grazing the sides of the column. Rock chips flew, cutting his face. He flinched wincing, and then ducked, running inside the hospital.

People screamed. He ran behind a counter, smacking the lady tending it. She bled from the heavy-handed blow.

"Get up." He set the .40 Caliber down on the counter. He lifted her, then grabbed the gun. "Find this bitch for me. Gabby Lee-Reyes. Now!"

The lady looked and wept. "Two-seventeen," she yelped.

People ran out of the lobby, clawing and grabbing at each other. He fired into the crowd. They screamed, mobbing themselves even more. He emptied the magazine, then slipped in another.

He hustled through the halls with his weapons. Into an elevator. To the second floor.

He looked down both sides of the hallway, then turned left. Marching. He looked into every room, not shooting the patients. Nurses and doctors in the hallway sprinted in the opposite direction, staying close to the walls. He stopped short of two-seventeen, knelt down, opened the case and pulled out the AR. He slid the .40 Caliber into its thigh holster.

Then he heard commotion. Voices of panic and murmurs of relief. He was resting on one knee when he saw the officers turn the corner. He raised the rifle in a hurry and fired at the end of the hall. The sound dropped like a stack of pallets. Three times over and rapid.

They fired back. He stood and walked toward them, shooting. Filled with adrenaline and the power of murder.

The butt of the gun nudged his shoulder as he kept firing. Right, left, low, central. Their army grew. A tactical team walled behind ballistic shields now advanced with bursting rifles. Bullets pelted his vest. Missiles whizzed by his head.

He turned and fired backward, ducking and running. The bolt locked to the rear.

Death was still coming.

He hooked right into a room and pressed a button on the side of the firearm to release the magazine. It fell to the floor as he slid in another. He slapped the bolt catch and ducked back into the hallway. Something bit into his arm, and then his shoulder. He turned and shot with his left as he backpedaled, dodging into two-seventeen.

Duck swung and connected, rocking Fats with an overhand right.

Fats stumbled and fell onto a chair. He pushed himself up and started to raise his rifle.

Duck threw himself, tackling him.

"Ruunn!" Duck screamed, pinning him down on the chair.

Gabby and Sarah ran out with the newborn.

Fats opened his mouth and bit Duck on the cheek and tugged. Duck screamed, grabbing his face, jerking back. Fats spat out a gob of flesh. He kicked Duck in the chest, firing wildly with the rifle. Bullets tore at the ceiling and walls.

Duck stumbled and fell backwards. His elbows hitting the floor. His head jarred by the bedrail.

Fats stood up and strutted to him.

Duck kicked Fats in the groin. Fats doubled over and dropped the rifle.

Duck got up fast. Fats tried to straighten, grasping his sidearm.

Duck heaved an upper cut, catching Fats under his chin as the pistol barked. Duck buckled grabbing his left thigh, yelping. Fats fired again. Disorientated. Missing.

Duck threw a right hook clear across his jaw. Fats saw triple and stumbled sideways across the room. Duck shadowed him, jabbing twice at his mouth. Fats dropped the pistol, feeling his lips split between teeth and knuckle. He fell against the vital signs monitor.

Duck grabbed him and threw him to the floor.

"What the fuck's wrong with you?" Duck shouted.

Fats crawled painfully across the tile, made it to a floor cabinet, and sat up against it, grinning. Blood covered his teeth.

Duck picked up the rifle. "Why'd you do this, huh?" He kicked at his foot.

Fats looked up at Duck and huffed. He licked the blood in his teeth and swallowed. "You never get any breaks in this life." He paused, still trying to catch his breath. "These devils—they always fuck it up for you."

Duck breathed hard. His right cheek burned and his left thigh throbbed. "You have to create your own breaks." He raised the rifle to protect himself, not sure if Fats had any more guns.

A mechanical whirring sound interrupted them. They both turned to see a robot wheeling itself into the room. It jerked awkwardly to a stop. It was two and half feet tall and had a Z-shaped arm with a gripper, and a 12 gauge shotgun mounted next to the arm. A camera was the head of the robot.

The robot inched closer to Fats and stopped, aiming the shotgun at his skull.

Duck backed away, lowered the AR-15, and then let it fall.

Fats spat at the camera and yelled, "Fuck you!"

Duck turned his head quickly and closed his eyes hearing the *blast*.

Turn the page for a preview of Marrico Gordon's thriller
Moses Lake
Available in paperback from Amazon

Gurpreet

No one enjoys being lonely. Yet many of us isolate ourselves for fear of being hurt, embarrassed, or rejected—usually by a ghost. We spend hours on social media, YouTube, dating sites, and video games, chatting, and trying to fill a void. And in those moments we may feel less lonely, but once we log off, sign out, or come out of the Youtube wormhole, we realize we're just as lonely as we were hours before. Despite video chats or constant inboxing, there is no substitute for real intimate, physical human interaction. Time well spent in solitude can make you crazy . . . or fatally desperate. This I know.

There's a party going on in my apartment. Cardi B thumps, competing with intoxicated young adults yelling frivolous conversations at one another. They're excited about tonight's boxing match between two undefeated competitors, both champions, whose names I don't know.

I'm alone in my dark room. The only light comes from my phone. I'm in bed, covered up to my narrow shoulders, looking at Instagram posts. I am comfortable but annoyed. Annoyed by the music. Annoyed by the heckling of horny youths. Annoyed by the choking mist of vaping, which smells like Cap'n Crunch's Crunch Berries cereal, by the weed smoke, coughing, and the sound of things being knocked over. My roommate is a dick and I want to choke him. I do not have to work in the morning, but I am waiting for Laura.

I consider touching myself but don't. I don't want to feel ashamed when I see Laura. She will know. She will detect signs of guilt in my long, crunchy peanut butter-like face and know that I have been dishonorable. No, I tell myself. I will not objectify Laura. When we meet, she will see that I respect her.

The music shuts off abruptly, but the living room is still loud for the TV. The main event must've just started. I hear people casting in their bets, making predictions on what fighter will win, what round. Men and women over-talk one another, equally trying to impress the room by stating how much they know about either boxer. The challenger starts his ring walk, I suppose, coming out to Takeshi69's "Bori." Instantly I think he is going to lose. Probably by knockout. Second round.

Thrilled, the girls express their excitement over the fighter. A gladiator, I imagine, showing how ripped he is once he is de-robed in the ring.

I get an alert from my phone and sit up.

Laura is on Live.

I want to see her on full screen so I get out of bed and sit down at my desk. I open my laptop. I never sign out on Tagged so all I have to do is open the page. And there I am. In Laura's pink universe. I see her room but she is not there. Not yet visible. I hear rustling in the background of her apartment. I see other guys joining in the livestream. Twenty-three and counting. Her white dog, a toy poodle, pads around. It looks into the camera, wags its furry stump of a tail, licks its chops, and then scampers out of view.

Her phone is placed in an awkward position for the room is sideways. It sounds like she is brushing her teeth now. It is 8 p.m. Her waking hour. Tap water runs. Moments after that, the toilet flushes. She coughs, taking her morning toke. Wake and bake. I don't mind her smoking marijuana. It's who she is. THC makes her happy. Finally, she appears, blessing us with her lovely presence.

"Hi, guys." She fixes her hair and pushes a blonde feather from her eye.

From my living room, there's yelling, cheering, stomping, clapping.

"Damnit." I turn the volume up on my laptop. One of the fighters must've gotten rocked.

"I just smoked," she says. She sips from a dented can of White Claw. Pineapple flavor. Again I do not judge. She has new nails, but I dare not comment on them. The guys will make fun of me. But I do like them. They're long. Squared at the tip. Purple."Mm." She sets the can down beside her. Leans forward, squinting at the comments and compliments, showered upon her.

"'Those eyes,'" she reads. "Thank you." She smiles and flutters her lashes, teasing us.

Reading on. "Omega, what's up?"

"Hi, Corey.

"Jasmine, DM me your IG . . ."

She gasps. "You guys! You've got to try those Pepsi-flavored Cheetos. They're so good.

"Oh no. What's wrong with my Spotify? It's not working."

She moves out of view, tinkering with her TV remote, I assume.

She reappears. "I have one of those smart TVs. I freakin hate this thing. You guys. Ugh. Does anyone know how to work this?"

What kind of TV is it? a guy asks.

She reads his question. "It's a Samsung, I think. I don't know. Anyway—Oh! I think I got it. I got it. Thanks. Oh, this is my song." She turns it up. She winds her neck to the music and closes her eyes. She smiles, doing a silent sing-along.

She's so beautiful—so mesmerizing—I decided to send her gifts. First roses, then hearts. They flood the screen, floating upward like virtual balloons.

"Thank yooou!" She makes a heart with her hands. Each gift has a diamond worth, which can be converted into real money. I feel proud.

The loud activity from the living room floods my bedroom. I whirl around.

My roommate comes in. "Dude, you're missing this fight!"

"What the actual fuck, Preston?"

One of his friends barges in behind him. "Are you in here watching porn?" The guy rudely turns on the lights.

Four of Preston's buddies are in my room now. They look around and grab things that don't belong to them.

"No, he's in here being a loser," Preston says. He leans over my shoulder. "On this damn dating site. This is what he does all day. Check it out."

His friends join him. They poke their heads into my personal space, staring into the monitor at Laura.

"Ah, dude," one of them says. "Are you fucking with these Internet hoes?" The guy reaches over to type something. I move my laptop and shut it.

"You guys, can you please leave my room?" I ask politely. "This is totally disrespectful."

"This is totally disrespectful," Preston mocks. "This is why you'll never get laid. There's a living room full of hot chicks—

"Hot bitches," one of his friends says.

"And you're in here, in the dark, chatting with some broad three hundred miles away. Dude, that's lame. Come out here and introduce yourself. Like a man. Hey, ladies!" he shouts over his shoulder.

"Don't," I say.

"Stop being a pussy," he says. "Come meet my roommate! Ladies! Come meet this exotic fuck!"

"I'm not—Preston, can you please stop." I turn around and dunk my head when the women enter. Gorgeous women, I glimpse. Petite model types. Girls you see working at Starbucks or dental offices. Girls you see leaving the tanning salon or 24 Hour Fitness gym. How he manages to meet these girls, I don't know.

I guess he's okay looking. Whenever I did have female company they would ask about him, which is why I stopped bringing girls over—whenever I did get lucky and meet one on a dating site. I repeatedly hear he's handsome, and he always has charm. Always talking, making women laugh—so naturally being himself.

He'd make a total fool of himself and not give two shits about it. Throwing himself in front of a passing car, getting hit, and laughing about it, just to stop traffic for a girl afraid to jaywalk. Dancing wildly without his shirt on. Letting a girl test her Taser on him.

Me? I could never do stuff like that.

"Ladies, meet Gurpreet," he says. "Or G. Turn around, G. Let 'em see you."

Reluctantly, I turn around in my swivel chair. "Hi."

The girls giggle. "Oh, he's shy," one of them says. "That's so cute."

Preston slugs me on the shoulder. "You hear that? Marylin thinks you're cute."

"Oh, look, he's blushing," another says.

Awed by my DVD collection, a guy drifts off to one of my shelves and plucks out a movie.

"Dude, your roommate has like a thousand movies." He turns around, holding a copy of *Fright Night,* the 2011 version. He faces the library again and selects another movie. "He's got all the *Fast and Furious* movies! All the *Saws*! All the *Screams*!"

"Do you mind?" I say.

"Are you like—a movie buff?" one of the girls asks. The guy puts the DVDs back, in the right spot, I ensure.

"Yes," I say.

"He wants to be a movie producer," Preston says. "They make big money. Maybe Sheryl can be in one of your pictures?" He elbows me, lifting his brow. His version of a wink.

"Gurpreet?" a pretty girl with braces asks. "Is that Indian?"

"He's Persian," Preston says. He always tells girls I'm Persian as if that makes me more exotic. "Look at his hair."

I slap his hand away. "It's—I'm Indian." I stroke my black hair back, becoming more comfortable yet still nervous. Most of the girls Preston brings over have never met an Indian guy before. Well, if anything I'm American. Third-generation Indian, totally assimilated, doesn't count for exotic. I don't even speak my native language. My parents refused to teach me, even though both sets of my grandparents had taught them Hindi respectively.

Marylin, the girl who said my shyness was cute, steps closer to me, and, without my permission, reaches over, and starts playing with strands of my hair. Another girl does the same. Preston and the fellas move out of the way. I feel hot and lean over, aroused. The girls comb their fingers through my mane, which climbs down my back to my waist.

Traditionally, I am not to cut it, but I have and do occasionally when length becomes a nuisance. Or when maintenance becomes a hassle.

The women began to braid my hair into twin tails. Another is recording. I feel like a superstar. A hot and horny superstar.

"Stand up," Preston says when they're done.

The girls look at me and giggle. They see my embarrassing dilemma.

"I can't," I say.

Everyone laughs, aware of the joke, then quietly—collectively—leaves the room.

I'm alone again.

I guess I wasn't cute enough for Marylin to stick around. My door shuts. And she is the one who closes it. I hear groaning—general disappointment. The fight is over. From the sounds of it, the challenger lost in an early round.

Music blares again. I open my laptop. Laura is on the screen. She wears a black dress, which shows her almighty cleavage. She is eating a powdered jelly doughnut, and stuffing her face with potato chips alternately. She has the munchies.

I want to type something, but I don't. I stare. I never know what to say to her. What if I sound corny? I follow her on IG. On one occasion, I came close to video chatting with her but chickened out when another guy boxed her. Some dude was in her box now. A black man. Attractive, high, and charismatic. Four things I'm not. Her profile says: **Black guys only. Sorry.** But somehow, I got an exception.

The guy in her box is rolling a blunt. "I would never have a threesome with my baby's mom if it involved another man."

I wondered what I missed. Things go left quickly on Live.

"You guys," she says, "I'm trying to go to this concert. Nas and Wu-Tang! It is going to be so lit. The tickets are like three hundred dollars. Oh, my gosh. And I'm going to need an outfit. I like, have to go to this concert, you guys. If I don't, I'm going to die. Nas and Wu-Tang! Here? In Seattle? That never happens. I need like three hundred dollars. You guys. Man . . ."

They were coming on my birthday. It'd be awesome if we could go together.

I message her, mentioning the former, leaving out the latter.

"Oh wow," she says after reading my line out loud. "Are you going, G?"

I don't know.

"You should go." She reaches for her bong. She takes a hit and coughs.

I notice her Cash App information at the bottom left side of the screen. Quickly, I jot the tag down. This is my chance to stand out. If I send her money, we will have something to talk about. Maybe, I can go with her—on my birthday—to the concert. She didn't say anything about going with girlfriends. I just got paid from work. Rent's not due for another two weeks. And she needs an outfit. I could send her $400.

I snag my phone. I Cash App her $400 and wait, staring at the screen for her reaction. Five minutes later, she picks up her phone.

"Oh my gosh!" She smiles. "Geeee." She stretches my name out. "Thank you so much." She blows me kisses. I blush. "Somebody was listening. You just made my day."

She reads a few comments. "Omega says, 'I get paid next week.' Mm. Where are you from, G?"

Bellevue. But I live in Renton, Washington.

"Oh, okay. Ren-tin." She sips from a new dented can of White Claw. Strawberry flavor. "So, do you live alone? I feel like—most guys on here don't live alone." She giggles. "They live with their girlfriends. You cheaters on here. No cheaters, guys." She waves at the camera as if to ward off the evil spirit of infidels. "No cheaters."

I'm not a cheater, I type. **I live with my roommate. And no girlfriend.** I hesitate. Is it too soon? Well, what the heck. **Who are you going to the concert with?**

I press return.

She reads.

I wait.

Instantly, I feel I made a mistake.

"Well, that's good," she says. "Nobody likes a cheater." She squints into the camera. "Um, I'm going to the concert with my girls. Girls' night out, but thank you. I'm so looking forward to this." She rolls her eyes. Sips White Claw. Guzzles three or four gulps. She burps, covers her mouth, and giggles. "Oh, my goodness. Sorry, guys."

That was sexy, someone types.

She makes a face, then laughs. I wonder if she would have had the same reaction if I had said that. Probably not.

I notice my apartment has quieted. Listening closer, I hear people leaving. The party is over.

Preston invades my room minutes later.

"Dude?" I swing around.

"Are you still on this?" He looks past my face at my laptop.

"Yes." I face the monitor.

"Hmph." I feel him lean over me. He puts a solid hand on my shoulder. "Marylin says you're a nice guy, which means she's not interested. I tried."

"I didn't ask, but thanks."

"Did you . . ." he squints at the screen. "Did you finally message her?" He stands straight and slugs me. "About damn time." He leans forward, reading more messages. "Wait. Tell me you didn't. Ah, bro, you're such a simp. You sent her money? Now, she'll never respect you."

I turn around. "She said she needed money for the Wu concert."

"You're a trick. . . . Or just an idiot. Dude." He rakes back his hair. "Move."

"What are you doing?"

"I'm getting you laid, you fuck." He reaches for the keyboard.

"Preston, stop."

He stands erect. "You don't get pussy being a simp."

"It's not about that. And—I wish you'd stop talking like that."

"My God, bro." He shakes his head. "You know our neighbor, Cliff—the mailman? Dude is like sixty years old. Never gets laid. You know why? Because he's a simp. He's going to die lonely, and so are you if you keep being nice and polite to these bitches. You have to be a dog, my friend." He howls. "Now watch this."

"Preston."

"Move and stop being a bitch." He shoves my chair out of the way and leans over the laptop. "Okay." He reads: "'Put yourself here! Tap the heart below!'" There's a red box in the upper right corner of the screen. And a heart below with the words: Date Me.

"Preston, don't." I stand up and reach for the keyboard.

He clicks on the heart.

"Fuck." I turn around and hide my face. I hear Laura's confused voice.

"G?"

"Nah, I'm his brother," Preston says. "What's up? You looking magically delicious over there. All I need is some milk and I'll eat you like some cereal."

She laughs. "Uh-uh. Who-are-you?"

"I told you, I'm his brother. Preston. Call me, P."

"Okay, Preston. I don't know if you know, but . . . I hate to burst your little bubble, but this stream is for black guys only. Sorry."

"Oh, I'm albino, babe. I told you, we're brothers."

She laughs again. "I'm so dead. G is not black, and *you* are not albino."

"What's wrong with your camera? You better clean the lens. Or maybe you need an eye doctor or something. G is black. And if he isn't black why is he here on your Live? Since you say, 'black guys only?'"

She shakes her head. "This man, you guys. I can't."

"Come here, G." He pulls me into view of the monitor. "Am I albino?"

I say nothing.

"You hear that?" he says to her. "He just told you I'm albino."

"I didn't hear anything," she says.

"Man, there's something wrong with your phone. You must have an Android."

She gasps. "Ni—" She stops herself. Swipes at the bangs covering her forehead.

"What was you about to say?"

"Nothing. You know what? You're too much. And—I don't have an Android, by the way. I have an iPhone. An iPhone 14, if you must know."

"Word? You *should* be balling. With all that Live and Cash App money you gettin'."

"Mm-mm. Who is this man? And why is your hand all in my pocket?"

"If my hand was in anything, it'd be in your purse. Don't be ashamed, though. Shoot, we all gotta get money."

"I'm not ashamed. If dudes wanna trick, then that's on them. That don't mean they getting something in return."

He turns his head and gives me a look, then faces the monitor again. "Right. I'm not judging. So you don't work?"

"How you gonna—" She laughs. "Yes, I work."

"Hold on."

He mutes the laptop, then searches the room for I don't know what. Digging into my hamper, he plucks out a dirty T-shirt and throws it over the monitor.

"What are you doing?" I ask.

"Watch this." He borrows my phone to pull up her page. "This girl is insecure, bro. She's got old pictures of herself from when she was in high school, and now she's fat. She doesn't work. Doesn't have a social life, and she's bored. If she's still there in five minutes, we got her. Right now, she's curious, wondering what we're doing. None of the guys on there are talking to her. They're lame, and now she's entertained. You're going over there."

"What? No. I can't. We haven't even been on a date."

"Dude. Yes, you can. Just watch."

Ten minutes later, not five.

He removes the T-shirt and unmutes the laptop.

Immediately, she scoots up. I see a few guys had messaged her but weren't saying much.

"What were you doing?" she asks. "Blanking your screen out like—

"So look," Preston says. "We 'bout to head out. I gotta do a show tonight."

"Oh." Her eyes widen. "Are you like an artist?"

"What? Follow me on IG. Are you serious? I'm 'bout to open up for the show at Climate Pledge Arena on October eighteenth. Are you stupid?"

Her eyes grow big. "You're opening up for Nas and Wu-Tang?"

"Anyways, man." He turns to me. "Is this girl slow or something?" Faces the monitor. "We 'bout to go."

"Wait. What's your IG?"

"I'm not about to say all that on here. Just DM your number."

"Okay. Dang. You're so demanding. Mr. *Preston.*" She sexualizes his name, I notice.

"That's right, babe. I'm a boss and call the shots. Now hurry up. I gotta go."

She DMs her number.

I don't go to her house. He does. Turns out, she only lives five miles away. I'm still on her Live when he arrives there. Her stream disconnects right before the lovemaking.

Then I meet the devil.

Made in United States
Troutdale, OR
03/09/2024

18118612R00216